Para
Mi AMIGA
Gobernadura,
con todo y
dedicación
de Davidow

4/12/04

D0820938

To Eduardo Bours
With appreciation
for your friendship
and for your
contribution
to Mexico's
development

Jeff Davidow

THE U.S. AND MEXICO
The Bear and the Porcupine

THE U.S. AND

THE BEAR
AND THE
PORCUPINE

MEXICO

Jeffrey Davidow

 Markus Wiener Publishers
Princeton

Copyright © 2004 by Jeffrey Davidow
Copyright © 2004 by Maria Madonna Davidoff for the inside spot artwork

All rights reserved. No part of this book may be reproduced or transmitted
in any form or by any means, electronic or mechanical, including photocopying,
recording, or by any information storage or retrieval system, without permission
of the copyright owners.

For information write to: Markus Wiener Publishers
231 Nassau Street, Princeton, NJ 08542

Cover photo: Courtesy of Jeffrey Davidow
Photo on pp. ii–iii: Courtesy of Jeffrey Davidow
Cover design and chapter illustrations by Maria Madonna Davidoff
Book design by Cheryl Mirkin
This book was composed in Goudy Old Style

Library of Congress Cataloging-in-Publication Data

Davidow, Jeffrey.
    The U.S. and Mexico : the bear and the porcupine / Jeffrey Davidow.
    ISBN 1-55876-333-3 (alk. paper)
    ISBN 1-55876-334-1 (pbk. : alk. paper)
    1. United States—Foreign relations—Mexico. 2. Mexico—Foreign relations—
    United States. 3. United States—Foreign relations—1989- 4. Davidow, Jeffrey.
    5. Ambassadors—Mexico—Biography. 6. Ambassadors—United States—Biography.
    I. Title: United States and Mexico. II. Title.
E183.8.M6D38 2004   327.73072—dc22   2004001548

Markus Wiener Publishers books are printed in the United States of America
on acid-free paper, and meet the guidelines for permanence and durability
of the Committee on Production Guidelines for Book Longevity of the
Council on Library Resources.

Contents

Acknowledgments
PAGE ix

Prologue ✧ In the Land of Aztlán
PAGE xi

Introduction ✧ Of Ignorance and Arrogance
PAGE xiii

Chapter 1 ✧ Clearing the Land
PAGE 1

Chapter 2 ✧ The Ambivalence
PAGE 11

Chapter 3 ✧ White House to Casablanca
PAGE 19

Chapter 4 ✧ The Flower Wars
PAGE 31

Chapter 5 ✧ Certifiably Insane
PAGE 45

Chapter 6 ✧ Running in Vicious Circles
PAGE 57

Chapter 7 ✧ Fingers, Locks, and Primaries
PAGE 67

Chapter 8 ✧ Dancing on Marbles in Chinatown
PAGE 81

Chapter 9 ✧ The Caribbean Three-Step
PAGE 97

Chapter 10 ✧ "Where Did All These People Come From?"
PAGE 109

Chapter 11 ✧ The Hole in the Wall
PAGE *121*

Chapter 12 ✧ Mexico Changes Course
PAGE *131*

Chapter 13 ✧ Incidents of Travel
PAGE *145*

Chapter 14 ✧ The Fox Presidency
PAGE *159*

Chapter 15 ✧ Fidel's Revenge
PAGE *175*

Chapter 16 ✧ Visits from Planet Washington
PAGE *187*

Chapter 17 ✧ The Mothers of All Visits
PAGE *195*

Chapter 18 ✧ Enrique
PAGE *207*

Chapter 19 ✧ The Negotiation That Wasn't
PAGE *217*

Chapter 20 ✧ The End of the Honeymoon
PAGE *233*

Epilogue ✧ 2025
PAGE *245*

Index
PAGE *251*

About the Author
PAGE *254*

President Fox and his wife watching fireworks with President Bush and Ambassador Davidow on the terrace of the White House.

Acknowledgments

This book is the responsibility of only one person—the author. But it could not have been written without the assistance of many friends. A number of former colleagues still in the U.S. government offered guidance, cautioned me, and stimulated my memory. But I will not name them because they should bear no burden for its contents.

I spent the 2002–2003 academic year enjoying Harvard University on a sabbatical from the State Department. At the Institute of Politics of the John F. Kennedy School of Government I was assisted by the students in my study group and by the staff of the Institute, notably Jennifer Phillips. At Harvard's David Rockefeller Center for Latin American Studies, its director, Professor John Coatsworth, provided a welcoming environment and insightful criticism as did longtime friend Professor Jorge Dominguez, head of the Weatherhead Center for International Affairs. Dov Ronen, an academic who for twenty years has harbored the secret hope that I would become less of an apparatchik, also used his pen to keep me honest. Steve Chaplin and Aaron Mihaly gave good advice. Luis Rubio, one of Mexico's most astute political analysts, read everything and gently corrected me.

Jerry Kammer, an experienced reporter with an affection for Mexico as great as mine, convinced me to publish the work. His careful reading and editing suggestions were enhanced by his own in-depth reporting on immigration and U.S.-Mexican relations and his understanding of the Mexican press and academia. He insisted that I remove some of my more outrageous statements and opinions. He was only partially successful, but he did try hard. Willa Speiser gave valuable editing assistance, and Susie Lorand carefully scoured the manuscript for inconsistencies, omissions, and errors. Miguel Juaregui and Andres Oppenheimer gave me good advice about publishing. Gaston Luken, chairman of the board of the Institute of the Americas at the University of California in San Diego of which I now serve as president, read the work and encouraged me to publish it knowing that many in Mexico will mistake its efforts at honesty for intromission.

Joan Davidow, my partner in all that I do, carefully read and corrected every page. She was as concerned about my careless grammar as I was unconcerned about it. For all of her help, and not just in the completion of this book, I dedicate this volume to her.

Prologue:
In the Land of Aztlán

In 2002, researchers reported that a previously unknown document had been discovered in a library in Seville. The fragment has not yet been fully analyzed, but it is already generating considerable academic debate. It may be an account of an Aztec creation fable as told to a Franciscan friar in Mexico in the mid-sixteenth century. Or it may be a recent fabrication without historical value. Whatever its provenance, it recounts the history of the arrival in central Mexico of the Mexicas. The friars later called them the Aztecs after the land they had left in the north, Aztlán.

The Mexicas came to the valley of Anáhuac and began the construction of Tenochtitlán less than two hundred years before Cortés arrived. In their travels from the north they had been guided by Xólotl, the brother of the great god Quetzalcóatl. Xólotl assumed the form of the evening star and led his chosen people to a place where they found, as had been prophesied, an eagle on a cactus devouring a snake. The new document provides the following additional, hitherto unreported, fable.

Before our grandfathers came to this land, they lived as children live in Chicomotzoc, the place of the seven caves, in Aztlán. They were happy. But in the years of the great dryness, their crops shriveled and burned. The fathers returned to the forest to search for food. The forest was a dangerous place. Our enemies were hungry and they chased us. We fought them. Many died. Even the creatures of the forest would not share the fruits of the trees or the seeds of the earth with the children of Aztlán. We could not stay in Aztlán and our fathers sent scouts to search for a new land.

One night in the forest the spirit of the porcupine approached one of the scouts.

"The children of Aztlán must follow me. I fear no man or animal. I am among the smallest of the animals of the forest. But I am feared by the biggest. My quills protect me from all. I travel the whole forest and eat the fruits and seeds I desire."

The scout laughed at the porcupine and said he was too boastful. "And what of the giant bear? Do you not fear him?"

"I will tell you a story. One day I walked in the forest. I must travel with my nose in the earth to search for seeds. I did not see the bear. And he did not see me as his eyes were looking upward searching for berries. He almost stepped on me. We startled each other. I made my quills stand up. He stopped, and he laughed at me."

"Do you think you can kill me with your little arrows?"

"No, but do you think you can step on me without suffering the pain of my quills?"

The bear responded, "Pain is the tribute we owe Huitzilopochtli for the privilege of life. I do not fear your little arrows. I will allow you to stay near me and serve me. You will bring me seeds and berries. I will protect you from the jaguar and the fox. I will give your quills to the men of Aztlán so that they may take their own blood as a tribute to Huitzilopochtli."

The porcupine kept his quills up. "I do not wish to live with you. You are careless and your step in the forest places my children in danger. I will not be your slave. I serve only Huitzilopochtli. I will lead the people of Aztlán to a better place. There Huitzilopochtli will vanquish the other gods and protect them."

The spirit of the porcupine gave each man one of his children to carry on his back as protection. The people traveled for a long time. They followed the star of the god Xólotl. They met many enemies in their travels. The men of Aztlán used the quills as spears and arrows to vanquish their foes.

Then they found the place next to the prickly pear cactus, the land that the gods had given them. And there the sons of the porcupine crawled from the backs of the scouts. The children of the porcupine stayed with the people and taught them to raise their spears and to be ever vigilant because the great bear might come again. And they waited for him.

Introduction:
Of Ignorance and Arrogance

I am relatively confident that the fable recounted in the prologue is not of sixteenth-century origin. In fact, I am more than relatively confident because I wrote it myself. I was looking for a parable that could describe the U.S.-Mexican relationship, and not finding a good one, I took the liberty of creating one.

Of course, the porcupine does not envision itself as a rather unpleasant rodent. And the bear does not think of itself as a blundering oaf. In their own minds both are as noble as the eagles that are their national symbols. Misperception is common in human and international affairs. But does it really matter? In most instances, no. But the lack of understanding between the United States and Mexico is important. It leads to errors in judgment on both sides and creates an environment in which important opportunities to build a better future are lost.

All American ambassadors suffer from a certain amount of "clientitis," a disease that places the country to which each is accredited at the center of the world and its relations with the United States in the column of the absolutely crucial. This view is rarely an accurate presentation of reality, but it does wonders for the ego. That said, I will make this flat statement: No nation in the world has a greater impact on the daily lives of average Americans than Mexico. What we produce in our factories and on our farms, the prices of many of our products, the wages we pay and receive, the language we teach in our classrooms and use in our schoolyards, the crime that afflicts us, the very demographic makeup of our country—who we are—and, in some locales, the air we breathe and the water we drink are all influenced by developments in Mexico.

This is not an argument to wrest importance from America's involvement in other regions of the world. Rather, it is a simple statement of fact—that for the average American going about his or her daily life, no country is more likely to have a greater influence than Mexico.

Conversely, and perhaps even more obviously, no nation more affects Mexico than does the giant to the north. The places that leap out from this morning's headlines—Kandahar or Basra or some other spot that most of us had not heard of until yesterday and will forget about tomorrow—cannot compare in long-range interest and importance to what kind of relationship the United States can construct with Mexico.

The weight of economics and demography is pushing the two countries closer together than would have been conceivable even a few years ago. Twenty years from now, the U.S.-Mexican relationship may have changed as much as it has in the past twenty years. Today, we cannot state accurately where the relationship is heading or how it will get there. It is a journey with no clear destination and without trustworthy maps. We will have to construct the road as we travel it. And we will have to build it together. This will not be easy. There are tremendous impediments to greater cooperation.

Perhaps the greatest impediment is ignorance. The people of the two countries really know little and understand less about each other. The ignorance allows resentment to fester and prejudice to grow. This is, of course, something of an overstatement. Many Mexicans and Americans have a clear vision of the other side of the border. But, in general, for nations that are so important to each other, there is an alarming lack of comprehension.

We are different animals—as different as the bear and the porcupine. The size and power of the United States make it loom over Mexico, and even when we are at our most benign, our very weight can overwhelm. We lumber through the forest unaware that we can inadvertently stomp on other creatures. And when we are at our worst—when a lack of vision or generosity leads us to narrow-mindedness or a stubborn unwillingness to confront the complex reality of the relationship—we can be a most difficult neighbor.

Generally, the United States has no intention to inflict damage upon Mexico. In reality, the greatest harm it does is by ignoring its neighbor—or, to extend the metaphor perhaps beyond its carrying capacity—by entering into periods of extended hibernation in which it insultingly pays little or no attention. The United States also inflicts harm by willfully ignoring the collateral damage of its own domestic policies and politics. When Washington passes legislation giving additional subsidies to

American farmers, or delays implementing an important transportation element of NAFTA to placate the Teamsters Union, it carelessly exacts a toll upon Mexico.

Mexico is frequently not the most attractive of neighbors either. Its hypersensitivity to the northern bear means that its porcupine quills are always at the ready, often making the simplest of cooperation difficult. And its poverty and weak institutions generate or aggravate problems that become ours to deal with—migration and drugs, to name but two. Also, for Mexican politicians there has traditionally been benefit in striking out against the United States. The aggression is generally controlled, usually highly rhetorical but occasionally real, a sharp poke in the eye, rather than a body blow. It is true that in some parts of the United States at some times Mexico-bashing has been a useful political gimmick, but it is one of limited utility. On the other hand, U.S.-bashing in Mexico is an important element of the country's political life.

In recent years, both sides of the dividing line have developed a greater willingness to recognize that they can only deal with many issues by cooperating. The old approach of standing at the border and pointing fingers at each other just does not make sense in the twenty-first century. This is especially so, if we believe, as I do, that we can and should move closer together to meet common challenges and improve the lives of our citizens. But to make the move we must better understand each other. And that understanding cannot ignore the fact that the U.S.-Mexican relationship is a complex and often difficult one. Nor can it ignore the reality that many of the issues we face together are also matters of heavy domestic political concern, a fact that further impedes rational discussion and action.

This book is an effort to use my experiences to shed some light on this complex and difficult relationship. It is not a detailed, chronological account of my service in Mexico. I cannot imagine that much of what I did on a daily basis as ambassador would be of interest to general readers. A fair amount of that did not even interest me. Nor is this an attempt to describe every strand in the twisted rope that binds us. It is part history, part political analysis, part memoir, part score settling, and fully of my own design. I would like to think that those who make the maps for the future might be able to extract some guideposts or directions from this account.

However, in the endeavor to provide some help to the mapmakers of the future, I am aware that as a futurologist and as a cartographer, I leave much to be desired. One example of my limitations will suffice. It comes from 1979, when I was on a temporary leave from the State Department and worked in the office of a senator whom I found distant and occasionally subject to weird ideas. At his direction, I organized what was probably the first congressional inquiry into the possibility of forming a free trade area for North America. I thought the concept was impractical and the hearings a waste of my time and effort. Dutifully, I assembled a list of witnesses who more or less shared the senator's biases. I attended the hearings. The senator attended the hearings. Hardly anybody else came to his party. At the time, conventional wisdom, to the degree that such things were being thought about, held that a trade pact with Canada might make some sense. But not with Mexico, a third world country with little to sell us and no money to buy our products. It just did not seem to be within the realm of the possible.

By the time I left Mexico in 2002, after serving four years as U.S. ambassador there, two-way trade between the United States and Mexico had reached $250 billion a year. Mexico was our second-largest trading partner, and projections indicated that it could move into first place, surpassing Canada within the decade. Free trade had profoundly changed Mexican society and altered the manufacturing base of our own. In 1979 I had not been able to comprehend the possibilities of the future because my understanding of Mexico was limited and I was arrogant. I dismissed the potential importance of Mexico because I was caught up in narrow views and biases. It is a mistake that both countries consistently make to our own detriment. Fortunately, in the years following 1979, there were others who had broader views and more open minds.

I do not want to see our two countries make the same kind of mistake in the coming decades that I made then. While the United States suffers from ignorance and arrogance, Mexico too is afflicted by incomplete or distorted knowledge about the United States. It also suffers from an arrested state of national psychological development that too frequently infuses the bilateral relationship with adolescent resentment and self-defeating posturing. Fortunately, the negative character traits of each nation are not held by all of their citizens. We now have an opportunity to create something qualitatively different in North America. We should move beyond the simple and impressive trade numbers to develop greater levels of integration that will involve new institutions and new perceptions and create new realities that will serve our respective national interests. To do so, both countries will have to mature, one abandoning the insensitivity of the bear and the other the defensiveness of the porcupine.

Friends in Mexico may object to some of my harsher comments. They should not take offense. The words are not meant to hurt, and, in any event, they are no sharper than some of my views on U.S. personalities and policies. To set the record straight, I stress that for my wife, Joan, and for myself, Mexico is and will remain a special place. In a lifetime of foreign living, no other country has so captivated us. No other culture has so impressed us. No other people have so befriended us. And no other nation has so filled us with hope for the future.

Friends in the United States, especially former colleagues in the government, might worry that I have revealed too much about sensitive topics. I can assure them that I have been very careful. Even matters that may have once been dealt with in classified documents have all been subsequently discussed in the press and can no longer be considered privileged material. In the writing of this book, I made no effort to obtain or use sensitive government sources.

Friends in academia, both Mexican and American, may be disturbed by the absence of the outward manifestations of scholarship such as footnotes and a bibliography. I did not think they were necessary or appropriate in a highly personalized account. With the exception of the prologue and a similar flight of imagination in the epilogue, I stand by the veracity and accuracy of this text. Of course, I have my biases developed with considerable effort in a Foreign Service career of thirty-five years. Some of my prejudices may be totally irrational, but I see no reason to obscure them.

Finally, I would ask the reader to approach this work as a compilation of incontrovertible fact and unabashed opinion. Any reader who finds a fact to controvert should immediately treat it as an opinion. That will make life easier for both the reader and the author.

Clearing the Land

We had just returned to Mexico City after a hectic ten days in the United States. We had traveled first to our daughter's wedding in California. Then we moved on to Washington, where President Bush feted Mexican President Vicente Fox during an elaborate state visit filled with pomp and ceremony and warm predictions of a new era of friendship and trust between the two countries.

While the trip had been exciting, on that morning in Mexico City, I felt a certain weariness. A life in the Foreign Service had accustomed me to frequent changes, and the three years we had already spent in Mexico were beginning to seem like a very long time. A feeling of emptiness was creeping in as I faced another heavily scheduled day. If the day had gone as planned, I would have had breakfast at the office of a prominent Mexican businessman, called on the president of Mexico's Supreme Court to protest that he was helping crooks by blocking extraditions to the United States, returned to the embassy to greet four new staffers, held a series of phone consultations with various federal bureaucrats I liked to call "the Wizards of the Potomac," had lunch with a member of President Fox's cabinet, given an early-evening speech, and finally gone out to dinner, arriving home at midnight or later.

While I dressed, as I contemplated the rest of the day, I thought of the book I had just read on the plane trip from Washington, Ian McEwan's novel *Amsterdam*. A passage about the frenetic but increasingly hollow existence of the main character, a newspaper editor, struck a chord with me:

Since arriving at [his office] two hours earlier, he had spoken, separately and intensely, to forty people. And not only spoken: in all but two of these exchanges he had decided, prioritized, delegated, chosen, or offered an opinion that was bound to be interpreted as a command. This exercise of authority did not sharpen his sense of self, as it usually did. Instead it seemed to Vernon that he was infinitely diluted; he was simply the sum of all the people who had listened to him...

Vernon clearly needed to be woken up. Perhaps I did as well.

I turned on the television and saw the first plane hit the World Trade Center. Not understanding the enormity of what I had witnessed, I left a few minutes later to begin my rounds. But by the time I reached my first destination, the horrible reality was coming into focus with reports of the second attack in New York and the bombing of the Pentagon. I bid a hasty good-bye to my host and headed quickly back to the office. My bodyguards were jumpy. By the time we got to the embassy, Mexican police had already beefed up their controls at the perimeter. I knew I needed to allay fears and calm nerves among the six hundred members of the embassy staff. I spent much of the morning walking around the embassy, talking, and just being visible. Then we called the staff together. With more visible emotion than I had expected to display, I told them that anyone who felt the need to be with family should go home. But the rest of us had to get back to work, or we would be letting the bastards win.

The terror of September 11, so damaging to the American soul, became a window on the Mexican psyche. It did not so much alter the U.S.-Mexican emotional terrain as it cleared it, thinning out the brushwood and revealing the fault lines and contours of the twisted land.

Just a week earlier, as Washington feted Fox like a hero for the stunning electoral triumph in 2000 that had ended seventy-one years of one-party rule in Mexico, he had issued a stirring call for a new era of understanding. In a speech to a joint session of Congress, he had declared, "We must . . . leave [behind] the kind of suspicion and indifference that have so often in the past been the source of misunderstandings between our two peoples." In his thirty-minute speech, he invoked "trust" twenty-nine times.

The initial Mexican reaction to the terror was one of horror. President Fox's office and other government departments faxed statements of grief. Ordinary citizens, politicians, and cabinet ministers called the embassy or friends in the United States to express sympathy. Millions of Mexicans sat stunned and numbed in front of their television sets. They learned of the probable deaths of Mexicans in the World Trade Center, where many worked in the Windows on the World Restaurant. (Much later, the deaths of sixteen Mexicans were confirmed.)

But quickly the reaction became muddled, degenerating into an unseemly internal political debate that revealed very little trust or understanding but much ugliness and a harsh insensitivity.

At the center of the storm was Jorge Castañeda, Fox's foreign secretary. Brilliant of mind, imperious of temperament, Castañeda was like an irascible professor who has no patience with those who do not appreciate his insights. His absolute conviction that he was smarter than almost everyone else was made more aggravating by the fact that he was right. A respected academic and the urbane son of a former foreign secretary, Castañeda speaks flawless English, French, and Spanish. He is convinced he would make a wonderful Mexican president, and he longs for the job.

Before joining Fox's cabinet, Castañeda had never served in government and had little talent for the give and take and compromise required in political life. In less than one year in office, he had managed to offend most of his government colleagues and every significant political group in the country. Fox's own National Action Party, the PAN, viewed him as a supercilious outsider. Years of fierce criticism of Mexican authoritarianism had earned him the animosity of the Institutional Revolutionary Party, the PRI, which Fox had booted from the presidency after seven decades of uninterrupted power. And Castañeda, having turned away from the Marxism of his youth toward the center, was bitterly estranged from the Mexican left, which was appalled that he had helped a former Coca-Cola executive win Mexico's dramatic presidential election of 2000.

Most troubling to Mexico's political and intellectual elites was Castañeda's habit of telling the truth. He was willing to slash through conventional and comfortable shibboleths of Mexican foreign policy and lay it on the line. As with many provocative people, Castañeda's strengths and weaknesses were simply different sides of the same coin. The remarkable glibness that made him such an interesting commentator also led him to careless, undiplomatic comments that his many enemies would pounce on with irate glee.

Having graduated from Princeton and having taught for years at New

York University, Castañeda must have felt the attack on the World Trade Center with a particular intensity. And as the architect of Fox's efforts to build a stronger relationship with the United States, he was not inclined to mask his outrage. So while I sat in the embassy crafting a careful statement that was full of statesmanlike moderation, stiff-upper-lip fortitude, and earnest calls for international cooperation, Castañeda told the press exactly what he thought in an impromptu interview as he hurried from a meeting with President Fox.

Castañeda said pretty much what I would have liked to have said: The U.S. has every right and reason to seek revenge; and in the face of such barbaric terror, the civilized world should stand shoulder to shoulder with America. "In difficult moments for a country, like those the United States is now facing, friends should not haggle over support," he said.

Such blunt talk was manna from heaven for Castañeda's critics. They screamed that he was offering a "blank check of support" to whatever plans of unilateral and unbridled force the Americans were hatching. The PRI led the charge, warning that the Fox-Castañeda policy of subservience to U.S. interests would cast the country into war.

Intellectual backing for the assault on Castañeda came from predictable sources. Carlos Fuentes, who has more talent as a novelist than as a political analyst and who has lived for years off the largesse of American universities and foundations, led the charge. Well before September 11, he had made a splash in the news by calling President Bush a moron. Now he resumed the offensive, wrapping his reflexive antigringoism in the elegant language shaped by the philosophy that there is no better time to kick an adversary than when he is on the ground.

Fuentes argued that the United States had brought the attacks on itself by recklessly pushing its own power throughout the world. His laundry list of American sins managed to convey the impression that Osama Bin Laden had somehow been spurred to action by Bush's renunciation of the Kyoto Protocol on global warming. He told his countrymen not to act as America's *achinchicles*—a wonderful Mexican word meaning "minions" and full of the onomatopoeia of clanking prisoners' chains. His defiant assertion that "we are not lackeys" became the battle cry of the Mexican "this is not our war" crowd.

Other critics blathered on with overwrought expressions of dread about the possibility that the United States would strike the terrorists who had just murdered three thousand innocents. When President Bush issued his "you're with us or you're with the terrorists" call to the world, Mexico's anti-U.S. contingent worked itself into a lather over the notion that the U.S. wanted to pull Mexican soldiers onto the battlefield, a prospect that Washington, knowing Mexican sensitivities very well, would never have considered.

Unfortunately, Castañeda added to the furor. When the Mexican press asked whether Mexico would send its boys to die for the United States, Castañeda could have simply responded that Mexico's constitution and established policy prohibit foreign military commitments. Instead, he answered that the United States did not need Mexico's military help and had not asked for it. Gratuitously, he added, "And if they did ask, we would not give it." The last part of his answer made news in the United States. Even though Washington had no intention of seeking Mexican military support, here was our neighbor turning an unnecessarily cold shoulder. President Fox only deepened Washington's discomfort with his strange public silence as the domestic Mexican political debate blustered on.

Washington's worries were compounded by another Castañeda misstep that had generally gone unnoticed. For me it had been a huge headache. In late August, several weeks before the terrorist attacks, he had called to tell me that when Fox addressed the Organization of American States (OAS) on the last day of his impending state visit to Washington, he would announce Mexico's withdrawal from the Rio Treaty. Signed in 1946, the treaty bound its Western Hemisphere signers to mutual self-defense in the face of foreign aggression. As a remnant of Cold War efforts to oppose the Soviet threat, it had not seen much action in recent years. I had never had occasion to refer to it in the years that I served as the chief of the State Department's Latin American Bureau.

Castañeda argued that if Mexico pulled out of a treaty that offered the possibility of joint military action, implicitly under U.S. direction, its military would somewhat ironically be able to become more involved in hemispheric defense. Once free from the potential political burden of theoretical Pentagon supervision, he argued, the Mexican military would have room to participate in joint training operations, cabinet level defense meetings, and other armed forces cooperative efforts. As far as I was concerned, this was theoretical sugarcoating for an unpleasant pill. While I could not personally get very worked up about a plan by a generally nonparticipating country to withdraw from an underutilized treaty, I knew this was the kind of nonissue that could generate serious heartburn in Washington, particularly in the Pentagon, which has a limited sense of humor when it comes to its defense treaties.

I told Castañeda that I did not like the timing. An announcement from Fox on the last day of his visit to Washington would be seen for what it was: a message that while Fox was Bush's friend, he would find ways to demonstrate Mexico's independence from the United States. Castañeda saw it as a masterstroke—a light, quick poke in Uncle Sam's eye that had little practical effect but would buy him political space back home and reinforce his position with the holdover PRI mandarins of the foreign ministry. It was a move in the time-honored tradition of that ministry—old thinking and reflexive antigringoism at work. For me, it threatened to provide an unnecessary and insulting end to what was clearly going to be an important visit.

After repeated calls back and forth among Castañeda, Secretary of State Colin Powell, and myself, Castañeda finally agreed to soften his position ever so slightly. Instead of announcing that Mexico was withdrawing from the treaty, Fox would state his government's intention to consult with other treaty members with the intention to withdraw. On such heads of pins not-so-angelic diplomats dance.

Castañeda banked on the move not getting much press attention in the United States, but playing well at home. He was annoyingly right. Fox's speech to the OAS received little coverage in the American press, but it was a decent-sized story in Mexico. But September 11 changed everything, as the State Department mobilized every international mechanism available for the fight on terrorism. While the Rio Treaty would have little practical effect in the battle, it was symbolically important at a time when the United States needed global support.

Sensing Mexican vulnerability, the government of Brazil, always looking for an opportunity to embarrass their rival for the role of most important Latin American nation, called on the OAS to invoke the treaty that took its name from Brazil's proudest city, the place where it had been signed. Suddenly, Castañeda's attempt at a minor insult became the stuff of high-level Washington conversation. Mixed with press reports of his "we will not send our boys to fight" posturing, it troubled many in the capital. Some were convinced that the Mexicans would now seek to block the invocation of the treaty. I argued that they would not stand in our way, but needed a ladder to climb out of the hole they had dug for themselves.

Building that ladder was classic ambassadorial work, using understanding of the local political terrain to help another government do something important to us without embarrassing itself. We agreed that Castañeda would attend the meeting of hemispheric foreign ministers that the OAS called to discuss terrorism, but he would be absent when the ministers decided by a consensus vote of all present to invoke the treaty.

The agitation and press play over the treaty obscured a more encouraging development in the U.S.-Mexico relationship. In the aftermath of September 11, as the United States looked frantically around the world for other possible attacks, Mexican agencies swung quickly into action. At our request, they checked immigration and travel records and were able to confirm that none of the suspects we had identified had come to Mexico or used its banks for financial transactions. We appreciated their cooperation and the concern that they demonstrated.

In the weeks after September 11, political commentators in both Mexico and the United States warned that Mexico was badly mishandling its response to the crisis by creating the impression that it was neutral in the war on terrorism. Respected Mexican historian Lorenzo Meyer criticized politicians and intellectuals for not understanding that the attack on the Twin Towers could damage the scaffolding of the new relationship that Fox was trying to construct with Washington. "They do not understand what is happening and are using the opportunity to attack Fox," Meyer said. "Mexico is coming out looking like an idiot. We suffer from an enormous historical weight and there is no way to change it." Meyer warned of "a childish anti-Americanism, very emotional, not rational, or well thought out" that would hurt Mexico. "The political class is very devious and they want Castañeda to pay [for his position], but we will all wind up paying," he wrote.

I was brutally frank with leading members of the opposition PRI. I called them and told them their bickering with Castañeda was being read in the United States as overt anti-Americanism. I asked Senator Silvia Hernández, a leading "Americanologist," to "please not conduct your family's fights at my family's funeral." The office of Senator Christopher Dodd, who is respected throughout Latin America for his understanding of the region, passed on the same message to Hernandez and others. The PRI responded by hustling a delegation of its senators to Washington in an effort to calm the troubled waters.

Even Mexican correspondents in Washington, not a preternaturally pro-American group, were puzzled by their country's seeming indifference to the American crisis. "Where is Fox?" asked a story by an influential reporter that noted the unease on the Potomac. While Mexico dithered, other nations had rallied to Uncle Sam's side. Canadian Prime Minister Chrétien had nearly broken his leg running to the White House to express solidarity. The Queen of England was having "The Star-Spangled Banner" played at Buckingham Palace. Even the French were being civil. Fox, who had spoken so earnestly of trust, was, after the first days' pro forma expressions of sympathy, invisible.

It did not help that September 11 came just before Mexico's *Fiestas Patrias* (patriotic holidays). They are part of a festive week when the country celebrates the beginning of its war for independence from Spain in 1810 and also honors the young soldiers who died during the 1847 American assault on Mexico City's Chapultepec castle. As patriotism in Mexico cannot be separated from saber rattling anti-interventionism—code for anti-Americanism—there could not have been a worse time to try to rally public sentiment in support of the United States.

But Castañeda had other ideas. He suggested that Fox ask for a moment of silence when he addressed several hundred thousand celebrating countrymen at the traditional *grito* celebration of Independence Day in Mexico City's main square, the Zócalo. It did not seem like a brilliant plan to me. The *grito*, literally a "shout" for liberty, is a lot like New Year's Eve in Times Square. By midnight, a good portion of the crowd would have imbibed a lot more than patriotic spirit. Quieting them for a minute for anything would have been impossible. But the most sharp-edged opposition to the moment-of-silence proposal came from Secretary of Interior Santiago Creel, the cabinet member most responsible for taking the nation's pulse. Creel said it would be inappropriate to bring the United States into Mexico's most sacred patriotic ritual. Such a gesture, he said, would brand Fox, at least with the political and intellectual elites, as a submissive Yankee bootlicker, as an "achinchincle."

The petty political debate and intragovernmental squabbling continued for nearly two weeks. Creel, whose ministry was also responsible for domestic security and who had just been named as the point man for antiterrorism, was designated to speak to the press. His fundamental message, condemning terrorism and pledging non-military cooperation with the United States, was reasonable. But as a politician with presidential aspirations, he succumbed to the siren call of nationalist rhetoric. Creel conditioned his antiterrorism pledge with the usual gobbledygook of "no submission" to the United States.

Naturally, the Mexican press picked up the patriotic hype and played it as the headline. So the U.S. media tuned in to another round of the ritualistic Mexican melodrama in which Uncle Sam is played as the historic bully. Creel sent me a message through his chief of intelligence to ignore the press. I responded by suggesting that it was time for his government to speak with one voice and a clear message. The advice was so obvious that it must have come from other sources as well. The next day Fox told his cabinet—Creel, Castañeda, et al.—to shut up. He, alone, would speak for Mexico, and he would take on the work of repairing the damage to the relationship that had seemed so promising that first golden week of September.

Soon Fox appeared on *Larry King Live*. Speaking from his office in Los Pinos, he delivered a message carefully crafted for an American audience. Emphasizing Mexican solidarity with its neighbor, he cleverly neutered the question of military participation. That was a nonissue, he explained, since Mexico "does not have a fighting army." Then he packed his bags for Washington, where he would take his damage-control tour to the White House and President Bush.

I flew to Washington to help prepare for the Bush-Fox meeting. There was a palpable tension in the capital city, a sense of imminent threat, of lurking danger. I witnessed a particularly dramatic moment in the Oval Office just before President Fox arrived. In a series of urgent phone calls, the president's National Security Advisor, Condoleezza Rice, received news that a person in Florida had contracted anthrax. This was the beginning of another national trauma that was to last for weeks and take several lives.

Less than a month after he had been the guest of honor at a state dinner in the White House, Fox returned to a very different city in a very different world. President Bush greeted him in the Oval Office, but with none of the backslapping, Texas good-old-boy charm of the previous visit. Bush was purposeful and grim. "We expect more attacks," he told Fox, who appeared taken aback by the president's certainty. Fox was statesmanlike as he expressed solidarity. "This is our fight as well," he said. Everyone understood that his pledge did not include a military commitment. The medium—his presence at the White House—was the message: despite the political posturing at home, Mexico would not abandon the United States in its hour of greatest need.

At the embassy, we received the same message in many individual gestures of kindness and concern. The most touching came in late October, when a group of Mexican women constructed next to the embassy a large flower-covered altar, the traditional way to commemorate the very Mexican holiday of the Day of the Dead. But one reporter found reason for ridicule, noting that not many people had come to see the altar dedicated, except for the few well-coiffed suburban ladies who had built it. The article included the sort of gratuitous swipe at the United States that has become obligatory for much of the Mexican press. The reporter could barely contain her outrage that at a ceremony honoring the dead of New York and Washington, "no mention was made of the victims of American terrorism in the Middle East."

I was struck by a great, sad irony in the tangled mess of misstatements, misunderstandings, and miscues that constituted the Mexican public response to September 11. Mexicans, even those who have a fondness for the United States and think that they truly understand us, believe that the greatest difference between our two cultures is that those of us north of the border are hardheaded, sharp-elbowed, flinty, unsentimental. Those who live south of the border, on the other hand, are graced by Latin gentility, compassion, and sentimentality. Most Mexicans failed to understand that what we most wanted from them in our lowest moment was nothing more than expressions of solidarity and concern. All we needed was a gesture of sympathy. A traditional Mexican *abrazo*, a hug, would have sufficed. Confined and confused by their own complexes and political games, they were unable to deliver.

C
H
A
P
T
E
R

T
W
O

The Ambivalence

Just before President Fox arrived at the White House, and while Condoleezza Rice was fielding telephone calls about the Florida anthrax case, I joined President Bush, his chief advisers, and Secretary of State Colin Powell on the yellow chairs in front of the Oval Office fireplace. "Why do they hate us so?" someone asked ruefully, obviously jolted by the fumbling Mexican response to September 11. It fell to me, as ambassador to Mexico, to respond. I wanted to come up with a thoughtful response. Three or four pithy sentences with a profound thought or two, seasoned with a touch of irony and a dash of humor, would have been enough to impress the president of the United States with my brilliance. But I blew it. I hesitated. I stumbled. I mumbled until others, recognizing incompetence, cut in and the conversation degenerated into a buzz of pooled ignorance and prejudice.

Finally, Powell put an end to the chatter. "They don't hate us," he said firmly. "They resent us. It's different."

Powell was right. The initial question was misstated. It reflected Americans' general lack of understanding about Mexico and the cliché, often heard on both sides of the Rio Grande, that the Mexican attitude toward their northern neighbors is a volatile blend of love and hate. That notion is off the mark. Instead, there is a strong ambivalence, a combination of attraction and revulsion, fascination and fear. There is a sense of the United States as a source of both opportunity and threat.

Mexicans themselves are often confounded by the emotional swirl.

Carlos Monsiváis, a Mexican political analyst and thinker, put it this way in a piece entitled "Yankees Come Home" in the June 16, 2002 *El Universal*:

> For two centuries Mexico and the United States have lived in a con-flictive relationship, dramatic, tragic on occasion, extraordinarily unequal, marked by the distances between imperial arrogance and the "good neigh-bor policy." We frequently confuse myth with reality, but (American) racism, the rape of natural resources, and the insolence that demands sub-mission and unconditional support cannot be forgotten. But we cannot minimize the contributions of American culture, the growth of tolerance, cultural development and freedom of expression. The relationship between Mexico and the United States is at once oppressive and liberating.

Most Mexicans view the United States through the bifocal lens of opportunity and threat. They recoil from the threat of cultural inunda-tion, political domination, and economic manipulation. At the same time, they are intrigued by the possibilities of imbibing the freedom of a dynamic society, emulating a democratic political system, and taking advantage of economic opportunities provided by proximity to the world's largest market. Mexicans are convinced that immigrants are treated poor-ly in the United States, but everyone has a successful cousin living in his own house and driving a late-model car in Los Angeles or Chicago. Intellectuals sniff about the barbarism of American culture but could not bear to live without frequent trips to New York. And the same father who worries about the influence of video games and McDonald's will save all he can to teach his son English and pray that he attends an American university. Anyone who has lived in the shadow of an immensely suc-cessful and occasionally thoughtless or bullying older sibling can under-stand the Mexican resentment.

The ambivalence is revealed time and again in polling data. Two-thirds of Mexicans generally hold a good opinion of the United States. The favorable rating rises along with the respondents' education and income levels, contact with individual Americans, and proximity to the border. Mexicans most admire America's economic stability, high standard of liv-ing, and the quality of government service. Eight in ten see the United States as a land of opportunity where anyone can succeed with hard work. But a large percentage is also sensitive to perceived poor treatment of migrants and American discrimination and racism in general. Almost half believe that the influence of American popular culture on Mexico is beneficial. Almost half believe that it is negative. And so on.

But beyond public perception, there is history, and few countries live as close to their past as does Mexico. History does not disappear as it often does in the United States. Joan and I spent a fascinating evening in the home of one of the members of the large Moctezuma family, discussing the genealogical lineage that they can trace back to the Aztec ruler who had the misfortune to confront Cortés. Mexican history reviles him as an inept sell-out. It is his younger relative Cuauhtémoc who is revered as the tragic and brave fighter who unsuccessfully took on the Spanish conquerors. But for the Moctezuma clan, five hundred years ago is as yesterday, and they vigorously defended their family's reputation.

We also talked that night about the myths surrounding La Malinche, the Indian woman who served as Cortés's guide, translator, common-law wife, and mother of some of his children. Without her, Cortés would have been unable to communicate and probably incapable of recruiting the indigenous allies he needed to defeat the Aztecs. La Malinche was an essential part of the Conquest. Nothing so dramatizes the contrast between the Mexican view of Spanish conquest as a protracted rape and the American view of Europe civilizing the New World as the two countries' differing mythologies about their archetypal Indian women. Pocahontas and Sacagawea are heroines. La Malinche is a victim at best, a traitorous slut at worst. As Octavio Paz noted, when the founding mother of the nation is seen as a whore, the psychological implications for her descendants are profound.

The durability of historical myth in Mexico is truly impressive. And, of course, when it comes to the role of the United States in Mexican history there are sufficient facts to stir strong feelings. Some of the earliest trouble began with Joel Poinsett, the first American diplomat to arrive after Mexico won its independence in 1821. He is generally unremembered in his own country except for his name, which he gave to the scarlet Christmas flower he brought home from Mexico. But in Mexico he remains infamous for his machinations, supporting one group of Freemasons against another in the battle for post-Spanish power. In that view, Poinsett established a pattern of interventionism that two decades later produced the American invasion of 1846 that cost the fledgling nation forty percent of its territory.

Few historians in either country portray that war as anything but a land-grab in which the United States seized California, Texas, the Southwest, and land as far north as Colorado. But while American textbooks generally give scant attention to the sordid but successful adventure, for Mexico it remains a national trauma. American meddling during Mexico's early-twentieth-century revolutionary struggles, along with its military interventions before and during World War I when Mexico was consumed in chaos, serve as further examples of American perfidy. No Mexican child goes through a year of school without reminders of the heroism of his ancestors in the face of American aggression. The young cadets who supposedly committed suicide rather than surrender while defending the Castle of Chapultepec against the army of Winfield Scott in 1847 are among the most revered national heroes. It is as if Mexico's version of Masada occurred yesterday.

The United States invaded Mexico twice in the twentieth century. In 1914, Marines landed at Veracruz on orders from President Woodrow Wilson, who took sides in the power struggle that followed the assassination of President Francisco Madero. Two years later, General John "Blackjack" Pershing chased the elusive Pancho Villa through the wild mountains and deserts of Chihuahua. However, once Mexico settled down in the 1920s after the bloodletting of the revolution, the United States generally kept its meddling to a minimum. The two countries arranged what scholars Jorge Domínguez and Rafael Fernández de Castro have called a "bargained negligence," a tacit agreement that the United States would not interfere as long as Mexico kept its house in order. After World War II, the United States also made it clear that it did not want Mexico to serve as a base for communist subversion in the hemisphere.

Although the United States has not invaded Mexico for almost a century, we have often acted in a dismissive or aggressive fashion. We have been unwilling to listen to Mexican concerns or so convinced of our rectitude that we have made overly harsh judgments. The mere act of judging, as in, for example, the notorious certification process in which we determined which countries came up to snuff in their antinarcotics effort, was profoundly insulting to such a prideful nation. It bred bitterness and resentment.

Enrique Canales, a sensible commentator based in Monterrey, was surprised to encounter so many well-educated Mexicans who took a certain satisfaction from the September 11 attacks. The Mexican schadenfreude came not from the grim sights of American suffering and death, but rather from seeing the mighty struck down. Canales identified four powerful emotional currents that flowed together to produce the unsympathetic response: bitterness over past confrontations with the United States; rejection of the crassness of American society; anxiety about the unrestrained use of American power around the world; and simple envy.

While such analysis is useful, it is incomplete because it omits an important point. There is no denying that America's historical mistreatment of Mexico is fact, but why is Mexican resentment so durable? Why do other countries that have been traditional enemies of each other—for example, Germany and France—been able to establish new, healthy, almost ahistorical relationships? Why do other countries that have also suffered at our hands—with cause or without—seem to have been able to move on with their national existence and build less conflicted relations with the United States? Why have other people who may be equally appalled by our excesses as a government or a society been better able to put those attitudes aside? Certainly, geography has played a role in the enduring resentment. It is hard to live so close to the actor responsible for one's greatest humiliation. But the answer is to be found not so much in the historical record or in geography as in the political use of the past. The political elite that created modern Mexico in the twentieth century conscientiously maintained and fed the image of the beast of American aggression. Most truly believed it. But more important than their convictions was their calculated understanding of the political utility of nationalist resentment.

One of the great achievements of the twentieth century in the Western Hemisphere was the creation of a politically stable, economically advancing Mexico. While the rest of Latin America suffered through periods of coup and countercoup, political repression, and horrendous state-sponsored violence, Mexico passed its own postrevolutionary years in relative peace. There were several reasons for this, including the nonintrusive but nevertheless permanent presence of U.S. interest. But beyond all else, credit for Mexico's growth and stability must be given to the PRI for its creation and maintenance of a political system backed by a nationalist mythology that served the nation well. This was not a foreordained outcome. Mexico is a land of profound divisions.

There is great wealth and abysmal poverty. There are strong regional differences. There is a wide ethnic divide between the majority mestizo population and the indigenous communities—both of which are separated in a myriad of ways from the small class who control the economy from behind the barrier of their heavily European heritage. The political panorama has all the makings for disruption, but Mexico did not head in that direction. Today, when the PRI is better known for its failings, the corruption of many of its leaders, and the arthritis of much of its thinking, it is all too easy to discount the pivotal role the party played in Mexico's development. In now much-quoted words, the Peruvian novelist Mario Vargas Llosa told a Mexico City conference in 1990 that the PRI had created "the perfect dictatorship." The PRI was repressive when necessary, but mostly benign; corrupt but with enough skill to promote the welfare of the many; autocratic but with a structure that allowed for new blood; and, though narrowly ideological, sufficiently dexterous to co-opt intellectuals.

Central to the PRI's hold on power was its establishment of a national mythology and ethos. This wasn't just a political act. The construct also grew organically from the work of intellectuals and the collective yearnings of the Mexican people to have a firm sense of national identity. Elements of the national self-conception include a celebration of the glories of pre-Hispanic civilizations, condemnation of Spanish exploitation of the Indians, and exaltation of the new race—la raza—formed by the mixing of the two civilizations. Other essential ingredients have been a fierce anticlericalism, toned down in recent years; ritualistic invocations of the Mexican Revolution and its icons, notably Zapata; and a fervent patriotism centered on the defense of national sovereignty and integrity.

The emphasis of the PRI governments on sovereignty, and their success in identifying the party as crucial to the defense of the nation, have made it difficult for the Mexican people to move beyond the legitimate grievances of the past when dealing with the United States. The PRI developed an ideology that blurred the lines dividing the concepts of party, state, nation, and people. The only political force that could be entrusted with the defense of all that was Mexican was the PRI itself.

It was never really necessary to ask, "Defense against whom?" The answer was obvious. For generations Mexican textbooks have been filled with patriotic calls to defend the nation from the interventionism of for-eigners. Every schoolchild within Mexico City's environs visits the Museum of Interventions, where displays recount multiple foreign attacks, including the Spanish conquest and two French invasions. But the bulk of the displays recount the multiple sins of the United States. As a result, Mexicans have a deep-seated conviction that they must remain vigilant against foreigners who are determined to defile their fatherland. When President Ernesto Zedillo attempted in the mid-1990s to have schoolbooks revised in order to reflect modern cooperation as well as his-toric confrontations, he was vilified as a traitor and had to give up.

A few Mexicans have dissented from the carefully crafted mythology. Octavio Paz, Mexico's Nobel laureate for literature, was one of the first to punch holes in the doctrine. He rejected the PRI's claim to be the legiti-mate heir of the Aztec empire and therefore to be justified in its auto-cratic mode of governing. Paz further argued that the bloodthirsty and imperious Aztecs were among the least laudable of the pre-Hispanic civi-lizations. He said the PRI's Aztec fixation did disservice to the Maya, Zapotec, Toltecs, and others that he believed had contributed far more to the growth of Mexican culture.

Even as other elements of the PRI's mythology started to collapse, Mexicans continued to accept reflexively the idea of a continuing exter-nal threat from the north. One morning a group of intellectuals came to the embassy residence for a talk by a scholar from a U.S. think tank. One attendee was an intense woman who presented me with her latest work—a refutation of that portion of the national myth that holds that Mexico is a country without racism. After documenting widespread discrimina-tion against indigenous Mexicans, she argued passionately that Mexico had to demythologize its past in order to understand its present and con-struct its future. I could not have agreed more. I suggested that she might also want to try to demythologize the U.S.-Mexican relationship, strip-ping away the myths of aggression and subjugation to reveal the essen-tially nonthreatening nature of the modern north. "Oh no!" she blurted out, still committed to traditional stereotypes. "All that is true!"

The ingrained suspicion of the United States became a double-edged sword for successive Mexican governments. Reality dictated that the two countries cooperate, and with NAFTA the trends are clearly toward greater integration. But for generations the most effective epithet that could be leveled at a Mexican politician or civil servant has been to call him or her "pro-American." The term carries a string of crippling connotations, branding the target as a sell-out, a loyal son or daughter of Malinche, the first turncoat. The straightjacket that is created by this is very similar to an American politician's paralyzing Cold War fear of being labeled "soft on communism." It distorts the relationship and causes enormous headaches for diplomats of both countries.

This is not to argue that corresponding complexes do not exist on the American side. There, especially in Washington, a lack of faith in Mexico's ability to deal straightforwardly with the United States frequently spins into a formulaic distrust that can damage the relationship. Ingrained prejudices and unthinking biases about Mexico's poverty, corruption, and culture color American thinking. And Mexico's hurt perception of this negativism serves to increase its own defensiveness. Those in both countries who want to work together, who understand that we cannot confront the problems we jointly face without close cooperation, are often torn between the desire to trust and the experience of disappointment. Heavy psychological baggage weighs down both sides.

Sometimes, as in the aftermath of September 11, the Mexican ritualistic anti-gringoism goes too far. Jorge Castañeda's blunt statement of support for the United States reflected his conviction that Mexico must transcend the old hostility in order to develop political, cultural, and economic ties that benefit both countries. But Castañeda's straight talk generated a backlash so shrill and ugly that President Fox had to come to Washington. Less than a month after his euphoric state visit that promised new commitments to cooperation and goodwill, Fox had to repair the damage inflicted by old grudges and lingering hostilities.

There is a personal footnote to the Fox White House visit that made me thankful once again to be stationed away from Washington. After Fox and his team left, Ari Fleischer, the President's spokesman, took me and Ambassador John Maisto, Condoleezza Rice's principal Latin American expert, aside. He cautioned us not to reveal what we had overheard about the Florida anthrax case. It was a totally unnecessary warning from a self-important public relations man to a pair of old-timers who had been in public service since he was a toddler. It reminded me once again why career professionals hold many political appointees in low esteem. It made me eager to get back to Mexico City.

White House to Casablanca

It was another encounter at the White House almost four years before President Fox's post-September 11 visit that put me on the road to Mexico. I was hanging around the small takeout counter in the West Wing's mess looking for someone to buy me a cup of coffee when Sandy Berger, President Clinton's National Security Advisor, came into view. Usually, I am not much of a mendicant. But since ability to purchase anything in the mess is limited to White House staff and their guests, I needed to latch on to someone. Berger took pity on me.

By that time I was fairly familiar with the White House. As head of the State Department's Bureau of Latin America, I was supervising our embassies in the region and spent a good deal of time at White House meetings. Latin America had been the focus of much of my thirty years in the Foreign Service. I had gone to Guatemala as a junior officer in 1970, arriving shortly after leftist rebels assassinated our ambassador. I served in Chile when the military overthrew President Salvador Allende. I had been posted twice to Venezuela, where I was ambassador from 1993 to 1996, before being called back to Washington to take on the job of assistant secretary for Inter-American Affairs.

Berger was a fine manager who provided adult supervision not only to the National Security Council but also to the horde of very young and bright Clinton staffers who swarmed through the White House. They often left me breathless with their glib assertions that domestic politics and spin must trump all other concerns. At one 1996 meeting in the Situation Room, the cramped space in the White House basement that has seen more than its share of high drama, one of the youngsters said that President Clinton should navigate through his upcoming trip to Mexico without mentioning NAFTA. He insisted the topic should be taboo because polls showed that the trade agreement was unpopular with American voters. I could not restrain myself from laughing out loud at the absurdity of the notion. Congressional passage of NAFTA after a long, dramatic battle for public opinion and Hill votes had been one of Clinton's most sterling first-term victories. NAFTA had altered, fundamentally and forever, our relationship with Mexico. Mexicans would be flabbergasted if he avoided the topic. Berger, a wise and patient man, let the conversation steam on for a few minutes. Then he looked up over the rims of his glasses and gently slapped down that particular bit of youthful amateurism.

During our 1997 encounter at the White House mess, Berger asked if I would be willing to go to Mexico as ambassador. Until that time, the Clinton administration had been intent on naming a political appointee to the post, which had been vacant for many months. Appointees from outside the Foreign Service head about one-third of America's embassies. Occasionally they have particular knowledge—stemming from academic, commercial, or philanthropic experience—of the country to which they are sent. But more often than not, they are politicians, campaign contributors, or fund-raisers who have helped the president reach the White House. They get their jobs through old-fashioned political patronage or because the president feels that their nomination would serve a particular political interest.

Some of the noncareer ambassadors to Mexico and other countries had performed exceptionally well. Others had failed because they didn't know the country, couldn't speak its language, or were ignorant of international affairs. Mexicans were puzzled that a relationship that was so obviously important would on occasion be turned over to people with no relevant experience or skills.

Jim Jones, an affable and effective former Oklahoma congressman, was one of the noncareer ambassadors who had performed well in Mexico City. Jones took the job in 1993 and helped forge support for NAFTA in the United States and business ties between the two countries. By late

1996, Jones had made it clear to Washington that he wanted to step down. But the White House prevailed upon him to stay on until after President Clinton's mid-1997 trip to Mexico. He waited for the visit and then resigned. But even after he had left the post, the Clinton administration continued to dawdle about naming a successor, although it knew that the process, including lengthy vetting and Senate approval, could take up to a year. By failing to focus on the issue of Jones's successor the administration guaranteed that there would be a long gap between ambassadors. Periodically, Secretary of State Albright would push the White House to decide and Berger would help, but the decision was in the hands of the domestic political advisors and they moved at their own, at times unfathomable, pace with little regard for foreign policy implications of their action or inaction.

Two months after his trip to Mexico, President Clinton decided to nominate William Weld, former governor of Massachusetts, to the post. Weld had resigned the governorship in 1996 to run for the Senate against incumbent John Kerry and lost. He was an attractive liberal Republican with an interest in Mexico and had been an important advocate of NAFTA.

As soon as the pending Weld nomination was leaked to the press, it was shot down by Senator Jesse Helms, the conservative Republican chairman of the Senate Foreign Relations Committee. Helms would not even give Weld a hearing.

As always, rumors swirled in Washington. Did Weld really want the job? Why hadn't the White House consulted with Helms before moving ahead? Was the president using Weld as a pawn in his efforts to paint the Republicans as obstructionists? The affair was bizarre even by capital standards. Knowing a little bit about all the players, including the immensely likable Weld, my guess was that Clinton really wanted him to go to Mexico and that he wanted the job. It seemed to me that Helms was not so much alarmed by the former governor's allegedly soft position on illegal drugs—the ostensible cause for his opposition—but angry because Weld had said during his unsuccessful Senate campaign that if he were elected, he might not vote for Helms to continue as chairman of the Foreign Relations Committee. That bit of electioneering for the benefit of Massachusetts's liberal electorate did not help him beat John Kerry. But it did seal his fate on Mexico.

For a few weeks, the Weld-Helms face-off was front-page news. Weld enjoyed being at the center of a major story, but ultimately he recognized reality and withdrew his name from consideration. But the White House did not give up easily on the goal of finding another noncareer candidate. The embassy in Mexico is considered a plum posting. One of our largest embassies, it comes with a beautiful home, opportunities for extensive travel, and an interesting political environment. Moreover it is close enough to the United States for quick trips back home.

When President Ernesto Zedillo visited Washington for a state visit in early November 1997, President Clinton dropped the name of an ex-mayor of a major Texas city in conversation, without specifically mentioning the embassy. Zedillo offered no reaction to the name and soon a White House emissary was on the way to make the formal offer.

But the elderly ex-mayor wanted answers to two big questions that revealed how unsuited he would be for the position. Would he have to involve himself in the fight against narcotics, and did the job involve much night work? It soon became apparent that he was less interested in becoming Mr. Ambassador than his wife was in becoming Madam Ambassador. As the search dragged on, even the White House became embarrassed by the long delay in getting an ambassador to Mexico. The White House does not embarrass easily. Finally, they threw in the towel and asked for the State Department to send over some names of career officials. Secretary Albright, Berger, Mack McLarty, who was the president's special envoy to Latin America, and others let it be known that the republic would probably survive my nomination.

A quick informal vetting on the Hill revealed that Helms was not interested in making more trouble about Mexico, and no other senators were intent on blocking my nomination. Still, there were a couple of protests before my confirmation hearing. A two-man left-wing think tank angry about everything since the Monroe Doctrine branded me "an incompetent mediocrity." I thought the criticism might have some merit, but it didn't get much attention in the Senate. A group of conservative House Republicans, or more precisely their staffers, wrote a letter to the Senate complaining about my unwillingness as assistant secretary for Latin America to approve the transfer of $36 million worth of advanced helicopters to Colombia's antidrug efforts. As the House was not prepared to provide additional funding and the money would have had to come from other, already underfunded, programs, the Senators paid scant attention to the House staffers' bleat.

My confirmation hearing in May 1998 was a relaxed affair. These events are rarely as dramatic as television dramas portray them to be. They are not statesmanlike searches for the truth. Rather they are opportunities for senators to score some political points about the issue at hand. The greatest mistake an executive branch witness can make when appearing at a hearing, confirmation or otherwise, is to see the event as an opportunity to educate the members. Congress cannot be educated when the press is watching. Only two senators, Chris Dodd of Connecticut and Paul Coverdell of Georgia, showed up to throw a few softball questions. A combination of obsequiousness and humor carried me through the relatively brief hearing.

By the time I reached Mexico in late July, the ambassador's office had been vacant for more than a year. The embassy had been well managed by chargé d'affaires Charles Brayshaw, the embassy's second-in-command and an experienced Latin Americanist. But that did not matter to the ever-agitated, conspiratorially minded Mexican press. It published article after editorial asserting that, at the very least, the absence of an ambassador had been an insult to Mexico or, more likely, a calculated effort on the part of the Clinton administration to express disfavor. This was one occasion where truth was no defense. The facts pointed directly to White House incompetence in delaying a nomination for so long after Jones had said he was leaving, in naming Weld without the sufficient political legwork, and in fiddling away months looking for another politician to reward. But with an acumen born of years of government service, I decided it best not to use the ineptitude defense. I simply said, in a self-serving way, that the president wanted to make sure he chose the right person for the difficult job.

The Mexican press published the requisite welcoming articles, reminding readers of the long tradition of nefarious interventionism by U.S. ambassadors. The first envoy, Joel Poinsett was dragged from his comfortable perch on florist shelves. He was coupled with the most notorious and hated ambassador of all—Henry Lane Wilson—to stir old fears and caution the young. Wilson had been William Howard Taft's ambassador in 1911 when Dictator Porfirio Díaz escaped the country in the face of a growing popular uprising. His departure ushered in the ten-year civil war that Mexico refers to as its Revolution. Initially understanding of the motives for Díaz's overthrow, the American ambassador became increasingly upset by the bumbling performance of Francisco Madero, who succeeded Díaz. Though Madero had been a heroic revolutionary, he was an incompetent president. Ambassador Wilson also saw him as hostile to corporate interests. He helped plot a coup that overthrew Madero and put him behind bars. When Mrs. Madero dramatically came to the ambassador's residence to appeal for help in getting her imprisoned husband out of the country, Wilson was unsympathetic and unhelpful. Madero and his vice president were taken from their prison cells and cold-bloodedly assassinated. Henry Lane Wilson remains one of Mexico's arch-villains. In the eyes of many Mexican editorialists, the blood of his crime still stains the street. He was my most famous predecessor, and still seen as the archetypal ambassador—sinister, manipulative, and arrogant.

While that ninety-year-old history remained fresh in Mexican minds, a series of much more recent events had poisoned the air when I arrived in Mexico City. A *Los Angeles Times* editorial observed that I faced a road "peppered with landmines." One of them involved Mexican reaction to a fairly innocuous comment a month earlier by Secretary Albright at a Senate hearing. Responding to concerns about the unresolved conflict in Chiapas, Albright said the United States was "pressing" the Mexican government to settle the situation peacefully. She should have used the softer and more accurate "encouraging." But the Mexican press twisted her words to read that she had demanded action, forcing Foreign Secretary Rosario Green to issue a ritualistic defense asserting Mexico's proud resistance to any kind of foreign interference.

More poisonous to the bilateral atmosphere were the lingering effects of an undercover U.S. anti–money-laundering operation called Casablanca, named after a fictitious casino. That operation generated a major diplomatic flap that the press seized on and would not let go.

The evolution of Casablanca revealed much about the intense suspicion and double-dealing among law enforcement agencies on both sides of the border. The U.S. Customs Service, locked in a bitter rivalry with the Drug Enforcement Agency, had the lead in the undercover investigation, which began in 1995 and exploded into public view shortly before my arrival. Customs belonged to the very large law enforcement wing of the Treasury Department, but its police ethos and law enforcement culture generally kept it off the radar screen of the secretary of treasury. In the Clinton administration, Secretary Robert Rubin had his hands full managing the economy and negotiating at stratospheric international levels. Meanwhile, his Customs Service was playing dangerous games in Mexico.

Customs learned in 1995 that the Colombian Cali cartel was using the branches of several Mexican and Venezuelan banks to launder drug proceeds. The agency decided to mount a sting operation, sending undercover agents to meet with the bankers and set up a scheme to wash funds. In postmortems of the operation, Customs contended that it had briefed Mexican Attorney General Antonio Lozano and asked for his cooperation. Lozano apparently never responded, so Customs took his silence as tacit approval. When the undercover agents arranged a meeting at a restaurant, the bankers showed up with local agents of the Attorney General's office. The bankers introduced them as providers of physical and political security for their money-laundering operations.

At that point, the disgusted Customs team decided to provide no further information to Lozano. While not passing judgment on Lozano's personal honesty, they were convinced his agency was riddled with corruption that could torpedo the operation. So the sting continued quietly for three years, as a unilateral U.S. operation in Mexican territory with no involvement of the Mexican government.

During those three years, Lozano was replaced as attorney general by Jorge Madrazo, who was widely regarded as an honorable man with little prosecutorial experience. An academic, he had been most recently the head of the government's Human Rights Commission. Since his appointment, Madrazo had established excellent relations with two key Washington players, Attorney General Janet Reno and retired General Barry McCaffrey, head of the Office of National Drug Control Policy. His relationship with Reno would become complicated in the Casablanca aftermath because Customs had brought the Drug Enforcement Administration into the unfolding investigation. While the DEA was ostensibly under Reno's control, it was actually run with cowboy autonomy by its director, Tom Constantine. It was unclear how extensively Constantine had briefed Reno on Casablanca.

On May 18, 1998, Casablanca leaped into worldwide headlines as Reno and Rubin announced its results. Over the previous month, twelve

Mexican and Venezuelan bankers and forty-three other conspirators had been arrested in San Diego, Chicago, New York, Los Angeles, and Las Vegas. The entire multiyear operation had resulted in the arrests of 112 individuals and the seizure of approximately $103 million, two tons of cocaine, and four tons of marijuana. Forty-two fugitives, including seven bank managers, remained at large. The decision to have two cabinet secretaries take Casablanca public in such a dramatic way was a matter of domestic and bureaucratic politics. It assured the American public that its government was hard at work fighting the drug menace. It also encouraged and validated the commitment of many Customs and DEA agents.

But the Casablanca operation nearly killed the very weak patient of U.S.-Mexico antinarcotics cooperation that Madrazo, Reno, and McCaffrey had nurtured. The Mexican government had been caught flat-footed. The success of a meticulously planned operation was undermined by a careless and unnecessary insult to the Zedillo administration. If Attorney General Madrazo had been brought into the picture even a few days before the announcement, and if he had had the opportunity to brief President Zedillo, the Mexicans could have developed a public line claiming partial credit for the operation. It would have constituted a ruse of sorts, but would have been infinitely preferable to being made to look untrustworthy before their own public.

Immediately, the Mexican press and political class began decrying the unilateral covert action that, by definition, had broken Mexican law. The U.S. agents, the press charged, had violated the country's sovereignty by engaging in illegal financial transactions. Even more violent was the response of the Mexican banking sector. Though no high-ranking official was ever implicated, the potential loss in prestige and share values and the risks of possible civil and criminal penalties in the United States were enormous. Several banks, including the largest, were in danger of losing their U.S. branches or agencies. It was a dire situation, and the reaction was intense. In the Mexican view, American interventionism had raised its ugly head once again. To American law enforcement officials, it was a good operation that once again pointed up Mexican corruption and inefficiency.

Secretary of State Albright was also caught unaware. She made this fact abundantly clear to me, her hapless assistant secretary for Latin

America. She may have suspected that I was spending entirely too much time preparing for my departure to the embassy in Mexico. She had to field the phone calls from Foreign Secretary Rosario Green, who had been ordered by a thoroughly piqued President Zedillo to spare no bleat in protesting Casablanca. The affair highlighted a reality of American foreign policy. While the secretary of state is charged with the conduct of our international relations, dozens of other governmental entities operate overseas, often with little or no coordination with the Department of State. It frequently falls to the secretary of state to push the broom behind the other agencies' elephant parades. For Albright, Casablanca was one hell of a parade.

Albright protested to Reno and Rubin on the phone and in writing. She argued with some passion that their agents' tactics and the cabinet members' public ballyhooing had jeopardized the cooperation we would need for future success. Reno got the message. But Rubin remained defensive, noting that voices on the Hill, including Republic Majority Leader Trent Lott, had already rejected President Zedillo's criticism of the operation. Rubin was, of course, defending his own bureaucracy. But his palpable belief in the essential corruption of the Mexican law and order apparatus justified for him the unilateral operation. "They're all corrupt," he told me when I met with him a few days before departing Washington. Several years later, once out of government, Rubin would guide the giant Citibank into paying $12.5 billion for one of the Mexican banks caught in the sting operation, though I doubt his views on the rectitude of Mexican law enforcement or banking regulators had changed dramatically.

I had been helping to manage the Casablanca fallout in Washington and knew what to expect upon arrival in Mexico. It was topic number one for the Mexican press. At an airport press conference I used the fact that I had not yet presented my credentials to President Zedillo as my reason not to comment on topics that I would not have commented on in any event. A few days later, as I presented the credentials, I lost that particular excuse for ducking the press.

Among their many gifts, the Mexicans do public events superbly. The Mexican ceremony to welcome me involved school children waving the U.S. and Mexican flags and tremendous pomp in the National Palace. Other newly arrived ambassadors presented their credentials to President

Zedillo on the same day and received the same treatment, but naturally it was the American ambassador who got the heavy press coverage. One sour note was the delight the photo editors took in using a photo of a smiling President Zedillo grabbing on to my arm. Though it was nothing more than a friendly gesture, the disparity in our heights made it look as if the towering new American ambassador was about to lift the president off the ground like a child—or better yet, like a puppet. The photo was accompanied in a half-dozen newspapers with a straight text. There was no need for interpretation. It was a warning that Mexico's president might be getting too close to this new heavyweight representative of the colossus of the north.

In the following days, I met extensively with reporters and editors. I would continue to do so over the next four years. I never saw much profit in stiffing them. They always had the last word. "Never pick fights with people who buy ink by the barrel" is a well-worn Washington cliché, no less true for being overused. The questions would remain essentially unchanged for my entire tenure. In essence they were variations on the theme of "How are you planning to violate our sovereignty today, Mr. Ambassador?"

Once the rules are understood, dealing with the Mexican press is a relatively easy game to play, but success is permanently elusive. My response to almost any question was to underscore the excellent relations between the two countries, assure the questioner that whatever temporary problem we might be confronting could be resolved by harmonic intercourse, and exalt the high level of cooperation in the battle against the scourge of the day (usually narcotics). I also emphasized the that United States sought no role in the internal affairs of Mexico, and that I recognized our neighbor's sovereign right to choose its leaders, find peace in Chiapas, and trade with whomever it chose.

I learned a few tricks with the press. I could generally score a headline with any statement praising Mexico. On the other hand, any comment that could be turned into criticism of the United States was rapidly hijacked. For example, I answered a question about corruption in Mexico by noting that corruption is a threat in all societies including the United States. I added that nations differ in how they attack the problem, with some responding more diligently than others. The headlines screamed, "Davidow acknowledges corruption in the United States." Even the most carefully phrased responses frequently fell victim to misquotes and purposeful reportorial distortions. I was a target for malicious reporters, hostile editors, and editorial cartoonists who greeted the advent of a 6'6" overweight gringo ambassador as a gift equal to a lifetime's supply of free crayons.

And, of course, I was not always perfectly careful. Sometimes I was too glib, too tired, too angry or inattentive to those around me. I paid the price for my lack of caution when I attended the massive celebration of Mexico's fight for independence. The grito commemorating Miguel Hidalgo's 1810 exhortation to overthrow the Spaniards culminates with a midnight appearance by the President of Mexico on the balcony of the National Palace. As I listened to President Zedillo lead the revelers in a series of rapid "Vivas!"—for Mexico, democracy, and freedom—I turned to another diplomat and said it appeared to be the president's most successful speech of the year. A sniveling piece of a reporter overheard me and ignored my insistence that it was an off-the-record joke. He made much of it the following day, finding me guilty of disrespecting the president, Mexico, the War of Independence, and every other national icon. A commentator in the leftist journal *La Jornada* weighed in with this bit of pitiful nonsense: "Maybe good manners have disappeared in the United States since the Lewinsky scandal, because Ambassador Davidow demonstrated here in the National Palace of a country in crisis the lack of respect that the U.S. gives a traditional speech by the weak president of a subordinate nation." I was wrong to be careless. But I still think that when a politician can get a quarter of million people cheering with twenty-five words he is having his best day of the year.

The Flower Wars

Rosario Green and Madeleine Albright belonged to an exclusive sorority of female foreign ministers. Before joining that club, they had served together at the United Nations, where Albright, as U.S. ambassador, had begun periodic just-girls meetings with the handful of other women ambassadors and some UN female officials including Green. Madeleine, Rosario, and the others would gather to dine, compare notes, and complain about their male colleagues. They also met on several occasions as foreign ministers. They had radically different views about many international issues, but they felt a kinship as women who had made it to the top. Once the formal business was done, they would kick out everyone else, take off their always-too-tight high-heeled shoes, and compare notes about the difficulties of life in the male-dominated world they had successfully entered.

Green probably had much to complain about. For all of the sophistication and worldliness of Mexican officials, sexism remained rampant. Green had once been groped under the cabinet table. She also said her principal male aide in the foreign ministry accused her of hormonal mood swings. My modern American mind could not give credence to this account of unabashed political incorrectness. But later I asked the person in question, and he blithely confirmed the story.

Green was a faithful representative of the old school of Mexican diplomacy in the Secretariat of Foreign Relations (SRE). Like all foreign ministries, the SRE used the tools of diplomacy to defend the nation's interest. For Mexico, those tools included a theatrical hypersensitivity to any intimation of U.S. interventionism or unilateralism, and a constant search for ways to differentiate Mexico from the United States in the international arena. Nothing so riles a Mexican diplomat as the charge that he or she appears to have more in common with the United States than with the rest of Latin America.

The SRE's determination to avoid the American client tag responded to domestic political imperatives with deep historical roots. After the upheaval that gave birth to the PRI, the Party of the Institutional Revolution became less revolutionary and more institutional. It turned away from many of the social-justice aspirations of its founders. Indeed, by century's end the revolution that formed the nation and gave the party its middle name had been replaced by a pragmatic, modern, not yet fully democratic but essentially liberal, capitalist society. But that evolution was accompanied by a growing need of the government to reaffirm its patriotic ardor in rhetoric and symbolism. President Zedillo ordered that enormous flags be flown throughout the country. They were especially powerful at the U.S. borders, where their presence, legitimate to be sure, presented a certain in-your-face attitude to anyone looking southward.

The government's acute nationalism and its corresponding determination to avoid any appearance of dependence on the United States often made the simplest of contacts difficult. When floods ravaged the state of Tabasco in 1999, Washington offered a $500,000 cash contribution. Simple enough, I thought. But I couldn't give the money away. To avoid the appearance of accepting charity, the Mexican government insisted that all aid be passed through the Mexican Red Cross. Our experience with that organization had been unsatisfactory, however. I had previously had to ask for the return of $300,000 that we had donated and that the Red Cross could not adequately account for. I finally worked out an arrangement with the president's chief of staff, Liébano Sáenz, to donate the $500,000 to Mexico's social security system for hospital reconstruction in Tabasco. But the story did not end there.

On a trip to Tabasco, Zedillo was criticized for his government's slow response to the disaster. As he waded through mud up to his knees trying to demonstrate his concern for his people, a young woman in the crowd shouted at him, "Ask the Americans to help us!" His reflexive Mexican response was to reject any American contribution. Once publicly challenged to seek our help, Zedillo felt that he had no alternative but to say that Mexico did not need it. Otherwise he would appear weak or dependent. What should have been an easy expression of neighborly support turned into a complicated mess. We were not allowed to deliver the funds to help rebuild the hospitals.

That sad episode in Tabasco reminded me of William Bayard Hale, a U.S. envoy sent to Mexico during the revolution by Woodrow Wilson. He left the country in disgust, denouncing the Mexicans, who "with admirable skill, prevent their friends from helping them." Hale had wanted to bring the U.S. military into the civil war that followed the revolution. It seemed to me that our offer to help flood victims was a far cry from suggesting an invasion. But the tortured history between the two countries did not allow for distinctions.

Despite such errant assertions of sovereignty, at century's end leaders in both countries understood that we had to help each other. Otherwise, a difficult relationship could become unmanageable. There were individuals and political forces on both sides of the border who were anxious to seize upon any misstep or error to prove that cooperation was impossible or a calculating ruse. But by establishing fluid working relations the two governments were able to speak candidly, help each other to avoid problems, and find ways to work to mutual benefit.

In August 1999, for example, an American nun wanted to take three children from Chiapas to the United States for medical treatment. The children had been wounded in a massacre in the pro-Zapatista village of Acteal in December 1997. The circumstances of the violence were debatable, but the government of Mexico was concerned that the children would be used for propaganda purposes by American groups supporting the antigovernment rebels. The Ministry of Interior declined to issue passports for the children, saying that if the nun wanted to provide medical treatment, she should bring doctors to Mexico. It was a knee-jerk and cruel response. It was also foolish. If the children were taken to the United States, they might be a one-day story in the press of one city. But the hard line in Mexico City would guarantee heavy and hostile international coverage, with the kind of focus on Chiapas that the government wanted to avoid.

The situation called for a deft diplomat using subtle and skillful language. Unfortunately for the annals of diplomacy, the task fell to me. I was exasperated. Fortunately, I knew Deputy Foreign Secretary Juan Rebolledo well enough to be direct. I called and suggested that it did not take a lot of intelligence to realize that fighting with nuns about crippled children was not an approach that would win Mexico many friends. He understood that I was attempting to keep the Interior Ministry bureaucrats from damaging Mexico's international image and—not incidentally—from compounding the suffering of three innocent children. The children got their passports and went to the United States. A messy public relations disaster was avoided. Rebolledo returned the favor on numerous occasions, steering the U.S. government away from similarly misguided statements or actions, often with similarly blunt language.

In foreign affairs, and especially in Mexico's relations with the United States, the PRI was vulnerable to its own left wing, the political opposition, intellectuals, and the press. The political system offered no counterweight, no vocal pro-American party even among more conservative elements of the opposition. In fact, Fox's conservative National Action Party (PAN) was as likely to attack the PRI government for some alleged lack of backbone vis-à-vis the Americans as was the leftist Revolutionary Democratic Party. Therefore, the PRI government had to posture itself as unshakably anti-interventionist. Given the reality that economic, cultural, demographic, and political forces are drawing the two countries closer together, the Mexican stance would often approach schizophrenic levels.

Though often instinctual and knee-jerk, there was a well thought out strategy behind the Mexican position. In 1988, Jorge Castañeda, the young academic who a dozen years later was to become Vicente Fox's foreign secretary, explained that Mexico's nationalism provided a necessary defense. In a book he co-authored with Jimmy Carter's former Latin American advisor Robert Pastor entitled *Limits to Friendship*, he wrote that:

> There are solid grounds for believing that a foreign policy which is high profile and assertive, always nationalistic and often contrary to American interests, constitutes a sort of shield for Mexico. Only behind such a shield can the country proceed successfully with the delicate and exceedingly difficult balancing act it must carry out opening its windows to the world

without forsaking its national integrity or losing its national soul, and changing all that is secondary to preserve what is essential. Mexico would betray itself if it did not try to build and nurture this shield, for it may well have no other.

Through the years, successive foreign secretaries worked out unwritten rules and tacit understandings of just how far they could go before they poisoned the entire well of the bilateral relationship. Indeed, successive Mexican administrations adopted self-imposed limits to avoid certain kinds of confrontation. For instance, until the election of Vicente Fox in 2000, Mexico had served on the United Nations Security Council on only two occasions and without much enthusiasm. Avoidance of a larger role in the UN helped avert possible tiffs with the United States that could have evolved into bilateral crises. But the Mexican strategy of friction without real confrontation did not apply to all situations. At times the two countries were at daggers drawn, notably in the 1980s when the Mexican Foreign Ministry actively undermined Ronald Reagan's Central American policies.

Just as the U.S. Department of State is called Foggy Bottom after the marshland that originally occupied its location, the SRE is commonly referred to as Tlatelolco for the pre-Hispanic part of the city in which it is located. The location was not the SRE's only pre-Columbian vestige. Much in the way Mexico conducted its relations with the United States was reminiscent of how the Aztecs maintained their domination until the Spanish arrived.

Historians note that the Aztecs had an insatiable need for prisoners of war to be used as tribute in their sacrificial ceremonies. But war was costly and time-consuming. Once they consolidated their power, they arranged with other states to provide the necessary manpower for sacrifice through a technique known as the Flower Wars. Armies were mobilized and battles staged, but all was arranged in advance to guarantee prisoners for the Aztecs in return for an Aztec pledge not to wipe out the other side. Historians differ on the origin of the term Flower Wars, but one version asserts that the leaders of the opposing states would be secretly brought to the battle sight and concealed behind a screen of flowers where they could watch their own soldiers fight and be captured by the superior Aztec armies. The defeated rulers would then return home, no worse for wear.

Foreign Secretary Green had a deep background in the ethos of the SRE. Moreover, as a woman she was especially committed never to be seen as weak, particularly in the face of real or perceived U.S. aggression or intervention. She gyrated between a confrontational rhetorical style and a more subdued private approach that recognized the need for the two countries to cooperate. She understood the basic nature of the war of the flowers but was frequently not skillful in its execution. Occasionally she inflated issues that could have been dealt with quietly. Sometimes, as with the Casablanca mess, she let a dispute drag on for too long.

Green might have felt compelled to present herself as tough in order to establish her credentials within her own government. She had replaced a dynamic foreign minister who remained very visible in the Mexican government as secretary of finance. For most of President Zedillo's six-year term, his foreign secretary was José Ángel Gurría, who was known to everyone as Ángel. Politically ambitious, competent, and supremely self-confident, Ángel was great fun to watch in action. As assistant secretary, I attended a number of meetings between him and, first, Secretary of State Warren Christopher, and then, Madeleine Albright. Christopher, a taciturn man of immense intelligence and civility, would rarely get to say more than hello before Gurría would open his briefing book and launch into a detailed recitation of his talking points. The allotted hour for the meeting would be nearly over before Christopher would have an opportunity to say but a few words. He made his points clearly and briefly and then would amiably bid Ángel farewell.

I suspected that Christopher really did not mind. He was a calm man by nature, and there was something almost restful about going on autopilot and letting Ángel do all the talking. But Madeleine Albright was another story. She was not about to allow a man to dominate the conversation. Her meetings with Gurría were always more of a debate, a contest for control of the playing field. I found them pretty amusing.

Adding to Secretary Green's problems was the fact that President Zedillo did not trust the SRE. No less a nationalist than Green, Zedillo was concerned that the old-thinkers in the Foreign Ministry could go too far in their flights of instinctive anti-American rhetoric. He insisted that his own man, Juan Rebolledo, who was not a foreign affairs professional, serve as Green's deputy and take day-to-day charge of the relationship with the United States. Rebolledo, a strong PRI-ista who had been one of President Salinas's assistants, maintained a direct line to Zedillo's political advisor José Luis Barros. Green repeatedly asked Zedillo to fire Rebolledo, frequently over some alleged transgression involving excessive cooperation with the United States or its ambassador. But Zedillo refused. Relations with the United States were, in his view, too important to be left solely to the professionals of the SRE.

Cooperation between the embassy and the Foreign Ministry was essential to both countries. There are probably few governments in the world with which the United States conducts more business. Given the historical baggage, and the ideological and political complications, it is striking how much gets done. Throughout the Zedillo administration, the two governments improved cooperation in almost all areas of the relationship: border security, law enforcement, narcotics eradication, environmental protection, labor, cultural and educational exchange, science and technology, agriculture, water management, customs, transportation, health, fisheries, tourism, and energy—to name only a few. We arranged new programs, agreements, understandings, and treaties, and we generally broadened communications. Often it was not easy. Potential achievements were frequently thwarted by political hang-ups on one side or the other. But the relationship thickened, deepened, and matured.

Contact between individual ministries—say the Departments of Agriculture, Energy, and Transportation in Washington and their counterparts in Mexico City—was fluid and continual as they dealt with the inevitable issues of coordination between two nations so deeply intertwined. But the SRE was the supervisor of the entire Mexican side of the operation. It followed what the other ministries were doing, occasionally vetoing activities, but often unsnarling knots and clearing the way for cooperation. The SRE's supervisory and intermediary roles were particularly crucial in our relations with the Mexican military and law enforcement agencies. (The SRE's centrality in regard to security issues would change with the election of Fox. Castañeda made it clear from the outset that he wanted little to do with such matters.)

Frequently, it appeared to me that the SRE was acting irrationally, but I discovered that there was always a reason for their action or inaction. Usually it had to do with some internal government or PRI concern. Rather than telling the embassy that it would not be possible to take a certain action, the SRE often would temporize, obfuscate, or just refuse to communicate. Another common tactic was to agree in principle on a joint course of action, but to delay forever its implementation. The SRE appeared to be following directions that Mexico's last dictator, Porfirio Diaz, gave his staff: with the Americans, say yes, but never say when.

At the embassy we opted for a policy of open communication aimed at avoiding surprises like the lingering disaster of Casablanca. We wanted to keep the Mexican government informed. Otherwise, its reaction to any press insinuation of American misconduct would be Mexico's traditional default posture of rhetorical huff and puff, with quills at the ready. That would produce a cycle of heavy breathing and heated headlines that could complicate matters well beyond the issue at hand.

Beyond the daily interchange of information and gossip at the ambassadorial level, others in the embassy were similarly engaged. And of course the Mexican embassy in Washington was managing its contacts with the State Department and other U.S. agencies. Communication was usefully ample and served to build trust and cooperation on issues of mutual concern. In addition to the informal exchanges, the two countries had established a series of formal mechanisms for consultation. The annual Bi-National Commission meetings, which are held in Washington and Mexico City in alternating years, brought together up to twenty cabinet members for a day or two of discussion.

The commission meetings were useful to both countries. For one thing, the search for concrete results, called deliverables, would throw the respective bureaucracies into high gear for several weeks before the event. Under the pressure of a deadline, they often produced a new set of nuts and bolts that reinforced the scaffolding of the relationship. From university exchange programs to cooperation on medical research to new methods of information sharing among law enforcement agencies to a streamlined system for inspecting Mexican fruits and vegetables at the border, they developed dozens of ways for the two countries to work together more smoothly on a daily basis. The meetings also provided an opportunity for the cabinet ministers to engage in informal discussions that led quite naturally to a certain amount of bonding. There were some cabinet members on both sides who I could not imagine wanting to bond with. But for the most part, the out-of-session gatherings were worthwhile, comfortable, and the best part of the meetings.

Organizing the Bi-National Commission meetings required enormous logistical preparation. The visit of just one cabinet member can tie up embassy staff for weeks as they plan dozen of details: Where will the sec-retary stay—at the ambassador's residence or in a hotel? How big a secu-rity detail will accompany him and how will we mesh them with Mexican agents assigned to the secretary? How many events will there be? Who gets to sit next to the secretary at dinner? The plethora of details can be overwhelming. For a Bi-National Commission meeting, when a dozen cabinet members may show up, the planning becomes fre-netic. Fortunately, the embassy had sufficient resources to handle the onslaught. I was lucky to have two seasoned professionals—Chuck Brayshaw and later Jim Derham—as my seconds-in-command. I left the planning to them, and they never let me down.

Mexico hosted the Commission meeting in June of 1999. It went off about as well as could have been expected, despite the fact that Madeleine Albright, piqued by Mexican criticism of U.S. actions on Kosovo and Cuba, cancelled her participation at the last minute. Attorney General Reno stepped in to head the delegation. The meetings were often tedious beyond endurance. A photo that appeared on the front page of La Jornada, Mexico's leading leftist newspaper, caught Rosario Green, Janet Reno, and me in various stages of exhausted yawn-ing and head holding as we listened to the final reports of the assembled cabinet ministers. The photo was a fair reflection of the boredom such gatherings induced. It was not the only time the photographers had their fun with me. Often they lay in wait to catch me shoving food into my mouth, scratching various parts of my anatomy, and dozing off when I should have been wide awake and earning my salary.

Two lengthy, politically sensitive negotiations revealed what could be accomplished when the SRE and the embassy worked together to con-tain the troublesome impulses of other elements of their respective gov-ernments. One of them undid a Mexican proposal that could have scut-tled all military cooperation between the two countries. The other secured the final settlement of the maritime border in the Caribbean. In both cases solutions were found that met the practical and sovereignty concerns of both sides.

Some background is useful. Over the years, cooperation with the Mexican Navy to intercept drug-transporting ships off its coasts had improved. But most of the work was ad hoc, because the Mexican government was unwilling to formalize procedures that, if made public, would be criticized by knee-jerk nationalists for whom cooperation meant submission to the United States. Such super patriotism was a self-defeating caricature of the real thing. It served only the interests of drug traffickers, who pose a much greater threat to Mexico than the United States does.

Mexico imposed some restrictions that were aggravating and expensive. U.S. planes used for spotting suspect ships were not allowed to overnight in Mexico on the grounds that this would violate the Mexican constitutional prohibition against stationing foreign troops in the country. The planes had to return to the United States every night, a major limitation on their surveillance time. The same rigidity limited visits to Mexican ports by U.S. Navy ships.

While most of the complications emanated from the Mexican side, the U.S. Navy and Coast Guard were also caught in their own web of suspicion, bureaucracy, and tradition. Repeated Mexican requests for equipment that would provide direct communication with U.S. Navy ships and demands for faster handover of raw intelligence were deflected by American officials. They were concerned that the information the Mexicans would derive from easier communications and faster intelligence passing would wind up in the hands of drug traffickers.

Military cooperation increased slowly and fitfully, and it nearly came undone with a decision by the Mexican Navy to codify its procedures for dealing with foreign, that is, American, naval forces. The military mind—Mexican or American—cannot abide ad hoc–ism. Procedures must be established, written down, dipped in bronze, and issued to the troops. In some ways the resulting "bases-of-cooperation" document was a step forward. But it included one absolute clunker that threatened to wreck the limited but growing naval cooperation between the two countries.

For years, Mexico had made it clear that it would not allow nuclear-powered or nuclear-weapons-carrying ships into its ports. This was well known in Washington. We had not sought such permission for decades and had no intention of doing so. There was no strategic imperative to bring a nuclear-powered carrier into a Mexican port, only a day's steaming from homeports in Florida or California. So there really was no issue—until the Mexican military decided to put its bases of cooperation in writing. If they had adhered to the strategy of no surprises before publishing the document in the *Official Gazette*, we would have been able to avoid a major problem. But they did not. And the problem became a crisis.

When the nuclear naval ayatollahs in Washington learned of the newly stated Mexican position, they went wild. The same kind of prohibition had led to a severe rupture in our military relations with New Zealand. The American military could simply not accept any nation declaring a priori opposition to transit or visits by our nuclear ships. Where would that slippery slope end, they huffed. Other governments might take similar decisions, eroding the value of the American nuclear fleet. While the U.S. Navy did not mind that its nuclear ships could not enter Mexican ports, it did not want to see the prohibition in writing. In other words, "if you don't tell, we won't ask."

The nuclear types threatened to retaliate in a way that would have ended the military cooperation that served our drug-fighting goals, harpooning ourselves in the foot. Sometimes an ambassador can step in to stare down a part of the U.S. government. But I soon learned that this issue was critical to the nuclear specialists who could sway the navy, and then the navy would prod the Department of Defense toward a truly horrible decision.

After several discussions outlining the theology of the issue, the Mexicans understood that the bases of cooperation had to be altered. But they had already been published in the Mexican *Official Gazette*. If the American concerns were made public, the political system would have geared up to preserve them as if they were a sacred text. The Mexican government would have been roasted in the press for giving in to the gringos. Deputy Foreign Secretary Rebolledo's task was nearly impossible. He had to negotiate with his own naval bureaucracy, obtain the necessary changes, and keep it all out of the public eye.

While he was doing that, I had to keep the U.S. Navy single-minders from scuttling the ship. They demanded nothing less than a public and full disclaimer of the Mexican position. They helpfully suggested language for the task that was clearly unacceptable. After many months, we were successful. An amendment, buried in the *Official Gazette* in June 2000, was incomprehensible to all but a handful of Mexican and U.S.

naval lawyers. No person who had not been deeply involved in the negotiations could possibly have deciphered the language. It did not mention the word "nuclear." It simply referred to the relevant provisions of the previously published bases of cooperation document only by paragraph numbers, but it effectively undid the written nuclear position. It returned the situation to status quo ante with absolutely no derogation of Mexican sovereignty. And, as such, it was acceptable to the Mexican Navy.

Because the SRE and the embassy grasped the intricacies and politics of the other government's position and were able to convey them to other agencies in their respective bureaucracies, a threatening situation that would have damaged the interests of both nations was defused.

Similarly, the ability to respect each other's neuralgic points led to the final demarcation of the maritime bilateral border. The boundary between the two countries in the Gulf of Mexico was based on internationally recognized territorial claims of two hundred miles from the nearest point of territory. But this left an area of about ten thousand square miles as no-man's water. It was known as the doughnut hole because it was fully surrounded by watery territory belonging to either the United States or Mexico. Under international law, the two nations controlling the surrounding waters could negotiate a division of the area. Strong pressures were building from the U.S. oil industry for permission to drill in the hole. But Interior Secretary Bruce Babbitt understood that granting permits in undemarcated land would be explosive and create an ugly international incident. He held the oil industry at bay.

By 1999, there was no real dispute over the division of the territory in question. Experts from both nations had determined that Mexico was entitled to 62 percent of it. But Mexican politicians were convinced that once the doughnut hole was divided, the U.S. oil companies would be able to drill horizontally under the surface and suck up the Mexican oil. Not important was the fact that this had not happened elsewhere in the Gulf and that experts from both countries agreed that the nature of the likely petroleum deposits in question would make it impossible. The sucking theory, like our nuclear vessel orthodoxy, could not be challenged. In this case, U.S. negotiators in the Departments of Energy and Interior were told that they had to accept the scientifically unsupportable Mexican position. They were not happy. However, with a good deal of persuasion by the State Department Legal Advisor David Andrews, they finally accepted reality, and a satisfactory deal was worked out. It established a nondrillable buffer area on either side of the new line that could not be exploited for ten years, thus preventing the imaginary straws from sucking up the still undiscovered and perhaps nonexistent oil.

Since the agreement fixing the boundary had to take the form of a treaty, the SRE expended significant effort in bringing along Mexican legislators. It took more than a year to convince the Mexican Senate, but ultimately the members were swayed by the argument that Mexico had triumphed by getting the larger share of the territory and by compelling the U.S. to accept the sucking theory. I did my part by grumbling in the press about Mexico having taken the lion's share of the doughnut hole. I gave the impression that we were grudgingly going along with the treaty simply because we had been bested by their superior science and diplomacy. The two Senates ratified the treaty in record time.

There were many in Washington who viewed the SRE under the PRI government as preternaturally anti-American. Indeed, there were Mexican officials who delighted in messing us over. And true enough, the general ethos of the ministry was one of constant vigilance against real or imagined slights and machinations from the north. In reality, we accomplished a great deal with fluid communication and a mutual willingness to understand and interpret the sometimes arbitrary or illogical positions of the other side. The differences in approach promoted by varying outlooks, ideologies, and histories did not inevitably overwhelm common sense.

C
H
A
P
T
E
R

F
I
V
E

Certifiably Insane

The Casablanca affair truly bothered President Zedillo, who had no difficulty in letting his foreign secretary fulminate publicly and privately. Despite his urbane, international gloss, Yale graduate education, and fervent support for economic globalization, Zedillo was, at core, a Mexican nationalist. Growing up in the "frontera" city of Mexicali in a middle-class family, he no doubt experienced both the threats and opportunities of El Norte and the personal slights endemic to the border region. In his view, Casablanca was but another assault on Mexican sovereignty by insensitive, arrogant, and uncontrollable American officialdom. I empathized with him. The operation had been poorly handled.

When I arrived in late July 1998, two months after the Reno and Rubin press conference, the Mexican government was mismanaging its reaction and had worked itself into a ridiculously hostile stance. It argued that the Customs and DEA undercover agents and sources involved in the sting operation should be identified and extradited to Mexico to stand trial. They had engaged in money laundering, the Mexicans claimed, and deserved to be punished. Extradition was never even considered in Washington. It would have been preposterous for American officials to contemplate handing over to a judicial system in which there was little confidence employees who had been doing their job—perhaps not wisely, but certainly not with criminal intent.

The government of Mexico understood that its public cries for extradition would go unheeded in Washington. In fact, it never submitted documents to begin the extradition process. But the demand served a domestic political purpose by demonstrating that it would not hesitate to stand up to Yankee aggression. The Mexican attitude, no matter how sincerely felt by President Zedillo and the political elite, also served the time-tested objective of refocusing public attention away from the corruption at the heart of the Casablanca story. With the United States available as a whipping boy, the government did not have to address the troubling reality of drug-related graft in the banking industry.

The government's public relations strategy may have been helpful at home, but it was becoming highly counterproductive in the United States. Moreover, Attorney General Reno had already taken steps to ensure better coordination with Mexico on future undercover operations. She met with her counterpart, Jorge Madrazo, in Brownsville, Texas, at the beginning of July 1998. There they agreed on new procedures and sent a joint letter to Presidents Clinton and Zedillo pledging that both governments would give written notice in advance of any major cross-border activities by their respective federal law enforcement agencies. Such notification would provide an opportunity to consult on legal or practical considerations before the work began. The Brownsville letter was later transformed into a memorandum of understanding that the two attorneys general signed when President Clinton visited Mérida, Mexico, in February 1999. It was a major and necessary step toward antinarcotics cooperation and helped calm the post-Casablanca waters.

The Mérida Memorandum of Understanding was intended to expire at the end of the Clinton administration. Both sides understood that Attorney General Reno could not commit her successor to the policy. When it lapsed on January 20, 2001, the new Fox administration, not understanding its importance, showed little interest in extending it. The Washington agencies, which had never been happy with it, were just as unenthusiastic. But as ambassador, I insisted that the law enforcement units in the embassy continue to conduct their work as if the agreement remained in force. I wanted to ensure that there would be no more Casablancas.

In practice, the principal activity of the U.S. Drug Enforcement Agency (DEA) in Mexico was to obtain intelligence on drug cartels and their shipments to the United States. Much of the information was developed by Mexican authorities and passed to the DEA office in the embassy. But sometimes the DEA would need to send a source into Mexico to obtain information, usually from narcotics dealers. We were always aware that any activity that included discussions with criminals could be portrayed as entrapment or misconstrued as a criminal offense. Therefore, it was important that Mexican authorities be aware from the start of such contacts so as to avoid problems down the road.

Prior consultation and coordination with the Mexican government placed the activities of the confidential sources under a protective Mexican law enforcement umbrella. The Brownsville-Mérida process, as we referred to it within the embassy, also opened the door for the Mexican government to conduct similar intelligence-gathering activities in the United States. We would have welcomed such operations, particularly in narcotics and alien smuggling, but Mexico never took advantage of the opportunity, mostly owing to the country's weak police system and flaws in its legal underpinnings for undercover operations. Another element implicit in the agreement was that the two sides would share information from confidential sources in order to pursue joint or separate investigations. Decisions on passing information were made in Washington, where suspicions about Mexican law enforcement were widespread. But as time progressed and confidence grew, more intelligence was passed southward, particularly after Vicente Fox's team came to power.

Brownsville-Mérida served as an important tool in managing the embassy's large law enforcement contingents. The DEA, FBI, Customs, and a half-dozen other federal police agencies maintained their largest overseas presence in the embassy building in Mexico City. All reported to the ambassador, but it was up to me to determine how involved I would be in their activities. I insisted that every proposal for undercover information gathering pass through me before it was sent on to the appropriate Mexican authorities.

I approved almost all. But some were poorly presented or not well thought out as to potential consequences. I put a stop to them. I did not mind being referred to as "a son of a bitch obstructionist" by some officials in the Department of Justice or the DEA who openly resented my efforts to keep them from stepping on Mexican sensitivities. My concern was to maintain the kind of contacts that would allow cooperation to continue. Attorney General Reno generally agreed with me and protected my flank from her in-house zealots. The internal embassy process also helped to improve the morale of the law enforcement officials by demonstrating a consistent ambassadorial interest in their work. I also insisted on frequent and open information sharing among the agencies in Mexico City. No longer would the DEA and FBI be able to fight each other with zeal almost as intense as their assault on narcotics traffickers. In years past the two organizations, both part of the Department of Justice, commonly refused to share information. And the CIA had refused to deal with either.

The continuing Mexican uproar over Casablanca made life extremely difficult for those in Washington preparing for the early 1999 antidrug certification effort. I conveyed the message to the Mexican government that even Mexico's friends in Washington, those who had stuck their necks out to push through the Brownsville agreement over the opposition from law enforcement agencies and several congressmen, were losing patience. It was difficult enough for the executive branch to receive a constant pounding from Congress and the press about being "too soft" on the Mexican government's antidrug efforts. But when that was coupled with a drumbeat of accusations and impossible demands from Mexico, what little support Mexico had for the coming congressional certification battle was in danger of meltdown. By early 1999, the Mexican government saw the light and quietly dropped its rhetorical demands for the extradition of the offending DEA and Customs agents.

The annual narcotics certification drama dominated U.S.-Mexican relations for years, causing untold grief for successive ambassadors and always roiling the bilateral waters. By 1998, certification was an idea that had outlived whatever usefulness it might have ever had. A dozen years before, Congress had passed legislation mandating that the president certify by March 1 every year the countries that were cooperating fully with the U.S. antidrug effort. The law provided for three possible grades—certification, decertification, and decertification with a national interest waiver. A decertified government would lose American aid. Decertification with a national interest waiver would allow the aid to continue, if it were determined that to terminate it would do more harm than good. Congress also gave itself the authority to override a president's decision by a majority vote in both houses.

In passing the legislation, Congress was seeking a greater role in anti-narcotics efforts. In theory there is nothing wrong with establishing guidelines to determine how taxpayers' money should be spent. But in practice the certification process was a very mixed bag. At times it probably did help to focus the minds of some governments—Peru, Bolivia, Colombia, and Mexico—on the need to do more against the drug trade. But the unilateral nature of the process was always highly resented, nowhere more so than in Mexico, with its historical super-sensitivity to the notion that the United States has the right to judge it.

Ironically, the threat to terminate assistance meant little to Mexico in a practical sense because it received very little financial help from the U.S. government. But the prospect of being branded as a noncooperating pariah state, with all that might mean for Mexico's international image and ability to attract investment, tourism, and American goodwill, meant a lot. Thus, while the Mexican government truly resented the certification process and publicly professed not to care about it, in reality, there was hardly any issue more central to and disruptive of the bilateral relationship than the annual certification follies.

For many on the American political right, certification was not only a way to grade other countries, but to keep the State Department from sacrificing the drug war to other international interests. When it came to Mexico, the congressional critics had a point: There was little possibility that any American president would decertify Mexico. Too much was at stake in the relationship. The impact that declaring Mexico a noncooperating nation might have on investment flows, for instance, could harm the U.S. economy as well as Mexico's. The relationship had become so intertwined on so many levels that neither country had full flexibility of action. An economically weak or floundering Mexico would not be in the interest of the United States. Moreover, if the president decertified Mexico, the United States would still have to find a way to obtain the maximum antinarcotics cooperation possible. Decertification of Mexico would be useful for one group only—the drug traffickers.

On several occasions the House or Senate took steps to overturn a presidential decision to certify Mexico as a cooperating country. The effort reached its high-water mark in early 1997. Just a few weeks before the president was obliged to announce his decision, Mexico's newly appointed drug czar, Army General Jesús Gutiérrez Rebollo, was arrested for being in league with the traffickers. Both houses responded by passing resolutions that opposed certification but stopped short of demanding decertification. The administration worked out a deal that avoided decertification but obliged the White House to provide periodic reports to Congress on Mexico's performance. The 1998 debate was equally conflictive.

The yearly certification fight had grown as predictable as a kabuki drama, with each actor playing an established role. During the Clinton administration, the congressional battle was led by conservative Republicans. They argued that the Mexican drug trade had not diminished over the past year and the government of Mexico was doing little to improve its performance. The White House would trot out its big guns, notably the drug czar Barry McCaffrey, to report that despite the latest evidence of corruption or incompetence, the Mexican leadership was fully committed to fighting the scourge of narcotics. For its part, Mexico would publicly blow hot and cold. It professed that it cared not one bit about what the U.S. government might decide, but worked its lobbyists in Washington to exhaustion in an effort to demonstrate proof of cooperation and success to a skeptical American Congress.

The press in both countries fanned the flames mercilessly. The Mexican media hounded me for my opinion about the process or predictions about what would happen. Usually, I simply responded that certification was the law of the United States, and, yes, the president would be making his decisions by March 1 as required. This would normally result in a story highlighting my recalcitrance and alleging that I had defended certification as a legitimate manifestation of American unilateralism. I found all of this pretty humorous, considering my private negative feelings about the largely useless process.

It was all the more ironic then that I became the focal point for the Mexican press as the 2000 certification decision neared. Anyone with a good feel for Washington, and this most assuredly did not include the Mexican press or most of the country's politicians, should have sensed by early 2000 that the president had already determined to follow past practice and certify Mexico. Moreover, 2000 was an election year. The politicians were already distracted and it was shaping up to be a pretty quiet session on the certification front. That is, until I stumbled into a major debate.

An important part of an ambassador's job is to be the visible presence of the United States government. He or she must deliver America's message to the local public. There was never a dearth of opportunities to do so in Mexico. The American ambassador is always news. There are daily opportunities to present the views of the United States through impromptu interviews, press conferences, or formal speeches. The basic message of all my public addresses for four years was that the U.S.-Mexican relationship was of extreme importance to both countries. The only way to confront shared problems was through shared responsibility and action. And, contrary to what the press might portray, the two governments were actually making significant progress. This was not just feel-good rhetoric. It had the added advantage of being true.

I refused far more invitations to make formal speeches than I accepted. But I felt a certain responsibility in February 2000 when I was asked to address a breakfast meeting of the University of Southern California alumni association. These Mexican men and women were precisely the kind of educated opinion leaders who could help carry the message of the need for increased cooperation and understanding.

The gathering in a posh hotel in the Polanco district of upscale stores and apartment houses was no different from a hundred others I attended. About seventy-five USC alumni were present. The breakfast was the usual enormous fare of eggs a la mexicana, refried beans, bacon, sausages, sweet rolls, tortillas, fruit, juice, and enough carbohydrates to keep an army marching through a small war. The press was there in full force, but of no particular concern to me. Normally, I would have spoken in English to a group of U.S.-educated businesspeople, but the sponsors had made no provision for translation. The monolingual Mexican press, most of whom were probably more interested in the meal than in my words, would not have had the opportunity to hear my profound thoughts. So, I spoke in Spanish. Nobody in Mexico ever mistook my accent for anything but that of a gringo, but after thirty-plus years in and out of Latin America, my Spanish was serviceable and adequate for off-the-cuff remarks full of bromides I could repeat in my sleep. This was going to be an easy walk in the park in front of a friendly audience. Or so I thought.

The event started out as I had hoped, with most attendees apparently impressed with some of the lesser-known elements of cooperation that I highlighted. Then I dropped a bomb in my response to a question I had fielded a dozen times. My answer was probably no different from what it had been in the past. But press reaction in Mexico is always a game of Russian roulette. This time I found the loaded chamber. One of the alumni gave a brief speech disguised, as often happened at such events, as a question. "All we see here are reports from the United States that the narcotics criminals are Colombians and Mexicans, never any American cowboys. . . . What are you doing to fight the American criminals? Who certifies the United States?"

The inquiry had a real edge, reflecting the damaged pride of Mexicans who resented both the image of their country as a drug lords' paradise and the annual certification process. It was based on the widespread perception that the drug business in the United States is too big and profitable to be run by foreigners. Americans must be the true masterminds, as they run everything else in the world. The mini-speech also revealed the generalized lack of understanding of serious antidrug efforts in the United States. It was not a difficult question to answer. I could have done so in a sentence or two. But I felt that the audience, with its American ties, deserved a more detailed response. That was a mistake.

I began by summarizing our efforts both to fight traffickers and to reduce the demand for their drugs. Noting that our prison population had grown enormously in recent years, I assured the questioner that we go after homegrown drug dealers in the United States, although the Mexican press paid no attention to our efforts in that regard. "No wonder you do not know what we are doing," I said snidely, hoping my tone would jolt the reporters present. They continued eating.

Then, I tried to explain how almost all, if not all, of the drug cartels in the United States are operated from outside the U.S., where they are less vulnerable to American law enforcement. In a rhetorical effort that few understood, I used an analogy to explain how the system works. "The man who owns a large automobile distributorship in Mexico City is probably wealthy and powerful," I said, "but the important decisions relating to the automobile industry—finance, style, production—are made in Detroit or Tokyo, and that is where the big profits go." The truly big fish in the drug trade live outside of the United States, just as the truly powerful in the automotive industry live outside of Mexico. Those who run the drug business within the U.S., as wealthy and treacherous as they may be, are relatively small players. Out of deference to the audience,

I did not note that in many places throughout the United States, the drug trade down to the street level is controlled by their countrymen.

I was aware that underlying the question was an aggrieved feeling, widely shared in Mexico, that the drug problem is made in the USA. This simplistic and erroneous view holds that without American demand, there would be no Mexican supply: Mexico is but a poor victim of geography, sitting between the world's largest producers of cocaine and the enormous American market. The idea of Mexico as victim ignores the reality of the aggressive Mexican cartels that are continually searching for new sources of supply and for new markets. Mexican criminals are major figures in the drug world. The country is not simply the victim of outside forces, no matter how comforting that thought might be to some.

"The fact is that the headquarters of the narcotrafficking world are now in Mexico," I said. "That's the truth. As the headquarters of the Mafia was in Sicily, now the headquarters of the narcotics traffickers are in other countries, and Mexico is one of them. For this reason we are collaborating with the government of Mexico, and we have seen an infinity of cooperation, every year much greater, in this common fight."

Press coverage of my remarks was intense and reverberated for weeks in editorials and columns. The March 1, 2000, certification deadline was much on Mexico's mind. Some reporters and headline writers focused on the general import of my assertion that Mexico was one of several of the world's narco headquarters. But others seized on my seemingly contradictory statement in the previous sentence that "the headquarters of the narcotrafficking world are now in Mexico." Here was the spokesman of the drug-consuming United States outrageously blaming his country's problems on Mexico. It was just another form of Yankee aggression. The headlines had me calling Mexico the new Sicily. Some of the reports were silly. More than one editorialist, for example, tried to figure out which Mexico City car dealer I had been obliquely naming as a drug dealer. But the assault from almost all quarters was serious and intense.

Many of the editorialists and cartoonists looked for the "true" motives for my "outburst." Several determined that I was consciously currying favor with the Republican right either for personal protection or as some part of a Clinton White House–orchestrated bow in their direction. The cover cartoon in the weekly magazine *Siempre* had a grotesquely oversized U.S. ambassador swinging a club into the head of an undersized

Mexican in a sombrero. The Mexican was holding a barrel of petroleum and I was standing on a box labeled "USA elections." Oil prices had risen sharply in the previous months. The cartoon's message was clear: I was warning Mexico to lower oil prices in an American election year or face decertification. The interpretations were endless, Machiavellian, and all wrong. I paid the price for being careless in an otherwise mundane presentation. Politicians, sensing blood (mine) in the water, reacted with theatrical outrage. Members of both houses of the Mexican congress demanded that that the Zedillo administration rebuke me publicly. The Secretariat of Foreign Affairs issued a statement expressing concern about my remarks. I had no defenders. Even those who might have agreed with what I said were not about to ally themselves with the criticism from the spokesman of the North.

Presidential candidate Vicente Fox told a reporter that I was simply speaking the truth. But Fox quickly withdrew from the debate as his own party joined the attack with the rest of the political and press elite. Fox was reluctant to take on the drug issue as a political theme. It was too hot to touch. It would remain too hot for all of the candidates in the entire 2000 presidential campaign.

The uproar caused no lasting damage. But I was truly upset. My ego, which I usually managed to keep in check, moved into high gear. I felt I deserved better treatment. After all, I had spent a great deal of my time putting the best face possible on the actions, inactions, and gaffes of the Mexican government for the Washington audience. I felt hurt and abandoned by a country I had defended. It was foolish and self-pitying of me to feel that way. I had enough experience in Mexico to know that the U.S. ambassador is regarded as fair game. I managed the embassy's fire control. We issued the full text of what I had said, in an effort to show how my remarks had been pulled out of context. We also sent out other statements I had made, all underscoring the fact that I had consistently praised the increasing level of cooperation in fighting drugs that the two countries were enjoying. All that fell on deaf ears.

But generally, I kept the embassy's response low key and I made no further public comment. Although I was sorely tempted to do so and perhaps engender a real debate about narcotics in Mexico, I could not come out swinging because my words had already made it into the U.S. press. Any more criticism from me would be grist for the mill of those preparing their attack on the president's forthcoming certification of Mexico. Several conservative U.S. congressmen had already congratulated me and contrasted my position with the "soft" approach taken by the White House and the State Department. I had to weather the storm, and ultimately it passed.

By late 2000, all but the most obdurate members of the U.S. Congress realized that the certification process was counterproductive. Encouraged by Vicente Fox's election in July 2000, Congress took up legislation to exempt Mexico from the judgment in 2001. That effort got lost in the legislative maw, but further initiatives followed. In 2002 both houses passed legislation that effectively terminated the process.

The most negative effect of the certification law was that for years it focused Mexican attention on an extraneous issue—the perceived American arrogance inherent in the process of judging others—and, in doing so, provided a pretext for Mexico to ignore the reality of its drug scene. That reality was ugly. It remains ugly. And threatening.

Running in Vicious Circles

In the public flailing I took for my comments about Mexico's central role in the international drug trade, the local press was simply acting true to form and playing its part in the annual drama of certification. Stories and commentaries about the United States criticizing Mexico on the eve of the certification decision were the stuff of their dreams. Since much of the press was also adversarial toward their own government, my comments served a double purpose. They could be used as an implicit attack on the country's PRI rulers for not doing enough to fight drugs. And they could be used to condemn the United States for besmirching Mexico's honor and intervening in its internal affairs. Talk about having your cake and eating it.

For the most part, American reporters were more responsible than their Mexican colleagues. But the two groups shared the antagonistic and skeptical attitude that modern journalism brings to all things governmental. If the U.S. government asserted that Mexico was cooperating in the antinarcotics struggle, it was up to the American press to find the truth, which, most reporters suspected, was likely to cast doubt on the government's assertions. Moreover, the reporters had a fine sense of just how good the Mexican drug story was. Full of violence, money, corruption, colorful figures, and government intrigue, it made great front-page reading.

The American reporters operated under difficult circumstances. They could not develop sources within the closed world of the drug cartels. They depended almost uniquely on law enforcement sources in both countries. At times, untested or dubious information strongly influenced what the American press reported. The trained manipulators of words sometimes became the manipulated.

The modus operandi of U.S. law enforcement agencies operating in Mexico is to vacuum up all the information available and pass it to Washington where it is stored in data banks and occasionally analyzed. There are few filters along the way. Mixed in among the wheat of accurate accounts is a great deal of bogus chaff. Confidential sources in the United States and elsewhere often provide what they know the American cops are willing to pay to hear. Mexican politicians or bureaucrats consciously pass information, true or false, to smear enemies. Drug traffickers know that squealing on their rivals or putting out bad news about honest cops or politicians is an effective way to neutralize or eliminate them.

In Mexico, the American cops got most of their information from police and prosecutors. No Mexican agency trusted another, so they often felt justified in discrediting each other. The most scandalous charges about corruption in the military, for example, came from the attorney general's office and vice versa. Mexican law enforcement personnel worked in an environment of conflict and suspicion. But all their charges and countercharges became grist for the American information mill.

The Washington analysts who received such raw intelligence usually had no experience in Mexico, so they had limited understanding of the world from which it came. They catalogued the information and misinformation they received and wrote summaries that strung together data that ran the gamut from barroom gossip to hard documentary evidence, often without making clear distinctions as to the genesis or value of the information. Their analytical reports were passed to their chiefs. On occasion, a piece of raw intelligence was deemed so important as to be brought to the attention of policymakers without any analysis.

The flow of information within government in Washington follows established paths. But there is a cottage industry in the nation's capital involved in passing information to journalists. The motives for this are not always clear, and the reporters generally do not care: they are interested in the information, not the informer. Lower-level officials sometimes pass the substance of confidential reports to journalists to make themselves seem more important or to pursue their own policy goals or to reveal that their bosses are incompetent. At the upper levels, information is used to pursue a particular line in a policy battle or to embarrass a bureaucratic foe.

Information about the Mexican drug scene was a particularly valuable commodity, but it was often flawed because of dubious details, suspect sources, and overeager or inexperienced officials. When information got to the press, the results were often unpredictable and damaging. The flow of information through and out of government was a vicious circle frequently punctuated by a good deal of ignorance and unexamined motivations.

On occasion, when I received an analyst's report pointing the finger of drug corruption at Mexican government officials, I asked to see the raw intelligence upon which the report was based. The information was sometimes difficult to obtain because the DEA or other agency would cite a need to conceal the identity of its sources. I felt that on many occasions they simply did not want to reveal how flimsy the information was. But I persevered in my efforts, and when I did get to read the raw intelligence, I often found the supposed evidence unpersuasive. Sometimes it was obvious that the analysts had chosen among a source's allegations, selecting information that supported a preexisting bias. Washington analysts worked on the assumption that a series of unconfirmed or implausible reports, frequently repeating the same rumor or bit of information, constituted sufficient smoke to assume a fire. Only after September 11 and the 2003 war in Iraq did the American public begin to understand that no matter how good intelligence gathering and analysis might be, it remains an inexact science, vulnerable to willful or unwitting distortion. But the intelligence game has always been that way, and it is vulnerable at many levels.

Much of the information leaked to the American press came from the Washington headquarters of the DEA. That agency's legendary animosity toward Mexico was sealed in the blood of one of its agents. In 1985, Enrique Camarena, a DEA agent assigned to the American consulate in Guadalajara, was kidnapped, vilely tortured, and murdered. The DEA was convinced that Mexican police and politicians worked hand in hand with the narcotics traffickers to kill Camarena. A year later another DEA agent was kidnapped in the same city but released after a week of torture at the hands of Mexican police. The bad feelings only worsened in 1990 when the DEA paid Mexican bounty hunters to kidnap and deliver to El Paso the Mexican doctor who was alleged to have kept Camarena alive so that his interrogation and torture could be prolonged.

Mexico furiously protested Dr. Álvarez Macháin's abduction. The doctor was found guilty in a U.S. court, but the sentence was later reversed on appeal. The Mexican response to the Álvarez Macháin kidnapping foreshadowed the furor over Casablanca. To be fair, the American public would have responded strongly if a U.S. citizen had been kidnapped from Chicago and taken south of the border by bounty hunters paid for by the Mexican government. But we probably would have been able to get over it more rapidly than did the Mexicans, whose government threatened to kick the DEA out of the country. The agency was only allowed to stay when it agreed to Mexican rules that limited its numbers, prohibited agents from carrying guns, restricted their operations, and denied them the diplomatic status they were entitled to under international law. It was a humiliating turn of events for the DEA for which it could never forgive Mexico.

Already cynical because of the continuing and abundant evidence of Mexican police and judicial corruption, the agency's Washington headquarters developed a strong antipathy toward Mexico. The hostility sometimes found an outlet with American reporters, who were eager for any new information about the Mexican drug world and governmental corruption. DEA sources leaked information that led to stories that made it more difficult for the president to certify Mexico. DEA Director Tom Constantine repeatedly asserted that he regretted the leaks, but the suspicion around Washington and in Mexico was that he either condoned or actively promoted them. At the very least, he never indicated that he was upset by them.

Sometimes the leaks undermined the agency's ability to do its job. In 1998, for example, the DEA began to advise the Mexican attorney general's office in the administration of polygraphs to members of its Organized Crime Unit (OCU). Only those who passed the exam could work in the unit that received DEA information and training. The trouble began when the OCU's second-in-command failed his lie detector test. The DEA had already suspected him and urged that he be detained and pressed for information about his presumed corrupt activities. Instead, he was quickly shipped off to a sinecure in the Mexican embassy in Madrid. We never knew what to make of his transfer. Maybe he was being protected by other corrupt officials. Or maybe his prior reputation as an honest cop convinced his superiors that he was the target of a vendetta by the DEA, which many Mexican officials viewed as untrustworthy. DEA sources in Washington told the press about the polygraph and the sudden assignment to Spain, angering Mexican Attorney General Madrazo. Of course, the fact that the results of lie detector tests had been leaked put an end to the vetting program and cooperation with the OCU for a period of time.

As tense as that story was, it produced a sequel with a plot worthy of an international crime thriller that combined professional jealousies, dubious accusations of massive corruption at the highest level of the Mexican government, and some questionable journalism by America's most influential newspaper.

Ultimately, Attorney General Madrazo fired the OCU's boss, but he did not go quietly. He told the DEA and others that he was being punished because he had been investigating an allegation of drug corruption against Liébano Sáenz, President Zedillo's chief of staff. His version of events, coming either directly from him or from Washington sources, made its way to the investigative section of the *New York Times*. During the 1990s the *Times* had focused a great deal of attention on the Mexican narcotics scene, winning a Pulitzer Prize in 1998 for its coverage. Underlying the *Times*'s approach was the suspicion that the U.S. government had been less than zealous in getting to the bottom of the endemic corruption within the government of Mexico. Once alerted to the charges against Sáenz, Tim Golden, a member of the award-winning team of reporters, returned to Mexico in early 1999 to track down the story. His trip came just a few weeks before President Clinton was scheduled to visit Mexico. A story involving allegations of corruption in President Zedillo's office would be a blockbuster, especially if it appeared on the front page as Air Force One touched down in the midst of a bitter certification battle.

Golden looked at the allegations, talked with Sáenz and others, and returned to New York. No story was published at that time. I had seen the raw intelligence that had prompted the *Times*'s interest. The central charge was based on a report from a low-level Mexican criminal. The source claimed he had been told that Amado Carrillo Fuentes, one of Mexico's most notorious drug lords, had told other narcotics bigwigs that he had paid Sáenz $60 million in protection money. Carrillo later died on the operating table, liposuctioned to death during an effort to change his appearance. His plastic surgeon wound up in several barrels. According to the source, Carrillo had wanted the other cartel leaders to pay their fair share of the protection money. The money had allegedly been passed to Sáenz one afternoon in a Mexico City restaurant in a half-dozen Samsonite hard-sides.

As I read the intelligence, the story seemed to me to be weak. It was hearsay. It had come from a questionable source who had not been present when the money was allegedly passed or when Carillo supposedly later spoke about it. The allegation that $60 million in cash was passed in a public place in daylight to a person whose job gave him no operational control over police or courts rang hollow. My presumption was always that criminals might be evil, but they are not necessarily stupid. Might not the story be a fabrication by foes of President Zedillo or of Sáenz, who had made many enemies as a no-nonsense broker of his boss's power? Sáenz had upset many in the military by taking the story of General Gutiérrez Rebollo to President Zedillo. The military hierarchy would have preferred to handle the problem in a quieter fashion. He had also made enemies in the attorney general's office by alleging that many officials were incompetent or corrupt. He had certainly made plenty of other enemies inside and outside of government. Or perhaps Amado Carrillo Fuentes simply had been trying to shake down his competitors with a clever ruse. Multiple explanations seemed more plausible to me than the source's allegation.

Sáenz himself asked Zedillo to order an investigation of the charges. Zedillo did so, even though he didn't believe that Sáenz had sold out to the drug traffickers. One day after learning that reporter Golden was coming to Mexico to look into the allegations, the government announced that a thorough investigation had found the charges against Sáenz to be without foundation.

As President Clinton prepared for an early 1999 trip to Mexico, the *Times* news staff reported on what it viewed as Mexico's dismal performance in the drug fight over the previous year. The newspaper also took an editorial stand, recommending that the administration challenge Mexico by opting for decertification with a national interest waiver. But the Mexican presidential palace and the White House spun back. The Zedillo administration announced a new multiyear $500 million program to buy antidrug planes, ships, radars, and police equipment. Vice President Gore, General McCaffrey, and the American ambassador to Mexico all praised the move as an affirmation of Mexico's commitment to the drug fight. Before traveling to Mexico, President Clinton certified the country's cooperation against drug traffickers.

Golden's information sparked a discussion within the *Times* leadership. Apparently, his editors were unsure what to do. As recounted in Jorge Capetillo-Ponce's *Images of Mexico in the U.S. News Media*, one later told a seminar discussing how the American press reports on Mexico:

> We had a huge ongoing discussion about a Mexican government official—I think ultimately we did not run this story—in which all kinds of allegations were made. And it was the old sort of story linked to narcotics trafficking, which can be almost anything you care to name. We said substitute the name of this person with that of the U.S. Secretary of State, of the Treasury or the Secretary of Defense—which was more appropriate in this case—or the Chief of Staff of the White House, would we run the story? Would this story meet our standard, not just of sourcing, but of relevance? And sometimes we decide not to.

Although this transcript of Andrew Rosenthal's February 2000 words could conceivably be read as recounting how the *Times* decided not to print a story about the Mexican secretary of defense, it does seem more likely, given the context and timing, that he was referring to the person with the equivalent position to the White House chief of staff, that is, Liébano Sáenz. The editor was apparently recalling the early discussions with Golden that resulted in no publication of the story after he returned from his January trip to Mexico. But six months later the *Times* published the story just as a large delegation of U.S. cabinet members was heading to Mexico City for the June 1999 Bi-National Commission meeting.

The hook for the story, which was written by Golden, was that American officials were still concerned about the allegations about Sáenz. Perhaps the key had been found to Mexico's endemic corruption—an official at the very center of power who could protect the traffickers. Golden probably heard this from DEA and Justice Department officials who had learned of a meeting in Washington that Madrazo had held with Attorney General Reno in which she asked him for a report on the Sáenz investigation. Madrazo had turned to one of his principal assistants to brief Ms. Reno. The Mexican official spoke no English. He read a stilted response. As his words were being translated, the overweight and nervous functionary began to sweat profusely. Whatever he might have said, his account of the Mexican government's investigative procedure in clearing Sáenz's name appeared insufficient. Soon Washington sources were telling the *Times* that the attorney general of the United States remained unconvinced that the government of Mexico's investigation had been sufficiently thorough.

And that became the basis of the June 2, 1999 story. The previous inhibition about naming the Mexican official to which *Times* editor Rosenthal had referred to in the seminar disappeared under the weight of the continuing Washington suspicions. Datelined Washington and carrying the headline "Mexico Clears a Top Official, but Doesn't Convince the U.S.," the article began:

> Earlier this year, as President Clinton prepared to visit Mexico, law enforcement officials there disclosed what they cast as an extraordinary break from the country's long tradition of immunity for those at the highest levels of power.
>
> For more than a year, officials said, they had been investigating allegations of drug corruption involving President Ernest Zedillo's closest aide, his powerful private secretary. After an exhaustive effort begun at the urging of the aide himself, investigators had found the charges baseless, they said.
>
> Yet to the Mexicans' dismay, the matter of the presidential secretary, Jose Liébano Sáenz, has not been so easily put to rest.
>
> In Washington, senior officials including Attorney General Janet Reno privately questioned the thoroughness of the Mexican inquiry, prompting her Mexican counterpart to insist that he would consider any new evidence that emerged. But American officials have stepped up their own intelligence efforts to learn about Mr. Sáenz.

Apart from the element of Washington concern, the article did not contain any information that had not been available a half year earlier. The two-thousand-word piece contained a summary of the various allegations against Sáenz, including the handover of the Samsonite suitcases full of money. It acknowledged that there was no hard proof for any of the charges. In the context of *Times* coverage of the drug fight, the story was another element of its focus on how poorly American and Mexican authorities investigated allegations of corruption. The *Times* did not—and indeed could not—mount an independent investigation to determine which of the allegations were true. Its story relied on the same raw intelligence that had traveled the route from informers, to Mexican officials, to the DEA, to Washington, and finally to their reporter. It was the same intelligence that I found unpersuasive and suspect in its motivations.

The *Times* reported that the difference between Washington and Mexico City about the Sáenz case "reflects the difficulty Washington has in handling reports of corruption that involve high-level Mexican officials." As far as I was concerned, the *Times* story also reflected the difficulties journalists have in handling stories based on information made available by individuals or organizations with axes to grind.

Cornered on leaving a meeting by the Mexican press, I said that the article was another scene in "the same old show." I did not spell out that for me the "show" was the publication of a hot story on the threshold of an important meeting. Reno ducked the issue of her own continuing dissatisfaction with the Mexican investigation. At a Mexico City press conference dominated by questions about the *Times* piece she said, "it is just unfair and plain wrong . . . to make judgments on the basis of fragmented reports." The *Times* article on Reno's comments failed to report this implied criticism of the Golden piece. It reported that "Reno said the allegations she had seen were fragmentary and added, 'I cannot conclude, based on the evidence that I know of that he is guilty of any wrongdoing.'"

Journalistic and official U.S. concern about Mexico's ability to investigate reports of corruption at the highest levels of its government are understandable. But did naming the official, in the absence of specific proof of his guilt, and given the newspaper's own earlier concerns, meet the canons of journalistic ethics? I had my own doubts. I still do. A man's reputation had been questioned in one of the world's leading newspapers on the basis of what I thought to be weak intelligence anxiously seized upon by those looking for an easy explanation for Mexico's corruption.

After Reno and her team returned to Washington, Sáenz asked me to breakfast at Los Pinos. The setting, with its scampering red squirrels from neighboring Chapultepec Park and its lush vegetation, was as tranquil as Sáenz's mind was troubled. He asked plaintively if there was anything he could do to clear his name. He was worried about the effect on his kids and on his political future. I could not give him any encouragement. I told him that Washington never cleans out its databases. He could be sure that the next time his name surfaced as a political candidate or as an aspirant for another important appointed position, a button would be punched and the intelligence, now given added credence by the *Times* story, would flow once again. It was now part of his life. There was no escape.

C
H
A
P
T
E
R

S
E
V
E
N

Fingers, Locks, and Primaries

While the struggle against illegal narcotics was my daily fare and certification was episodically the hottest topic in the bilateral relationship, Mexicans, especially those in public life, had their attention focused elsewhere during the first half of 2000. For them, there was really only one issue—who would succeed Ernesto Zedillo as president.

Within weeks after presenting my credentials to Zedillo in August 1998, I had met many of the important political actors. Topics of conversation varied. Often we dwelled on the morning's headlines or political columns, sometimes on important issues in the bilateral relationship. But politicians are politicians whatever their nationality, and they were focusing their attention on the presidential election scheduled for July 2000. Who was in, who was out, who was up, who was down—the usual political gossip—filled my meetings with the politicians. But it was already clear that this would be an election unlike any other in Mexico's history.

I justified the time I spent with the politicians by telling myself that I had to be well informed in order to keep Washington up-to-date on political developments. But the truth was I hardly ever reported anything from conversations back to headquarters and Washington had many other sources of information, including the embassy's active political section. I spent time with the politicians because I enjoyed their company, and talking with them was a lot more fun than dealing with the myriad of other issues or problems that crossed my desk on a daily basis.

Fortunately for me, most politicians in Mexico were open to meeting with the American ambassador. This had little to do with my personal qualities. It was the result of a widespread perception that the representative of the United States is an important and powerful actor in Mexican politics. It was a gross exaggeration of reality, based largely on Mexico's inability to transcend the stereotypes of its entrenched mythology about its northern neighbor. True, some of my predecessors had played important roles in domestic Mexican developments. Joel Poinsett and Henry Lane Wilson were reviled. Nineteen-twenties ambassador Dwight Morrow, who became Charles Lindbergh's father-in-law, and Josephus Daniels in the 1930s were not as badly treated in Mexican folklore. But they were seen as meddlers at crucial points in Mexican history. The truth is that most modern U.S. ambassadors to Mexico have generally not been much involved in domestic intrigue. This does not mean that American ambassadors are devoid of influence in Washington or in Mexico itself. But as with so many other elements of the relationship, the reality is less colorful than the myth.

Mexicans continue to believe the mythology, because it fits well with their view of the United States as preternaturally interventionist. It also plays into their highly developed sense of conspiracy and intrigue. Even those who do not hold such views know that other Mexicans do. So contact with the American ambassador becomes part of the political game. Moreover, those who hold or seek power see the ambassador as an interlocutor with the U.S. government and leaders of American public opinion, so they often hope he will be useful in the furtherance of their own careers. The high profile that the U.S. ambassador enjoys (or suffers) in the Mexican press makes him someone that important people—or people who want to be important—feel they should know.

The very fact that the American ambassador has a relatively free field to roam is fairly new and reflects the changes in Mexico's political landscape. In the 1980s, Ambassador John Gavin caused a political furor when he met with a group of PAN party members. There was nothing surreptitious about the meeting, but the press and the PRI went wild. It was seen as interference in the political life of the country. The president of the PRI warned that the meeting was part of the "dark conclaves of the reactionaries." Some politicians demanded that the ambassador be declared persona non grata and be expelled from the country. The government, which disliked the outspoken Gavin, orchestrated much of the uproar, but wisely abstained from kicking him out. The episode highlighted just how closed and tightly run the PRI ship of state was at that time. Periodically, I would be criticized in the press for alleged interference, called a proconsul, and accused of favoring one party or politician over another. But for the most part, by 1998 the Mexican political elite and press had learned that talking to people is what diplomats do, whether they are Mexicans serving in Washington or Americans in Mexico.

The presidential election of July 2000 was a national earthquake, but the tectonic plates of Mexican politics had been slowly moving for the better part of two decades. Mexico is a textbook illustration for the argument that economic reform can generate political liberalization. As the country entered into the world economy with force during the 1980s and 1990s, the old ways of doing business began to change. Under Presidents De la Madrid, Salinas, and Zedillo, thousands of state-run companies with their padded payrolls of cronies were privatized, thus reducing the power of both the state and the PRI. International trading partners demanded clearer rules of the game and a more transparent political and judicial scene. Mexico's goal of attracting foreign investment was incompatible with an international image of a one-party autocracy. The speed of change accelerated with the advent of NAFTA as Mexico was compelled to modernize to join its two northern neighbors as a full partner.

The burgeoning middle class, international scrutiny, and a more aggressive, less controlled press all demanded a more open political system. In 1989 the PAN won a state governorship for the first time, and President Carlos Salinas demanded that the local Baja California PRI warlords accept the voters' decision. By the time the 2000 elections came, a majority of Mexicans lived in states or municipalities governed by parties other than the PRI. This included the nation's capital, the Federal District (D.F.) where Cuauhtémoc Cárdenas, leader of the leftist PRD and a former and future presidential candidate, had won the first popular election for governor in 1997. (Until then, the president had appointed the D.F.'s mayors.) In elections the same year, the PRI lost its congressional majority in the lower house of Congress.

The PRI's decline was in large measure the result of the public perception that it had become a nest of corruption. While that perception was not new, the greater openness of society and of the press allowed the discontent to be ventilated.

Adding to the political malaise was strong public opposition to the "neoliberal" economic reforms of the De la Madrid, Salinas, and Zedillo administrations. The reforms, some required by NAFTA, were preparing the country for the twenty-first century, but a lot of twentieth-century people were getting hurt in the process. These steps had been generally popular at first. But the collapse of the overvalued peso shortly after Zedillo took office eradicated the savings of the middle class, causing the public mood to turn against the reforms even though they had not caused the peso crisis. An effort to save the banking system added to the cynicism. For many, it seemed that the government was more concerned about saving the bankers' wealth than their depositors' assets.

Finally, public suspicions about the integrity of elections continued to simmer. For years Mexicans had doubted the honesty of vote counts. Most believed that Carlos Salinas, the PRI's presidential candidate in 1988, had actually lost that election. They were convinced that large-scale vote tinkering and a convenient computer blackout had stolen the victory from Cuauhtémoc Cárdenas. Though Zedillo won decisively in what appeared to be clean elections in 1994, suspicion of the electoral process remained strong.

The PRI was not impervious to the public's mood or the need to respond to it. Its responses were designed to portray the party as more democratic than in the past, more in tune with the people. Central to the effort was President Zedillo himself, the very model of the modern PRI-ista. As a Yale-trained economist, he understood the link between economic liberalization and political reform. He also understood the value of both for national development. Zedillo's contributions to the political opening of Mexico were multiple, not the least of which was his acceptance of the election results on July 2, 2000, when some in his party were still looking for a magic way, legal or illegal, to deny Fox his victory. But even before election night Zedillo had demonstrated his democratic inclination, most notably by amputating his finger—figuratively, not literally.

The PRI tradition had been that the outgoing president selected his party's candidate, and thus his successor. The *dedazo*, in which the president pointed his finger (*dedo*) at the newly anointed in much the same way as the Sistine Chapel represented God and Adam, was an instrumental part of the PRI's long-term success. In a country where the constitution prohibits reelection, the resident of Los Pinos needed a way to keep ambitious politicians with presidential aspirations in line. The dedazo also, at least in theory, guaranteed the outgoing president a certain amount of gratitude and political protection from his successor. It all worked pretty well for the party. Political infighting was, of course, a way of life, but public competition among likely successors was frowned upon. This maintained the image of party unity. Over the years, the dedazo came to be seen by many Mexicans as symptomatic of a closed, self-satisfied political elite that needed a good airing out.

In practice, the process was less autocratic than it seemed. Most presidents consulted widely within the party leadership before making their selections, who were generally chosen from a short list of consensus candidates. Nonetheless, the president retained the absolute right of dedazo. Zedillo's disavowal of it was a bold and honorable attempt to democratize Mexico's ruling party. He had made the decision to open the democratic system as wide as Mexico could accommodate. If this meant that the PRI might lose the next presidential election, so be it.

Though publicly abdicating the right of selecting his successor, Zedillo did not withdraw from the political game. Even without the dedazo, he maintained significant power, which he utilized during the PRI's primary campaign and the election itself. The man who would become the PRI's candidate in the 2000 election, Francisco Labastida, was a close associate of Zedillo and one of the few cabinet members he listened to. Labastida's name was on Zedillo's list of potential successors from the outset. These were not simple coincidences.

But while Zedillo was opening the process, the party as a whole was closing it. Insiders had grown resentful that Zedillo and his two predecessors, Salinas and de la Madrid, were not professional politicians. Rather, they were well-trained, highly educated technocrats who had built careers in government service by molding modern Mexico with their technical expertise. They were often disdainful of the less educated party hacks. When their reforms earned the wrath of the public, the party machinery struck back. It adopted an internal rule that barred from presidential candidacy anyone who had not previously been elected to public office. The old school had had enough of the technocratic presidents.

The professed justification of the new locks (*candados*) on the political process was that only those who had risked themselves in the public arena and had served at the will of the people merited the highest office. The PRI presidential candidate must be someone who had dirtied his shoes walking through the dust of Mexico in search of votes. This was a pretext. In reality, the move was the party hierarchy's payback for being marginalized from important decisions, particularly by Salinas and Zedillo. The theory behind the candados was not outlandish, but its adoption was laced with personal political interests, as potential candidates and their supporters eliminated technocratic competitors.

One star who fell from the heavens was Finance Secretary José Ángel Gurría, who might very well have been Zedillo's choice as successor, if the president had decided to keep all of his fingers and if the candados had not been adopted. Gurría had never been elected to public office. Still, well into 1998 he harbored the hope that the party would eliminate the locks that were keeping him out. His fate was ultimately sealed when he blew up at a congressional hearing late in the year and called some of the assembled legislators idiots. That judgment may have been correct, but it was politically unfortunate. In my conversations with his political rivals, they tried to express concern about "poor Ángel"—without, it seemed to me, a great deal of conviction.

High on the list of people I began meeting with shortly after my arrival were the leading presidential candidates. There were four declared PRI "pre-candidates," three of whom were considered to have a chance. I had difficulty establishing contact with one of them, Governor Manuel Bartlett of Puebla. But the other two likely contenders, Minister of Interior Francisco Labastida and Governor Roberto Madrazo of Tabasco, were accessible. Also willing to converse were the PRD's Cuauhtémoc Cárdenas and the PAN's Vicente Fox, the undisputed designees of their respective parties.

With the exception of Fox, all the leading candidates were sons of political families. Bartlett's and Madrazo's fathers had been governors. Cárdenas's father, a national hero, had been a revolutionary general, governor, and president and was still revered as a political saint for having nationalized Mexico's oil industry. Labastida's family was active in politics in the state of Sinaloa. The transgenerational lines drew an accurate portrait of Mexico's political elite as a small family. While Fox had served as a congressman and as governor of Guanajuato, he was a relatively new entry into the political game, and his personal style was contrary to the essentially buttoned up, controlled approach of the others. The former Coca-Cola executive sold himself as the un-cola, a rough-hewn, straight-talking man of the people.

Without high expectations, I invited Fox for breakfast at our residence. The press play had led me to expect an ego in cowboy boots, with few thoughts beyond the script of his election strategy. Instead, I encountered a man who had obviously thought carefully about Mexico's future. He was committed to pursuing liberal economic reform, and serious about changing the country's political dynamic to give the people faith in their government. He was also humorous, sometimes in a self-deprecating fashion, and possessed the greatest gift a politician can have, the ability to see himself from a distance. I had been prepared to run into a media creation of flash and filigree and found someone who could offer Mexico a concrete plan for the future. Whether he had the political skills or the running room to implement that plan was another issue. But clearly Vicente Fox was going to be a formidable candidate.

While Fox liked to talk about broad political and social themes, Labastida's conversations were often studded with imposing renditions of fact and detail. His mind was as organized as an accountant's spreadsheet. He would note ten important factors relating to a given topic, tax policy, for instance and then reel them off with extraordinary facility and attention to statistics, names, and dates. Though a very pleasant man, he came across as more somber, more serious, more battle-hardened than Fox.

Several of our early conversations dealt with issues Labastida managed as interior minister, including the conflict in Chiapas. I made a strong pitch for him to take a more aggressive public posture in the search for peace. I urged that the Mexicans invite the UN human rights commissioner, Mary Robinson, to visit Chiapas so that the bad press Mexico was receiving, more in Europe than in the United States, could be addressed. Chiapas had taken center stage once again in December 1997 when forty-five peasants were killed in the pro-Zapatista village of Acteal by members of a rival campesino group. Labastida, who had taken over the Ministry of Interior when his predecessor was removed for bumbling the massacre investigation, told me that the incident had little to do with the Zapatista cause. He asserted that it had actually exploded over a land dispute. But that message, true or not, was not getting an international hearing. There was broad suspicion that the peasants who committed the murders were members of an illegal anti-Zapatista paramilitary force that had been armed by Mexican authorities.

Labastida and others left me with the impression that the government believed the Zapatistas would not come back to the negotiating table before the elections of 2000. I did not find fault with their analysis. But by acquiescing in that delay, by not presenting the government as energetically searching for a solution, Mexico was damaging its international reputation. This was a concern to Washington. The United States wanted a Mexican neighbor that was, and was seen to be, actively promoting the kind of social order that would attract international investment and promote support among its own people for a dynamic, modern democracy. I suggested to Labastida that there was value in being seen trying to solve the Chiapas crisis, even when the probability of success was remote. He paid no attention to my advice.

Under Mexico's election law, Labastida had to resign as interior minister by mid-1999 in order to become a presidential aspirant. Before his resignation, we had many discussions about his personal history, law and order, and Mexico's response to the narcotics trade. Labastida made no effort to hide his doubts about the trend of the economy. Trained as a traditional Mexican economist, he questioned many of the approaches of Zedillo and his two predecessors. Labastida's knowledge of the drug scene was impressive. He had been given a pot of money—intended to reach $500 million over a three-year period—to buy new equipment and otherwise improve federal and state antidrug activities. But his brushes with the narcotics problem long preceded his administration of those funds. He had been previously targeted in the U.S. press with a DEA leak alleging narcotics ties. During the 1998 certification game, the Washington *Times* had reported that while governor of Sinaloa, Labastida had worked out an agreement with the narcos. According to the story, Labastida had pledged not to challenge the traffickers, if they kept their traditional violence out of his state. I had seen no credible evidence to support that report, and said so at a congressional hearing when I was assistant secretary. General Barry McCaffrey, the White House drug czar, said the same thing.

Labastida went to considerable lengths to clear his name. He gave a detailed account of his antidrug activities to a friendly American academic, who faxed it around Washington. Labastida told me how several of his closest collaborators in Sinaloa had been assassinated because of his tough stance against the traffickers. The threats against his family had become so severe that he was sent to Portugal as Mexico's ambassador.

I also enjoyed talking with the PRI's other leading pre-candidate, Tabasco Governor Roberto Madrazo. He had a distinguished political pedigree. His father had also served as the state's governor and was later elected to the PRI party presidency. There, his attempts at democratic reforms in the 1960s ran up against the hierarchy led by President Gustavo Díaz Ordaz. When he died in a commercial plane crash, many Mexicans were convinced that his PRI opponents had killed him. The younger Madrazo never mentioned his father's death to me, but clearly there was a highly personal dimension in his effort to pick up the mantle of opposition to the party leadership. An immensely disciplined man— he would rise at dawn for hours of running and exercise—Madrazo was emerging as the most likely beneficiary of a more open PRI selection process. Because Madrazo was governor during most of his campaign for the nomination, he had an advantage over Labastida. As a cabinet minister, Labastida was obliged to defend, or at least not criticize, the federal government's policies. Madrazo faced no such constraint and presented himself as a vocal populist. Although he frequently condemned Zedillo's neoliberal economic policies in public, in our conversations his views on social and economic issues seemed indistinguishable from those of the president.

Zedillo distrusted Madrazo, whose election as governor in 1994 had allegedly been tainted with dirty money. Zedillo tried to have Madrazo removed from office. He assigned a member of his cabinet, Esteban Moctezuma, to lead that effort, which ultimately failed. In a remarkable illustration of the intricate world of the PRI—where everyone has a history with everyone else—Moctezuma became Labastida's campaign manager in 1999.

I first called on Cuauhtémoc Cárdenas in his mayor's office near Mexico City's central square, the Zocalo. The son of one of the country's most revered presidents, Cárdenas had spent six years of his childhood living in Los Pinos. Long an important PRI member, he had broken with the party in the mid-1980s and formed the leftist Partido Revolucionario Democratico (PRD). Under that party's banner, he ran for president in the disputed 1988 election and again in 1994. His concern for the poor was real and his personal popularity was considerable, especially in Mexico City. But his party had yet to pose a significant threat to the PRI. Cárdenas had become the icon of the left. This suited his persona, which was wooden and serious and distinctly different from the traditional gregarious Mexican politico. Cárdenas actually looked pained most of the time, especially while campaigning. After our initial meeting in his office, we had chats at my home periodically, but less often than I talked with the other three candidates. As a traditionally polite Mexican, he did not tell me of the strong suspicions I knew he harbored about the United States, its role in the world and its intentions toward Mexico.

One presidential contender absent from the list of frequent guests at the ambassador's residence was Manuel Bartlett, governor of Puebla and a man generally recognized as one of the PRI's leading old-line thinkers—"dinosaurs." As minister of interior in 1988, he was in charge of the government computers that failed during the presidential vote count. Political cartoons bitterly portrayed him yanking a computer plug from its socket.

But it was not Bartlett's antediluvian views or his checkered political past that made it difficult for us to have personal contact. Rather, it was his alleged involvement in the most infamous narcotics-related incident in the history of U.S.-Mexican relations, the kidnapping and murder of DEA agent Enrique Camarena in 1985. The DEA was convinced that the cartel would not have dared go after Camarena without high-level government approval. Though he maintained good relations with a series of American ambassadors, Bartlett was viewed by the DEA with smoldering suspicion.

That suspicion was based in part on statements from two low-level criminals who were interrogated in Los Angeles five years after Camarena's death. They said they had seen Bartlett, who was then serving as Minister of Interior, as well as a number of other high-ranking Mexican officials, enter the Guadalajara house where Camarena was being tortured. The DEA had been looking for the high-level connection for years, and now they had it. The DEA did not factor into their thinking that an accusation like this would also be useful to a wide range of

Mexicans who hated Bartlett for various reasons. Moreover, whatever crimes, political or otherwise, Bartlett may have committed, no one ever accused him of being stupid. For a cabinet minister to travel to Guadalajara to visit the house where a U.S. government agent was being tortured just did not seem very likely to me. But U.S. investigators believed that they could make the case against Bartlett. A grand jury in Los Angeles issued a subpoena for him to appear and answer questions about the allegations. Over the course of several years, his representatives engaged in quiet negotiations with the U.S. Department of Justice. Ultimately, he was offered the opportunity to come to Los Angeles, testify, and be guaranteed that, no matter what was revealed in his testimony or in other evidence, he would be allowed to return to Mexico. Bartlett refused. Perhaps the well-paid American law firm that he had hired to clear his name advised him to stay away. To my knowledge, he never traveled to the U.S. again.

When asked about Bartlett by the press or other politicians, I would simply lay out the facts, always being careful to note that I had no view about his guilt or innocence. That simple recitation was taken in some quarters as proof of American intent to veto him as a presidential candidate. Bartlett's opponents in the PRI used my words politically. As 1999 moved along, Bartlett's candidacy sputtered and died under the weight of the Camarena scandal, the 1988 election, and his dinosaur image. Nevertheless, he remains a powerful political force within the PRI.

Throughout much of 1999 there were two major questions about the selection of candidates for the following year's presidential contest. How could the PRI, without the definitive presidential mandate of the dedazo, avoid a schism and unite behind one man? And would the opposition parties unite to take on the ruling party, or risk diluting the strength of voters who wanted to kick the PRI out of Los Pinos?

It would have been traditional for the PRI to hold a nominating convention to choose its candidate. Such events were the practice even though they were little more than coronations of the already chosen candidate. But Madrazo, understanding that Labastida would likely dominate a convention because he was the choice of the party establishment, demanded a primary election. Moreover, he said that since the party wanted to be more democratic, it should open the primary to all voters, not just to PRI members. The Labastida forces took a calculated gamble and accepted the primary, hoping to energize the party for the general election. It was a rough affair. Madrazo presented himself as a forceful agent of change ready to make necessary reforms. He painted Labastida as a dull remnant of the old, discredited PRI. Meanwhile, Labastida struggled to find ways to differentiate himself from the government without appearing treacherous or alienating the party leadership. Certainly his alliance with Zedillo, and Zedillo's disdain for Madrazo, must have helped the internal workings of his campaign in ways still unknown.

Labastida was confident when he arrived at the polls for the November election. A few days before, he had predicted to me that he would win 230 of the country's 300 voting districts. In fact, he won 270 and carried the election by a six-to-four margin. Some observers claimed that the final results fraudulently inflated the turnout, but few doubted Labastida's victory. Madrazo acknowledged to me a few days later that he had lost even though the numbers had been altered. Two years later, however, he told me he had really won the vote but chose not to challenge the results because he knew the PRI candidate was destined to lose in 2000. To me, the lack of a formal challenge by Madrazo or others in the party suggested that the PRI was more concerned about unity in a tough general election than it was about democratic reforms.

Some irresponsible press coverage of the primary stirred a fuss and briefly made President Clinton a story. Asked what he thought of the PRI primary results, the president responded by congratulating Mexico and President Zedillo for taking another step toward full democracy. Some articles distorted his words to give the impression that Clinton had endorsed the PRI and Labastida. That generated the usual indignant huffing and puffing about American interference. Vicente Fox told the press that he had complained to me about American partisanship. He and I had met the evening before, and our conversation included not one word of concern. We had not discussed Clinton's comments. I chose not to respond in the press, but let it be known to Fox's staff that I did not appreciate his comments. To my knowledge, he never misrepresented our discussions again.

Among the leading opposition parties, it was clear that Fox would be the choice of the PAN, and that Cárdenas would represent the PRD. But would either one stand a chance in a three-way race involving the PRI? Most observers thought no. So for several months the PAN and PRD engaged in very public negotiations aimed at an open primary in which Fox and Cárdenas would compete for the combined support of the two parties. On the face of things, this was not a bad idea. But there was no chance that two such radically differing philosophies could unite behind a single man. The PAN's leader, the charming lawyer and power broker Diego Fernández de Cevallos, spluttered to me at breakfast one morning, "Can you imagine me marching in the street, cheering for Cárdenas?" I could not, and neither could I imagine Cárdenas and his leftist support-ers taking to the streets in support of Fox. Ultimately, the negotiating charade ended and the PAN joined with the minuscule and corrupt Green Party, while the PRD put together an alliance with several small and insignificant leftist parties.

As 2000 began, it was clear that Labastida, Fox, and Cárdenas would somehow divide the vote in the tensely anticipated presidential election. Most smart money was betting that the machine strength the PRI would apply against the divided opposition would carry it to victory. Labastida seemed to have the best chance of becoming Mexico's next president.

C
H
A
P
T
E
R

E
I
G
H
T

Dancing on
Marbles in Chinatown

The jellybeans were for the attorney general's daughter. It was a beautiful Sunday morning in June 2000. I did not want to intrude upon his home without bringing something for the two-year-old. Their house was a modest one. All the windows had been replaced with bullet-proof glass, and there was a small army of guards at the gate. As Mexico's chief law enforcement officer, he was a target of assassination.

I enjoyed the company of Jorge Madrazo (no relation of PRI politician Roberto Madrazo), but this was not a social visit. It was another run of the ambassadorial fire engine, rushing to put out a brushfire before it became a conflagration. The often bitter suspicion between U.S. and Mexican law enforcement authorities and the never-ending resentment engendered by the certification process meant that whatever cooperation we could carve out on a day-to-day basis was always fragile. The Mexican press and political opposition, forever ready to wave the sovereignty flag, thoroughly complicated the scene. The PRI government was always skittish, fluctuating between cooperation and threats that it would retreat into self-defeating isolation. We were dancing on a floor littered with marbles. Madrazo was my dancing partner.

Much of my work as ambassador was crisis management. More often than not, it had to do with drug-related law enforcement incidents, trying to keep some real or perceived American transgression out of the press so that we could continue to build the shaky infrastructure of cooperative action. The embassy had a large enforcement staff in charge of liaison with Mexican authorities. But there were some things only the ambassador could do. The Sunday morning visit was one of them.

This particular flap was another case of American law enforcement overstepping its bounds. American cops, this time Customs agents operating on the American side of the border, had grown frustrated after more than a year of noncooperation by Mexican officials with their efforts to capture a wanted criminal. The man in question, let's call him Juan, was a naturalized U.S. citizen. He wholesaled drugs in the Mexican border town of Mexicali, from where his carriers took them northward. After repeated requests that he be arrested and deported to the United States went unanswered, the Customs agents decided to take matters into their own hands. They obtained the assistance of some Mexicali cops to pick up Juan and deliver him across the border.

American courts traditionally rule that the way a suspect is returned to the United States is not a matter of juridical concern. "Knock him on the head, put him a sack, and drop him on the other side," had been a long-standing practice in frontier communities. American police did similar favors for their Mexican counterparts. But the world had changed. The outrage about the kidnapping of Álvarez Macháin, the doctor who helped torture Camarena, had altered the border's free-wheeling style. The two countries had even signed a treaty in 1992 specifically prohibiting cross-border abductions. But the treaty met resistance in the U.S. Congress, where influential conservatives warned both the first President Bush and then President Clinton not to submit it for Senate ratification. They did not. But both wrote to President Zedillo affirming that the U.S. would not allow further abductions.

The Customs agents' deal with the Mexicali cops had clearly violated the presidential agreement. To make matters worse, the cops had bungled the assignment. They had picked up and delivered the wrong man—let's call him Pablo—a Juan look-alike who was a Mexican citizen and worked in the same dirty business. Pablo's family immediately demanded his return. Customs took a hard line, vowing that even though they had the wrong crook, they would keep him because he was wanted on other charges. I knew we had to give Pablo back, and do it fast before the protests of Pablo's family made it to the press and unleashed a firestorm. The Mexican government was not going to sit still and allow one of its citizens to be kidnapped and spirited out of the country. If the circumstances had been reversed, we certainly would not have remained quiet. The Mexicans, with their heightened sense of sovereignty, would be furious. Besides, there was too much at stake in the law enforcement relationship to risk future cooperation for a small-time hood. If the incident were made public, the Mexican press would go wild, politicians would beat their chests, and the government would raise high-level protests while lowering street-level law enforcement cooperation. We would stumble into another period of Casablanca-like recriminations.

I called Attorney General Reno, who agreed that that we had to move quickly to cap this fire by returning Pablo. But the Customs Service had strong allies in high places in the Treasury Department and insisted on keeping him. It was the same stiff-necked attitude that had given us the Casablanca mess. To hell with Mexican sensibilities. There were times when I shared their frustration and anger, and was inclined to quit the exquisitely choreographed dance that protected the pride of the Mexican government to the benefit of narcotics traffickers. But this was not one of those moments. The U.S. blunder was blatant. We did not need another blowup, especially just two weeks before a Mexican presidential election in which we had avoided becoming an issue.

Pablo had been delivered to the Customs agents on a Thursday night. By Friday night, I had worked out a deal with Mexican officials in the Foreign Ministry and the attorney general's office to solve the problem. It was apparent that the Mexican government wanted to avoid another high-profile confrontation with us, but for that they needed Pablo back home. We worked out a multipart, complex agreement. In essence, Pablo would be returned and Mexico would try him for crimes committed in the United States, a process provided for by the Mexican penal code. The Mexicans also agreed to look for the initial target, arrest and deport him. I understood that there was a fundamental imbalance in the bargain. We had committed to a specific, concrete action while the Mexicans were making promises about the future. I doubted that they would be able or willing to carry through on them, but at least we would be able to work our way out of the current mess.

On Saturday, the agreement came close to falling apart several times. The first problem came when the Treasury Department, also doubting Mexico's willingness or capability to carry through on the bargain, insisted that the Mexicans put the understanding in writing. I said that they would not be able to go on the record committing to anything that could be portrayed as a negotiation for the return of one of their citizens who had been kidnapped. While I was fighting with Treasury, Eduardo Ibarrola, Madrazo's chief deputy, called to say that his boss had not accepted the deal. I chose not to tell Treasury that for the moment they were simply negotiating with me.

I refined my tactics during a sleepless Saturday night. If I couldn't get Treasury to cooperate, I would ignore them. After all, Pablo was in the hands of the U.S. attorney in San Diego, who took orders from the attorney general of the United States. She would play ball, if I could get Madrazo back on the team. Thus the trip to his house.

He was upset. He had invested a lot of time and personal prestige defending cooperation with the United States. He had been the target of vicious attacks by critics who claimed he had cooperated too much. Now, once again, U.S. law enforcement had done exactly as it pleased without deference to him or to Mexico's laws. Madrazo and I discussed the incident, Janet Reno's desire to set it right, and the proposed agreement. But he still needed some stroking, so by applying much cellular telephone wizardry—his, not mine—we got Reno on the phone. Her security detail tracked her down at a wedding. The two attorneys general spoke briefly and agreed to put the plan into action. The next day the U.S. attorney in San Diego told a federal judge that the charges against Pablo were being suspended. He was returned to Mexico and sent to prison in Mexico City. Much later, when Pablo came to trial, his lawyers demanded to interview the Customs agents who had arranged to have him brought to the United States. American authorities naturally refused, so Pablo went free. At last report, he and Juan were still dealing drugs in Mexicali.

The incident had many of the elements common to the binational drug scene: U.S. cops, frustrated by Mexican inaction and corruption, fell into excess that indignant Mexican authorities took as another example of roughshod intrusiveness. The situation turned ugly, but (and this did not happen all of the time) Mexican and American officials found a way to patch things together—at least until the next crisis came along.

In the last years of the Zedillo administration, antidrug cooperation with Mexico improved. But the two governments' law enforcement agencies had little foundation upon which to build a lasting relationship.

The threat of a blowup like the one Casablanca caused—and the Mexicali incident nearly engendered—brought a heightened sense of precariousness to the relationship. On the American side, that unease was magnified by the knowledge that we could be sure about very little. The corruption and double-dealing in Mexican law enforcement were immense. Time after time we saw cases dissolve as criminals paid off the cops or judges issued suspect rulings. Rumors about high-level politicians and cops on the drug dealers' payrolls flowed incessantly, and the Washington headquarters of the law enforcement agencies tended to believe them all. Fortunately, their agents in Mexico were more savvy, picking and choosing collaborators among Mexican police. But they always had to be ready to jettison yesterday's friend, if today's intelligence turned up damning data.

Statistics are unreliable, but experts agree that about 70 percent of the cocaine coming north from South America passes through Mexico. Most of the foreign marijuana (domestic growers produce about 50 percent of what the U.S. consumes) is grown and transported from Mexico. In recent years, Mexico has also become a major source of methamphetamines and other chemical drugs like ecstasy. Mexican cartels, as I had noted in my ill-fated speech to the USC alumni, are major players in U.S. crime.

I debated constantly, with myself and with others, the issue of legalizing narcotics. There are no easy answers. I would certainly prefer to concentrate our resources on other national needs. But, at base, we cannot ignore that we also need to fight the narcotics trade. Those who disagree give little attention to the "what if" costs of turning away from the fight. What if some or all drugs were more readily available with no threat of punishment for their sale or use? Would fewer young people experiment with marijuana and then move on to other drugs? Would we be better off if we made drugs as easily obtainable as booze and tobacco? I do not think so. Legalization of drugs would lead to greater use, and government has an obligation to avoid such a tragedy. Every serious law enforcement official involved in fighting narcotics believes that we must spend much more to promote demand reduction, education, and treatment. But we cannot stop trying to interdict the flow from abroad, and for this we need Mexico's active cooperation.

It fell to the embassy to thread the needle of cooperation between the zeal and suspicions of Washington and the resentment of Mexico. Attorney General Reno was indispensable to that effort. Her interest in Mexico never flagged. And though often frustrated, she worked hard to give cooperation a chance. The general attitude of the Washington cops—DEA, FBI, Customs, and a half-dozen others—was at best skeptical about dealing with Mexican authorities. There was a grudging acknowledgment that cooperation was necessary, but rarely was there enthusiastic acceptance.

The attorney general's job was made particularly difficult because she did not have full control over DEA Director Tom Constantine or Louis Freeh of the FBI, even though both ostensibly reported to her. Nor did she supervise the chief of the Customs Service, the once and future New York City police commissioner, Raymond Kelly, who reported to the secretary of the treasury. All of the Washington agency heads were extraordinarily strong personalities. They were frequently at odds with each other and had varying degrees of public relations skill. They were, at heart, tough cops, fiercely devoted to their subordinates and impatient with the diplomatic niceties that are indispensable to international cooperation.

Another key player was the U.S. drug czar, General Barry McCaffrey, whose formal title was director of the White House Office of National Drug Control Policy, the ONDCP. Wounded three times in Vietnam and a commander in the Gulf War, McCaffrey was a legitimate military hero and had the presence to go along with it. President Clinton had chosen him to put new life in the ONDCP and to provide a White House that was often accused of being soft on drugs with a strong, unassailable public persona. McCaffrey was always aware that his presence served a political need for the president and that his departure would be damaging. He used that leverage and his strong personality to exert his influence, at times with uncommon ferocity, even by Washington standards. A born enthusiast, McCaffrey knew that his image as a war hero fighting another kind of national security battle with help from our friends was an important part of generating public support in the drug fight.

Sometimes his enthusiasm would get the better of him, as with his effusive praise for soon-to-be-arrested Mexican drug chief General Jesús Gutiérrez Rebollo. In late 1996, McCaffrey described Gutiérrez, who had recently been appointed to his position and whom he had just met, as "a guy of absolute unquestioned integrity" and an honorable and successful warrior. A few weeks later Gutiérrez was in jail. His enemies revealed that his vaunted success against one drug cartel was based on information he had been given by competing drug dealers. In return for the information, a luxurious apartment, and other gifts, he turned a blind eye to the helpful cartel's crimes. The U.S. press delighted in dragging up McCaffrey's praise for the jailed general, but he just soldiered on. Immensely articulate and forceful, he had a sometimes-difficult relationship with Attorney General Reno. Together, however, they made a good team, though they may not have realized it.

Combating the drug trade was difficult in Mexico for many reasons. The country was plagued by corruption, inadequate laws, weak police, and inefficient (at best) judicial structures. There were immense and bitter suspicions among Mexican law enforcement agencies, and there was a massive web of politically motivated complicity. All of this bred distrust and discomfort in Washington. That unease found its mirror image in Mexico, where honest officials were riled by Washington's reluctance to share information or otherwise cooperate with Mexico and by its politically motivated leaks to the press.

This turbulent environment made it difficult to distinguish truth from falsehood. Sometimes I believed everything I heard and then criticized myself for being gullible or naive. Other times I distrusted everything and everyone, and later faulted myself for cynicism and suspicion. I often thought of the movie starring Jack Nicholson, set in the Chinatown of Los Angeles, in which there were no answers for many questions simply because it was "Chinatown," impenetrable and enigmatic to outsiders.

There are honest policemen, judges, and prosecutors in Mexico. The problem is knowing who they are. As I traveled around the country and met with state governors, I always made a point of asking if they could depend on the local or state police to fight the narcotics traffickers. Some would stutter and dissemble, but most looked at me with an "are you crazy?" stare. Most of the governors had no confidence in their own law enforcement officials. Most were also absolutely convinced that the representatives of the central authority—the district representatives of the federal attorney general (the PGR) or the Mexican Customs Service, for example—were even more corrupt. Indeed, at the embassy we knew this to be the case in many instances. After all, it had been PGR officers who accompanied the corrupt bankers to the Casablanca meetings with the undercover operatives. In 1998, the year I arrived in Mexico, every major investigation in which the DEA cooperated with the federal PGR was blown by well-remunerated leaks to the drug dealers from inside the Mexican government. Public employees corrupted by drug money are one of Mexico's greatest tragedies.

Reports of corruption were rampant, and even if only partially true, painted a picture of a system gone wild. We heard that Mexican customs officials would pay their superiors up to a million dollars to be appointed agent-in-charge at a busy border crossing post. It was a good investment because the job gave them the chance to make arrangements with the local narcotics, migrant, and contraband smugglers. Though Attorney General Madrazo and several of his immediate team were honest, the PGR was rotten with corruption. In one instance, Mexican army operatives using DEA information captured two big drug fish in Cancún. But since the army had no right of arrest, it turned them over to PGR officials, who, we were told, released them for a reported payment of one million dollars.

We also suspected corruption when criminals went unapprehended or unpunished. In November 1999, an FBI agent and a DEA colleague assigned to our consulate in Monterrey were waylaid on a road near Matamoros by Osiel Cárdenas, a nearly insane rising star in the drug firmament who sported a gold-plated AK-47. Accompanied by fifteen of his men, Cárdenas threatened to kill the Americans. He probably would have done so if not for the cool heads of the two agents, who informed him: "If you think the U.S. government is causing you problems now, just imagine what would happen if you murdered us." Cárdenas saw the wisdom of that point of view and released them. Indeed, it was only the fear of massive American retaliation that provided a thin shield of protection to American law enforcement officers assigned to the embassy and the consulates. After the incident the embassy swung into high gear. I ordered the two agents in question out of the country for their protection. The first PGR team sent to search for Cárdenas at our request was bought off within days. That team was pulled out, but others who were sent in had no better luck, perhaps for the same reason. Osiel Cárdenas remained free for more than three years by intimidating or buying off the local police and federal agents. Three Mexican military men were ultimately convicted for providing him with protection. He was captured in a Wild West shootout with the Mexican army in early 2003.

The halfhearted Mexican response to the Cárdenas incident outraged the Washington agencies, particularly the DEA. Haunted by the memory of Enrique Camarena's 1985 murder, the agency chafed at the Mexican rule that denied the agents permission to carry weapons for their self-defense. The Mexican government argued that armed foreigners would constitute a major breach of national sovereignty. The issue had been kicking around quietly for years before DEA Chief Constantine and others inadvisedly brought it up publicly in 1997, obliging President Zedillo to repeat publicly the official Mexican position. That dug the two sides further into their trenches and demonstrated that some issues are better left undiscussed.

Unlike U.S. authorities, who responded with alarm to any threat against American personnel, high-ranking Mexican officials in the PGR and elsewhere appeared to be relatively unmoved even when their own men were killed. Most Mexicans believe all police are corrupt, so when an officer is killed they assume it is the result of a falling out among thieves. They apply similar cynicism to reports of the death of a judge or prosecuting attorney. Frequently they are correct, but the disservice to the memory of the honest is tragic.

There was an exception to the general rule of disrespect for the fallen in the death of Jesús Patiño in 2000. He was killed shortly after he became the new PGR delegate in Tijuana and began to work with the FBI office in San Diego. The FBI provided Patiño with a list of properties known to be owned by Ismael Higuera, a Tijuana drug heavy. Within hours, the list was in Higuera's hands, obviously leaked by someone in Patiño's office. A few days later, as he returned to Mexico after driving to San Diego to discuss the leak with the FBI, Patiño and two associates were forced off the road and killed. The FBI was convinced that the same corrupt PGR associates who had passed the property list to Higuera were the ones who set up Patiño's death. No one has been prosecuted for the murder. In this instance, the PGR, prodded by the FBI, held a memorial service, which I attended to show my respect for Patiño.

As the century closed, it seemed that Mexican law enforcement was actually becoming more corrupt. PRI political control had kept at least some order among corrupt public officials. But as that hegemony weakened, an every-man-for-himself situation emerged. Yet the connection among PRI political stalwarts remained strong, as demonstrated by the case of Mario Villanueva. Known as El Chueco ("the Crooked One"), for both a facial distortion and his rampant corruption, Villanueva was governor of Quintana Roo, the beautiful state on Mexico's Caribbean coast where Cancún is located. According to an indictment filed in a U.S. court, Villanueva essentially rented his state to narcotics traffickers, taking a cut of each shipment that came ashore. Attorney General Madrazo had a strong case against Villanueva as early as 1998 but could not arrest him because the Mexican Constitution provides governors with immunity against prosecution. The immunity could have been lifted by a congressional vote, but that would have embarrassed the PRI. Madrazo would have to wait until Villanueva left office.

All of this played out in the press, so it was not a big surprise that in late April 1999, just a few weeks before his term was scheduled to end, Villanueva disappeared. His last known meeting was with Governor Cervera Pacheco in the capital of the neighboring state of Yucatan. Then he vanished. Madrazo was convinced that Villanueva had been flown out of the country in a government plane commandeered by his cousin, a high-ranking military man who, ironically, remained an excellent antidrug collaborator of the embassy. Villanueva stayed on the run for two years. The DEA actively searched for him outside of Mexico while the PGR covered the local scene. Finally, two years later after a confidential source gave him up, he was arrested in Cancún, looking much the worse for wear. Villanueva awaits trial in Mexico and is also the subject of a warrant in New York for laundering millions of dollars. His case was symptomatic of the cronyism that protected high-level PRI criminals.

Even when not encumbered by corruption or cronyism, Mexico's legal system is not up to the challenges of modern law enforcement. Part of the problem is historical in origin. Government abuse of power is a long-standing Latin American tradition. Police brutality and torture remain commonplace in Mexico. But alongside that tradition, another has developed to protect individuals from abuse. It has had the unfortunate consequence of providing suspected criminals with rights well beyond anything available in the United States. Any person can seek a judicial *amparo*, an injunction to prevent the state from taking a specific action. While the amparo is most often used by the wealthy in tax and property cases, in recent years criminals have actually obtained court orders to prohibit their arrest. Of course, the government can try to overturn the amparo. But like much else in the legal system, that can take years.

Criminal suspects also have the right to impede efforts to collect evidence against them. They cannot be required to provide blood, saliva, hair, or handwriting samples. They can decline to give police a handwriting sample. If a booking photograph or a fingerprint chart is somehow misplaced (not too difficult a trick for a crooked lawyer to arrange), a second photograph or set of prints cannot be taken without the individual's consent. It is generally impossible for police to obtain statements from an uncooperative witness, and police are also obstructed in efforts to subpoena business records or private documents from an uncooperative individual or company.

In November 1996, Mexican law was changed to authorize the use of tools essential for breaking into closed organized crime rings. Undercover operations, telephone interceptions (long practiced, but illegal), plea agreements, and witness-protection programs were made legal. But the definition of organized crime remained so restrictive that investigators were reluctant to use the new tools because they expected the courts would strike them down. In the summer of 2002, six years after the new legislation was passed, the Mexican Supreme Court ruled the changes were constitutional. However, most judges continued to regard sting operations as entrapment and as a governmental abuse of power. Moreover, the judicial system itself lacks transparency. Trials are not public and pleadings are not delivered orally. There are no juries. The system is Dickensian in its delays. Judges commonly take years, especially in amparo or appeals cases, to render their decisions.

In April 2002 the United Nations Human Rights Commission reported that corruption in Mexican courts had increased in recent years owing to expanding drug traffic. It noted that there was no system of accountability for lawyers and that intimidation of human rights attorneys by government officials was common. The UN investigator, a Malaysian judge, expressed surprise that in spite of widespread allegations of corruption, few judicial officials had been disciplined. Corruption and other forms of abuse thrived because there was no effective system of vigilance and punishment. Mexican law enforcement agencies and courts lacked internal affairs divisions. Investigations were few and far between. When police agencies did launch an investigation, they did not utilize the tools—secret cameras, sting operations, etc.—that are necessary to break into the world of organized corruption.

The Mexican legal system also made it extraordinarily difficult to extradite criminal suspects to another country. For years, the foreign ministry (the SRE) had refused to approve the extradition of Mexican citizens to the United States, even though that was clearly authorized in a 1978 treaty. Mexico was willing to extradite only Americans and citizens of third countries. In 1996, under immense pressure from the annual certification process in the United States, the SRE changed its interpretation of Mexican law to allow the extradition of Mexicans in exceptional cases, usually horrific crimes of child abuse or multiple murders. But big narcotics dealers, whose crimes might be considered exceptional, got amparos to prevent their extradition. Their lawyers argued successfully that extradition was not necessary since Article Four of the Mexican penal code provides for trying Mexican citizens in Mexico for crimes committed out of the country. After more than a year of deliberation, the Supreme Court ruled—just a few weeks after Vicente Fox took office at the end of 2000—that the penal code did not preclude extradition.

A handful of drug kingpins were sent to the United States in the year after that decision. But in late 2001, the Mexican Court ruled that since Mexico does not impose life sentences, no one could be extradited to face charges that risked such a sentence. The ruling caused considerable consternation in the United States, which had already accepted that Mexico, like many other nations, refused to extradite individuals facing a possible death sentence. Most American prosecutors requesting extradition pledged that the individual would not be put to death, but many were unwilling to give up the life sentence option, especially when they had already forsworn the death penalty.

The American legal profession generally saw the Mexican position as hypocritical. They wondered how principled it was to take a stand against life imprisonment when Mexican courts routinely issued sixty-year prison sentences. However, Mexico stuck to its absolutist position that a lengthy sentence is not necessarily a life sentence. That effectively stopped extradition of major narcotics traffickers. Other criminals also benefited. In one ridiculous instance, a Salvadoran woman wanted for murder in the United States escaped punishment. Because U.S. prosecutors refused to renounce pursuit of a life sentence punishment, Mexican authorities let her walk. If she had been a Mexican, she might have been eligible for trial in a Mexican court under Article Four of the penal code, but as a foreigner she was not. Particularly alarming for American prosecutors was that the Mexican Constitution, like its U.S. counterpart, guarantees foreigners the same rights as citizens. It is conceivable that an American citizen who commits murder in the U.S. and then escapes to Mexico would be set free, if an American prosecutor refused to go along with Mexico's position on the death penalty and life imprisonment. I was reminded of this after I left Mexico, when Scott Peterson, a Californian suspected of killing his wife and unborn child, was arrested just a few miles north of the border. If he had made it to Mexico, and had American prosecutors asked for the death penalty or life imprisonment, he could have successfully fought extradition.

The most frightening tool American law enforcement can wield against drug traffickers and other criminals is the threat of trial in an American court. But the Mexican legal profession views extradition through the rhetorical haze of national sovereignty. The Mexican argument seems to be: "They are our citizens; we should be the ones to try them and punish them for their crimes." That approach is unrealistic. It ignores the fact that some acts that are crimes in the United States are not considered offenses in Mexico—criminal conspiracy and racketeering, to name two. The approach is also impractical. It ignores the common-sense fact that suspects should be tried where they are alleged to have committed the crime—so witnesses can be assembled to testify and victims can see justice done.

For Mexico, working with the behemoth to the north in the fight against narcotics or in other law enforcement issues is often not easy. Often our attempts to be of assistance caused more problems and greater friction. The bear's embrace can be as uncomfortable as the bear's attack. In October 1995, three years before I became ambassador, William Perry became the first U.S. secretary of defense to visit Mexico. Neither our embassy nor the Mexican military was thrilled with the prospect of his visit. Over the years, the Mexican armed forces had maintained a fairly distant contact with their U.S. counterparts. The U.S. military had, for the most part, kept its distance as well, respecting Mexican sensitivities.

But given the greater role the U.S. military was playing in the fight against drugs and the increased cooperation it was stimulating in Latin America, Perry wanted to visit Mexico.

One result of his visit was an agreement by the Mexican Army to revamp its drug interdiction effort by using U.S.-supplied helicopters. The new plan, devised in Washington, envisioned company-sized units spread over the country with their own mobile air capacity. Upon receiving intelligence about an impending drug delivery by small plane—the favored tactic of the dealers at the time—the helicopters with troops aboard would swoop down on the bad guys like a scene from *Apocalypse Now*.

The agreement looked good on paper, but it never really worked, principally because the helicopters provided by the U.S. Army were the famous Hueys of Vietnam. They were thirty-year-old cranky machines that needed constant care and spare parts that were either unavailable or too costly. The Mexican Army also resented that the Hueys came with strings attached: they had to be used principally for antinarcotics efforts and could not be sent to Chiapas or any other locale of civil disturbance. The machines broke down, and within a couple years most were unflyable. Disputes developed over which country would pay for repairs, and both alleged bad faith. Ultimately, a plan was agreed upon for Mexico to turn its seventy-two Hueys over to the United States for cannibalization of spare parts at an air force base near Phoenix. Then twenty of the rebuilt craft would return to Mexico. However, once the helicopters were delivered to Arizona, the Mexicans informed us that they did not want any of them back. This did not surprise me in the least. Working with the U.S. on this issue was just too much trouble for too little reward.

Another example of good intentions gone bad was an ill-designed FBI operation to look for the bodies of narcotics dealers reportedly buried near Ciudad Juárez. The Bureau offered its help in late 1999, when Ciudad Juárez, the border city that faces El Paso, had become the unofficial capital of missing persons. Scores of young women drawn to the city to work in its factories had been raped and killed. Their murderers remained at large. In 1997, the American press also reported on the disappearance of scores of other persons presumed to have been involved in the narcotics trade. The story that Sam Dillon wrote for the *New York Times* helped him win the Pulitzer Prize. He reported that many on the border felt that the Clinton administration was ignoring the problem, even though some of the disappeared were American citizens.

In late 1999, an FBI informant in Texas reported that he knew of a ranch on the Mexican side of the border where as many as a hundred bodies were buried. Some of the murders had occurred on the U.S. side near El Paso. The source appeared to be credible. He even admitted that he had actually participated in some of the executions. The FBI shared the information with the Mexican PGR and elicited an invitation from Attorney General Madrazo to join the search for the bodies. I approved the plan but did not ask the right questions. I assumed that the Bureau would send a few forensic investigators to work with a much larger number of Mexican police in excavating the supposed burial ground.

Instead, the FBI sent enough men and machinery across the border to build a six-lane highway. What should have been a quiet effort in law enforcement cooperation became a media circus. FBI Director Louis Freeh made a special trip to the area to buck up his troops and to inform the press of the splendid example of U.S.-Mexico cooperation. But in Mexico the press attention led to attacks on Attorney General Madrazo on the old charge of ceding sovereignty. The effort was portrayed as an American ploy to once again besmirch Mexico in the months before the certification decision. In the end, a few bodies were found, including those buried by the informant, but certainly not the hundred he had talked about. The political fallout at a time when President Zedillo was planning a trip to Washington was severe. Zedillo was engaged in a budget battle with his own Congress, which threatened to deny him the constitutionally-required permission to leave the country. He withdrew his request. He probably could have pushed it through the legislature, but he had no desire to spend his time in the United States answering questions about the supposed mass graves in Juárez. As in the case of the helicopters, we had tried to do too much. Our attempt to impose our plan on the Mexicans backfired. Generally speaking, the U.S. military and law enforcement agencies lack rheostats. They are either on or off. And when they are on, they are on—big time. A little more restraint and a little less zeal would make their efforts a lot more effective.

Narcotics will continue for the foreseeable future to be a major issue in the U.S.-Mexico relationship. For years, U.S. congressional and public opinion tended to reduce our infinitely complex ties with Mexico to that one issue. The inordinately heavy focus on the certification debate was a mistake. It ignored the real progress we made. The focus from the U.S. side has broadened in recent years. At the same time, increasing levels of consumption in Mexico, rising incidents of drug-related crime, and a fear that illegal narcotics may do to Mexico what they have done to Colombia have led to greater concern on the part of the Mexican government and public. In Mexico, policemen, prosecutors, and judges are threatened or killed every day. Entire areas of certain states are off limits to the forces of law and order. They are controlled by narcotics dealers. The most important institutions of government are being undermined. Mexico's national security is at risk.

For all of the daily friction and the PRI government's fear of being branded sellouts, cooperation increased measurably during the Zedillo administration. The positive trend continued to expand with the election of Vicente Fox in July 2000.

As long as the United States provides an enormous market for illegal drugs, narcotics dealers will find a way to meet the demand. Mexico's weak institutions and its porous border with the United States are easy targets. Efforts to confront the criminals, to interrupt the chain of supply, and to arrest and punish the guilty will inevitably depend on how well the United States works with foreign police forces and judicial systems. Mexico offers sometimes overwhelming challenges in that regard. But cooperation is imperative. Experience has proven that success is possible.

C
H
A
P
T
E
R

N
I
N
E

The Caribbean Three-Step

Fidel Castro is a symbolic and political force in Mexico. He is part of the local political stage, and, occasionally, he becomes the lead actor. The Castro-Mexico tie of nearly fifty years would make a rich novel—replete with a shifting cast of colorful characters, spies, and treachery.

Successive PRI governments used Mexico's ties to Cuba to balance the country's ever-strengthening relationship with the United States. Mexico's relations with Castro's Cuba were not a traditional bilateral link. Instead, they were a complicated trilateral balancing game that always involved the United States.

One of the drama's most intriguing characters was a Mexican who knew Castro before Castro was Fidel, that is, before he became one of the few political figures in the world instantly identifiable by just one name. When I met Fernando Gutiérrez Barrios, he looked like an aging Latin film star, always faultlessly dressed and groomed, with brilliant white hair. By 1998, he had assumed senior statesman status within the PRI. In 1999 he supervised the PRI primary between Labastida and Madrazo, and in 2000 he ran for senator from his home state of Veracruz. Gutiérrez cultivated the image of a man who knew much more than he could ever reveal to a mere civilian. That is a common syndrome among spies, but I found it acceptable in him because he was such a pleasant conversationalist.

We met periodically in my home or at his, which was crowded with a lifetime of gifts received for favors given. Gutiérrez still enjoyed his contact with the American embassy. That relationship had been much deeper when he was a member of Mexico's spy agency. He had been a key player in managing his country's covert relations with both Cuba and the United States.

Gutiérrez's history with Cuba was long and deep. In 1955, as a recently graduated military officer and a member of the Directorate of Federal Security (DFS), he was assigned to supervise the exile of a young Cuban revolutionary. Castro's failed attack on Cuba's Moncada Barracks on July 26, 1953, had led to nearly two years in prison before his release and exile to Mexico. During his Mexican stay he refined his revolutionary zeal and prepared for his armed return to the island. He also met another young revolutionary, Ernesto Guevara, known to everyone by the standard Latin nickname for Argentines as "Che."

Gutiérrez, about the same age as Castro, treated his charge well. He turned a blind eye as the Cuban and about eighty of his friends left Mexico on the small boat, the *Granma*, in 1956 to reinitiate their struggle against the Batista regime. It was a skillful gambit for Mexico. Without breaking its relations with Batista, Mexico placed what turned out to be a winning bet on the future. Gutiérrez stayed in contact with Fidel and his government for decades. As the new century began, Castro was still in power. Gutiérrez died shortly after winning his 2000 senatorial race.

From the outset of Castro's regime, Mexico's attitude toward Cuba was a pastiche of romantic Latin American revolutionary rhetoric, domestic politics, and international realpolitik; it was also to pursue the themes of sovereignty and nonintervention. Gutiérrez was always circumspect when he and I talked of Cuba. He gave away no secrets. He left no doubt, however, that in Cuba, Mexico had found its own porcupine that needed careful handling. For the PRI, Castro was useful but also potentially dangerous. Support for the Cuban dictator burnished the PRI's revolutionary image with important domestic constituencies.

But Mexico had already had its revolution and did not need another one. Its desire for stability ran counter to Castro's plans to promote an anti-imperial, communist hemisphere. So Mexico's strategy was to maintain friendly ties to ensure that Castro would not support Mexican insurgents. In the 1970s, Mexico mercilessly wiped out its own guerrillas in a dirty war that saw hundreds "disappeared" by security forces. Gutiérrez Barrios was actively involved in that campaign, the details of which are only now coming to light. Castro may have given some support to the Mexican guerrillas, but he had to weigh his relationship with the Mexican government carefully in all that he did.

That was precisely the goal of Mexico's Cuba policy. Among Latin states, only Mexico did not go along with the United States in forcing Cuba out of the Organization of American States in 1962. It left open its commerce, industry, ports, and airports to the Cubans and those visiting or trading with the island. Mexico's official ties with Castro served to redirect his revolutionary zeal to other states whose governments were less helpful to him. But just in case, Gutiérrez Barrios and his colleagues kept a close watch on the Cuban embassy. They also passed information about its activities, as well as information about travelers passing through Mexico on their way to or from the island, to the U.S. government. They probably performed similar information-gathering services for the Cubans concerning the American embassy and the Cuban exile community in Mexico.

In Mexico, as elsewhere in Latin America, Fidel became an icon not only of the political left, but of the general public, which saw him as a hero confronting the American Goliath. That was a particularly attractive image in a country trapped in its own permanent David-like self-conception. Mexicans made much of their solidarity with the Cuban people. But the Mexican government supported the Castro regime, not those living under its tyranny. For decades it turned a blind eye to Castro's suppression of political liberty or accepted the argument that democracy on the island would have to wait until the threat from the United States ended. The Mexican political class, which vociferously denounced dictatorships elsewhere in Latin America—Chile under Pinochet, for instance—hypocritically ignored Castro's denial of freedom to his own people. It was a pitiful performance. Castro's defiance of the United States was heroic enough. More, it was thought, should not be demanded of Fidel.

The net effect was that for many years Castro was generally unassailable. He used his considerable personal charm to reinforce Mexican affections. In late 1998, I met with a group of conservative PAN senators who had just returned from Cuba. They were starry-eyed after experiencing one of Fidel's traditional seven-hour marathon monologues. They acknowledged, in response to my question, that they had not raised any human rights concerns. They had, however, found Castro immensely knowledgeable about the forthcoming Mexican elections. I suggested that they should have asked him when he was planning to hold his own multiparty elections. They did not appreciate my irony. Perhaps they did not even understand it. They could not conceive of challenging the Latin hero.

Over the years, any hint of a lessening of Mexico's official support for Cuba provoked protest from the leftist PRD, much of the PRI, and political commentators. In addition to cultivating the genuine affinity expressed by many Mexicans for Castro and his revolution, the Cuban government spent heavily to recruit spies and agents of influence. Some of them still occupy positions of importance in the Mexican bureaucracy and on the political stage. They can still be depended upon to deliver when asked.

In the 1990s, as Latin American governments moved closer to the concepts of open markets and liberal democracy, they vaccinated themselves against the domestic left by espousing friendship for Fidel, readmitting him, step by step, to the organizations of the Latin American family. Only continued U.S. opposition kept Cuba out of the Organization of American States and the Summit of the Americas meetings.

Despite its own vaccination efforts, as Mexico negotiated, prepared for, and then entered NAFTA, the contradictions of supporting a communist state in the Caribbean became ever more obvious. Tears appeared in the fabric of solidarity. When Mexican President Carlos Salinas traveled to Miami in 1992 to seek support for NAFTA in the Cuban-American community, he left the impression that Mexico's ties with Castro were loosening. A year earlier, and as part of the same Salinas effort, Mexico had abstained from voting on a U.S.-sponsored resolution, which the United Nations Human Rights Commission ultimately approved, to censure Cuba's human rights record. The abstention was a move (minor, to be sure) away from Mexico's traditional support for Castro, which was based on a firm adherence to the policy of noninterventionism. It surprised Cuba and much of Mexico.

In subsequent years, as the United States continued to introduce condemnatory resolutions on Cuba at the annual meeting of the Human Rights Commission in Geneva, Mexico's abstention was never a sure thing. The Foreign Ministry no doubt enjoyed watching us squirm as we sought to eke out yearly victories from a commission whose members over the years included the Soviet Union, Libya, Sudan, Iraq, and Cuba itself. But in 1999, Mexico shocked Washington when it broke its chain of abstentions and voted against the resolution. Some in Washington angrily asked why had our ambassador in Mexico City not read the tea leaves and told them what to expect? Good question. No good answer, though I assumed that Foreign Secretary Green had pulled a fast one.

In the following months, still stung by what had happened in Geneva, I tried to piece the story together. Finally, Green revealed what I was able to confirm elsewhere. She had not decided how to vote. It was President Zedillo who had made the decision. According to this version, a week before the Geneva vote, Castro cornered Zedillo at a meeting of Latin American presidents in the Dominican Republic. Sitting in the back of a bus that was taking the heads of state from one session to another, Castro pressed the Mexican president. The U.S. had just begun its bombing campaign in the former Yugoslavia, and Zedillo responded to the flexing of U.S. military muscle in the traditional Mexican defensive manner—indignation mixed with anxiety. What would be the next target of American interventionism, Castro asked. Havana? Chiapas? Zedillo agreed. Mexico would vote no in Geneva to show its concern about the United States pushing its weight around.

In deciding Mexico's position at Geneva, Zedillo may also have been trying to patch things up with Castro and restore balance to the relationship after the chilliness caused by a series of critical remarks Castro had made about Mexico. In December 1998 Castro told a Havana meeting that Latin Americans were losing their cultural identity. He said, "You can do the test. You can ask a lot of Mexican kids, for example, who were the founders of their nation, and it is possible that many will not know. But they know Mickey Mouse and the other principal characters of the cartoons that come from the United States. It is a fact that leads to a tremendous loss of identity."

The Mexican press handled Castro's remarks mischievously, presenting them as a commentary on Mexican patriotism, not as a criticism of American cultural imperialism. The words rankled in Mexico, though they were probably true, at least for younger kids. Zedillo recalled his ambassador for consultations. More incidents followed. In January 2000, Castro told the press that Mexico, Colombia, and a few other Latin states were really being run by the American ambassadors. It was too ludicrous a charge to even be flattering. Not wanting to get caught in the middle, I responded to press questions by noting that I could no longer comprehend what Castro was saying.

The back and forth between the two governments raised the predictable pro-Cuban defenses within Mexico. Zedillo was criticized by much of the political elite for over-reacting to Castro's comments. He was accused of somehow being responsible for messing up the historical tie. So when the Human Rights Commission vote on Cuba came up a few months later, he may have thought that a no-vote would get things back on an even keel. Green told me that once Zedillo had given his pledge to Fidel on the bus, she could not dissuade him. Zedillo was apparently surprised by the strength of the American response: Secretary Albright abruptly cancelled her participation in the Bi-National Commission meeting that brings cabinet officers together every year. Moreover, Mexico's ambassador in Washington was called in for the strongest protest he had heard in his years of service there.

The Cuba-Mexico relationship continued to oscillate wildly. In late 1999, Zedillo insisted that a clearly uncomfortable Green meet with Cuban dissident Elizardo Sánchez during her visit to the island. It was the first time that a high-level Mexican official visiting Cuba had met with a well-known opposition figure. The Cubans reacted furiously. A few months later Zedillo took Castro on again in their final meeting. With other Latin heads of state present, Zedillo, who was about to risk his party's future in the service of democracy and clean elections, refuted Castro's longtime assertion that Cuba was a democracy because the will of the people was reflected in the decisions of its government. Zedillo rejected the claim. Democracy exists, Zedillo bluntly said, when the people have a fair opportunity to choose their leaders in free and open elections among competing parties. His words were a startling challenge to Castro's self-justification and Latin American hypocrisy.

So much of the Cuban-Mexican relationship was played out below the surface that it was impossible to know what had triggered Fidel's attacks on Zedillo and the Mexican government. But there was a wealth of speculation. After the Mickey Mouse comment, Zedillo's private secretary, José Luis Barros, spun a view that the Cuban was trying to chill relations with Mexico because he wanted to move closer to Brazil, Mexico's traditional rival for the role of the preeminent Latin American nation. Two leading advisers to the Fox campaign, Jorge Castañeda and Adolfo Aguilar Zínser, suspected that former President Carlos Salinas was behind Castro's various comments. The suspicions about Salinas were fascinating.

In one of the ironies of the Cuban-Mexican relationship, Salinas, who had done so much to move Mexico closer to the United States by championing NAFTA, was living much of the time in Cuba. He had been welcomed by Castro after leaving Mexico, where he was generally vilified for the corruption of his administration and where his brother was in jail for a hugely scandalous murder. His relationship with the Zedillo government ran a narrow gamut from chilly to hostile. Certainly, over the years there had been other, less visible, favors traded between Castro and Salinas. Castro's welcome to Salinas to live on the island was only the latest. For staunch anti-PRI-istas like Castañeda and Aguilar Zínser, Salinas was still very much a presence in Mexico, something like Napoleon on Elba. It was natural for them to cast suspicion on him for the decay in the Cuban-Mexican relationship.

I offered the thought that Castro had spoken without being prompted and that he was simply frustrated at seeing Mexico, with its close economic ties to the U.S., advance while Cuba, now without the Soviet Union to rely on, remained in the socialist doldrums with no major international backer. Explanations aside, as Zedillo left office at the end of 2000, Mexican-Cuban relations were suffering a real chill. They were about to get much colder.

Generally, Cuba was not a topic of daily concern at the embassy, except for the hectic weeks preceding the annual Human Rights Commission vote. But the island was never far from our conversations when I met with Castro's most charming and dedicated apologist, Gabriel García Márquez. The Colombian novelist, one of the great writers of the century, had made a home in Mexico for many years, spending more time there as his own country spiraled downward. We had first met in Washington a few years earlier, where we conversed over breakfast in the Jockey Club. The topic was Cuba, and we essentially repeated the same conversation at intervals over the next five years.

Castro's repression had ultimately cost him the support of some, but certainly not the majority, of important Latin American artists and intellectuals. Mexico's Octavio Paz had been among the first to label Castro as the Caribbean tin-pot dictator that he is. Others followed. In 2000, for instance, ninety leading Mexican intellectuals signed a petition to their government, asking for an affirmative vote in Geneva. But García Márquez never wavered in his support for Fidel. Over the years, he had used his influence to secure the release of many political prisoners in Cuba. But he never publicly criticized the regime that imprisoned them.

In our conversations, García Márquez's consistent line was that the unremitting hostility of the United States had cornered Castro. The only way out of the stalemate was for the U.S. to end its embargo and reestablish diplomatic relations with Cuba, he said. With Americans and their goods flooding in, Cuba could become a different place. I countered that several U.S. administrations had searched for some sign of liberalization from Castro that would give them political cover to move toward normalization. I pointed out that Castro had repeatedly rejected any move that might put a crack, no matter how small, in the dam of communist control. García Márquez brushed the argument aside. He said it was America's responsibility, as the larger and more powerful nation, to demonstrate its strength by changing its policy.

On several occasions in the previous four decades, American administrations had used García Márquez as a channel to Castro. He recounted carrying a message from President Carter to Castro during the U.S. presidential campaign of 1980. Carter, according to García Márquez, wanted Castro to intercede with the Iranian government to release the American hostages. His motivation, García Márquez asserted, was that their release would ensure his reelection and enable him to restore diplomatic relations with Cuba in his second term. The Colombian insisted that Castro tried but failed to convince the Iranians. Carter lost. The hostages were released only as Ronald Reagan was taking the oath of office on January 20, 1981.

Our conversations did not focus exclusively on Cuba. As we talked about his family, I learned that he and his wife Mercedes were proud parents—their son was a Hollywood cinematographer and director—and typical grandparents. But mostly we talked history. He encouraged me to think of Mexico as a civilization, not as a country, with a history and cul-ture as rich and deep as those of Egypt or China. And we gossiped at length about Mexican, Colombian, and U.S. politicians. We met less fre-quently as he began to spend more time in Los Angeles, engaged in an apparently successful fight against cancer. But he was one of the first people I wanted to talk to when I arrived in Mexico. And I respected him enough to visit his house as I was rushing around on the last night before I left the embassy in 2002.

I wondered constantly how a man so brilliant, and so dedicated to unleashing human imagination and freedom, could turn a blind eye toward tyranny. There might have been multiple motives for García Márquez's dedication to Castro. Perhaps he acted out of political affinity, Latin solidarity, gratitude for the comfortable home and welcoming reception he had been given on the island, or respect for Castro's perse-verance. But I came to believe that he had been seduced by Castro's charm early on and rather enjoyed his association with another famous personage.

I saw the same star-struck quality in García Márquez's view of President Clinton. He and Carlos Fuentes had been introduced to the president at the home of novelist William Styron on Martha's Vineyard in the summer of 1994. Clinton overwhelmed them with his knowledge of their writings, his devotion to William Faulkner—from whose work he quoted verbatim—and his contention that much of the Western Hemisphere, from Arkansas to São Paolo, shares a broad Caribbean cul-ture, the product of a common African heritage. The transgressions for which President Clinton was dragged through the congressional mud were beneath García Márquez's consideration. But if Clinton had kept an entire population in ideological chains, repressed human rights, and oth-erwise violated the precepts of modern democratic society, he still would not have drawn a harsh word from the creator of Macondo. To García Márquez, Clinton and Castro were noble victims, gods from Olympus, too good and brilliant to be understood or appreciated by mere mortals or judged by their mundane standards.

Even as the complicated Cuba-Mexico game was showing signs of enormous stress, the Havana–Mexico City axis was strong enough in the final days of the PRI government to claim yet another victim. On October 4, 2000, halfway between Fox's victory and his inauguration,

Pedro Riera Escalante was put on a plane to Cuba, where he faced certain prison and probably worse. Riera's story revealed much about Cuban espionage and influence in Mexico. Regrettably, it also demonstrated American ineptitude.

Riera approached the American embassy in late 1999 with a compelling tale. From 1986 to 1991, he had been assigned to the Cuban embassy in Mexico City, then, as now, one of Havana's largest outposts of espionage. As a major in Cuba's military intelligence organization, he had knowledge about Cuban efforts to penetrate the U.S. embassy. Additionally, while previously posted in Havana he had been one of the handlers of defector Phillip Agee, an ex-CIA agent who in 1975 had published *Inside the Company*, a damning account of some fact mixed with numerous lies. While serving in Mexico, Riera had been known for his more or less open contacts with the local Cuban community, which was generally far less strident in its anti-Castroism than the Cuban contingent in Miami. But perhaps he had gotten too close to them or was caught in some other real or perceived vice or crime. On his return to Cuba he ran into trouble, and in 1993 he was fired from the Cuban intelligence service. Somehow, for the next half-dozen years he eked out an existence in Cuba, but then he returned to Mexico.

Riera appeared to be someone we should listen to. All he wanted was help in getting his family out of Cuba and resettling in the United States. In early 2000, an embassy officer met with him frequently. His immigration status in Mexico was technically illegal. He had probably entered the country with false documents, or, if he had used his own, had overstayed the period of stay allotted to a tourist. He knew that gave the Mexican government the right to detain and deport him at will. He lived in hiding and fear. At any point during those months Riera could have taken a bus to any northern border crossing and walked or rushed into the United States. Once declaring himself as a Cuban citizen, he would have been immediately paroled into the United States with no threat of being returned to the island. But he did not want to do that. He wanted to wait and get his family out of Cuba.

Our appreciation for the urgency of his situation grew as the embassy officer who debriefed him became convinced that he was telling the truth and as we corroborated much of his story. But the embassy could not convince Washington. The established interagency committee there that determines how the U.S. should handle potential defectors bobbled the case. True, the decisions are not easy ones to make. Not everyone who approaches the U.S. government with a story of espionage is telling the truth. Or the truth they tell may have little value because it is already known. Getting a decision out of Washington was particularly difficult because the CIA, the leader of the interagency process, had been burnt so many times by false Cuban defectors that it seemed to have been traumatized into inaction and dithering.

The excuses were multiple and contradictory. I urged that experts be sent to interview Riera. I stressed that he was in danger in Mexico because of Cuba's considerable penetrations of the government. But skepticism and inaction prevailed. It was a difficult day for the embassy officer when he had to tell Riera that he was on his own, that we could not help him. But it was not the toughest day of his life. That came a few weeks later when he learned that the Mexicans had detained Riera and turned him over to Cuban intelligence, just as Riera had feared and just as the embassy had warned Washington.

After being dropped by the embassy, Riera had tried to find support elsewhere. He went desperately and dangerously public, meeting with intellectuals known for their anti-Castro views, U.S. reporters, Mexican editors, and ultimately with the Secretariat of Foreign Affairs, where he asked for political asylum. He was shuffled off to the Ministry of Interior, which is responsible for migration matters and, not incidentally, the home of the Mexican intelligence service, known as CISEN. Riera thought that going public would provide some protection. He was wrong.

On the afternoon of October 3, 2000 he met with two American reporters who were preparing a story about him. He then met with CISEN agents in a Sanborn's restaurant in the Colonia Roma area of Mexico City. He was accompanied by a Cuban émigré journalist with legal residence in Mexico. As Riera left that meeting, six armed men intercepted him, took him to a hotel, and interrogated him. The next morning he was flown to Cuba. The government of Mexico, under some pressure from reporters who smelled a good story, said he had been deported on a commercial flight after a study of his immigration documents revealed that he was in Mexico illegally. Other sources reported that that it was either a CISEN or a Cuban intelligence plane that flew him back to Havana under armed guard.

The Mexicans responsible for Riera's deportation started spinning the story furiously in the press. Riera had probably been a U.S. agent, they said, adding that he had met with the U.S. ambassador. False on both counts. The embassy issued a statement, noting that whether Riera had approached us or not, the Mexican government had a responsibility to comply with international law. A person seeking asylum, we pointed out, is not supposed to be summarily deported back to the persecuting nation.

From there the story played out in a depressing fashion. I asked the government of Mexico to determine Riera's whereabouts in Cuba and attend his trial. At first the SRE stated that it would but later denied that it had ever said anything to that effect. Falling back on traditional formulations, the Foreign Ministry said Mexico would accept no pressure from a foreign country regarding its dealings with Cuba.

Riera remains in a Cuban prison. In Washington, an internal CIA review of the handling of the case brushed over the fact that much of Riera's information had proven to be accurate and generally whitewashed the sad facts of our own inaction. There are a number of theories to explain what propelled the Mexican government to act as it did. Riera may have become a piece in a complicated exchange in which someone of interest to Mexico or to an influential Mexican politician was released from a Cuban jail or simply allowed to leave the island. Or perhaps Havana blackmailed persons in high places with threats to disclose unpleasant information. Maybe high-level Mexican officials feared that Riera would start telling the press what he knew about Cuban spies and agents of influence still in the Mexican government. In any event, as the PRI prepared to cede power to a new government, it was inconvenient to have Riera around. His life became another file for the government to shred on its way out the door.

C
H
A
P
T
E
R

T
E
N

"Where Did All These People Come From?"

The State Department is headquartered is a dull, utilitarian, mid-twentieth-century office building, but its diplomatic reception rooms on the eighth floor are a national treasure. They are beautifully appointed with wood paneling, cornices, moldings, gold leaf, and crystal chandeliers. There are graceful eighteenth-century paintings, china, and furniture donated by wealthy Americans anxious to express their national pride and obtain healthy tax deductions. I never tired of showing visiting foreigners the desk where Thomas Jefferson sat in 1803 as he signed the documents to buy the Louisiana Territory from Napoleon. That famous purchase made the United States a neighbor of the dominion of New Spain, soon to rise up in its own independence struggle. At mid-century, the new nation of Mexico would lose much of its northern territory to a voracious young United States. On an evening in June of 1999, I rubbed my hand along the top of the desk, wished Tom a good evening, and went into the secretary's private dining room for dinner with Madeleine Albright and Janet Reno.

Albright's staff had suggested the dinner so that I could brief her and Reno on the upcoming Bi-National Commission meeting in Mexico City. About ten U.S. cabinet members were planning to attend discussions on a broad range of issues, but narcotics and law enforcement would take top billing. The attorney general arrived for dinner right on time but we had to wait more than an hour for Albright. Anxious staff aides kept popping in to tell us that she was caught in a White House meeting on Kosovo but would be arriving soon.

Over drinks, Reno and I talked about DEA Administrator Tom Constantine's announcement of his retirement plans. The attorney general was not dismayed that he was leaving. I suggested that she choose someone with political experience and savvy who would avoid the public relations disasters that we had recently suffered. But she wanted another cop. (Ultimately, she chose Constantine's deputy, Donnie Marshall, a DEA veteran as hard-nosed as his departing boss, but without his theatrical and confrontational bent).

Madeleine Albright arrived looking weary after a four-hour meeting. She explained that she had had to fight to convince some of her cabinet colleagues of the need for strong U.S. action in the Balkans. She was winning the argument, if at a tremendous cost to her own energy. As the conversation jumped from one topic to another, I raised one that I regarded as particularly important: immigration.

"Our laws are not working," I said. "We are alienating the Mexicans without making our borders more secure or increasing our ability to keep out undocumented aliens. And we have big problems with visas. Our consulates in Mexico will interview two and half million visa applicants next year, but they are understaffed and the employees are underpaid and overwhelmed." They allowed me to prattle on while they toyed with their green salad and roast duck. At one point they perked up, and their eyes widened. I thought I had struck a nerve or made a particularly brilliant point, but they were only responding to a waiter entering the room with an especially elaborate dessert.

Their unspoken response was not surprising: immigration is too difficult an issue for an administration to take on during its last year. The next president—Al Gore, they assumed—would have to decide where to put it on his list of tasks. But for now, "coffee or tea?" We departed with kisses all around and plans to continue our conversation three days later in Mexico City. But I suspected that Albright had already decided not to come to the meeting there. There was a lot for her to tend to in Washington, and she was genuinely angry about Mexico's no-vote on the Geneva Human Rights Commission resolution to censure Cuba. The dinner, I understood, was her way of saying "I'm sorry" in advance to Janet Reno, who would learn the following day that she would have to fill in for Albright as the chief of the delegation.

During the Clinton years, Washington generally kept as far away as possible from the thorny issue of immigration reform. This was unfortunate, because the policies regarding the admission of foreigners into the United States are so sensitive that they are best discussed when the country is at peace and prosperous. But perhaps President Clinton understood that there was something strange about America's prosperity in the 1990s. The statistics and the stock market said we were getting richer. Our enemies were defeated, and our power was unchallenged in the world. Yet we were not as satisfied with our lives as we should have been. Life for the middle class became more difficult. Family incomes had not increased appreciably, and the income disparity between the very wealthy and the rest of America was widening. While race-baiting and violent anti-immigrant sentiment had largely disappeared from the American political vernacular, there was a nagging anxiety about the growing number of foreigners in the United States. Americans were asking, "Where did all these people come from?"

The numbers had grown astoundingly. The census of 2000 revealed that the United States had the largest population of non–native born residents in its history. The 31.3 million foreign-born figure was 11.3 million more than it had been ten years earlier—a 57 percent increase. They accounted for 11.1 percent of the nation's population, the highest proportion in sixty years. There were more foreigners living in the United States than Canadians living in Canada. More immigrants arrived during the 1990s than had lived in the country in 1970. Latinos led the way. In 1970, they were less than 20 percent of the foreign-born population, but now they accounted for more than half of the vastly larger immigrant pool. American-born and immigrant Latinos had surpassed African-Americans as the nation's largest minority. And Mexicans dominated the Hispanic influx. About 800,000 natives of Mexico lived in the U.S. in 1970. Thirty years later there were about ten million.

Everywhere they went, the new immigrants found work in the expanding American economy. Fifty percent of the jobs created in the 1990s were filled by newcomers to the United States. The lower end of the service industries had an insatiable appetite for housekeepers, janitors, and maids willing to work for minimum wage to keep the booming hotel and restaurant industry growing. In some cities, certain construction trades—roofing, painting, plastering—had become almost entirely dominated by immigrants. Agriculture continued to need its stoop laborers. The vast majority—one estimate put the figure at nearly ninety percent—of American farm workers were foreign-born, most living in the U.S. without proper documents. And the profound changes in American manufacturing provided additional opportunities. Factories moved to nonunion states and found immigrant labor willing to work for wages below what previous employees had earned.

Federal Reserve Board Chairman Alan Greenspan admitted that low-wage immigrant workers played an important role in controlling inflation. Other experts said they provided a boost to economic growth and consumer spending. Besides, Americans were told, immigrants took jobs that the native-born no longer wanted to do. That was only partially true. For a higher wage, many native-born workers would have made hotel beds, packed hams, or lugged carpets through the mills. But they would not sign up for the same jobs for wages so low as to appeal only to desperate immigrants with no opportunities for public assistance.

The internal migration of American manufacturing meant that immigrants started to arrive in great numbers in new places. While the traditional portal states—New York, California, Texas, and Illinois—continued to receive most of the newcomers, North Carolina, Utah, Indiana, Maine, a dozen other states, and even Alaska also became home to large numbers of immigrants. For more and more Americans, the faces of their own communities were changing. July Fourth orators and the public in general continued to exalt our open society as "a nation of immigrants." But many Americans became increasingly concerned. Some even felt threatened, as they considered the potential of the newcomers to change the nature of American society, or, more importantly, to change their lives.

Some Americans were angered by displays of Mexican nationalism, such as a parade in Los Angeles against Proposition 187, in which Mexican flags greatly outnumbered U.S. banners. In the Southwest, jesting by Mexican-Americans about the "reconquista" raised hackles among some Anglos. Academic screwballs, such as the university teacher of Chicano studies who asserted that the future Hispanic majority of California and the southwestern states would vote to secede and form a Spanish-speaking nation, alarmed the more gullible and impressionable.

America's face began to change in 1965, when Congress passed a sweeping immigration reform that eliminated the preferential treatment that European immigrants received. From that point on, Latins, Asians, and Africans could compete with Europeans on a level playing field for the limited number of immigrant visas. The 1965 law also changed the basis for deciding which individuals had preference in the long line of those waiting to come. Family reunification, rather than education, employment skills, or wealth, became the dominant criterion.

The tremendous influx of Mexicans into the United States in the 1990s was facilitated by another major piece of legislation, the Immigration Reform and Control Act (IRCA) of 1986. That law tried to deal with two radically different concerns. Many conservatives regarded IRCA as a remedy for what some, including Reagan's attorney general, William French Smith, characterized as a loss of control over the nation's borders. The law was designed to stop illegal immigration, primarily by beefing up the Border Patrol and by making it difficult for employers to hire undocumented aliens, thus reducing the magnet of employment. Liberals were pleased that IRCA offered amnesty to illegal aliens and promoted greater family reunification.

The bill, sponsored by two serious and respected legislators, Republican Senator Alan Simpson of Wyoming and Democratic Representative Rom Mazzoli of Kentucky, went through a multitude of versions and five years of legislative wrangling. Compromises to satisfy various interest groups were hammered out. An important element of one of the first drafts of the bill was vigorously opposed by a strange coalition of agricultural, business, Latino rights groups, and church organizations. These groups, joined by libertarians and conservative Republicans, resisted the proposal for a national identification card that was intended to be the foundation of a new employers sanctions program. If every adult had an identity document, employers could not argue that they had not known that someone they had hired was undocumented. But the American fear of Big Brother, that is, what the U.S. government might be able to do if it possessed detailed records about everyone, was overwhelmingly strong. The Simpson-Mazzoli law that finally passed included watered-down employer sanctions that would inevitably fail to stem the flow of illegal migrants.

Although not uniquely directed toward them, the amnesty provision was most utilized by Mexican nationals. An estimated 2.3 million Mexicans took advantage of the various amnesty provisions in the following years, augmenting the already large Mexican population in the United States and creating an even more welcoming environment for the undocumented who continued to arrive. The strengthening of the Border Patrol did not have a great effect in stemming that flow. The employer penalties proved over the years to be unenforceable. In reality, they were designed to fail. Regulations required that employers simply ask job applicants for identification to prove legal residence or citizenship in the United States. Further employer investigation or inquiry was not required, expected, or delivered. Employers were conveniently able to keep hiring workers whose documents they knew or strongly suspected were false.

Obtaining false documents was never difficult for an immigrant intent on giving an employer some minimal form of identification. It became even easier with the advent of computers, high-quality photocopying, and organized rings of document falsifiers. Sixty dollars was the going price for a false Social Security card in the 1990s. Also making life easier for the undocumented to find work was the fact that by the mid-1990s, the Immigration and Naturalization Service had all but ceased roundup raids at factories, restaurants, and other places of work. The raids were too disruptive, angered employers, and raised difficult issues of civil liberties as legal residents and citizens, who were frequently caught up in the dragnets, loudly objected. The INS concentrated its "interior enforcement effort" on targeted criminal aliens, those who had committed serious crimes and were a danger not only to the community, but also to native-born acceptance of newcomers.

The most significant long-range effect of IRCA was that by regularizing the status of so many foreigners, a new pool of legal residents and citizens was created that in turn sought to bring their family members, legally or illegally, to join them. For millions of Mexicans, particularly amnestied farm laborers, the ability to stay in the United States meant that they stopped returning home periodically. Instead, they petitioned the INS to allow their wives and children to join them. All the while, the influx of undocumented aliens continued unabated.

The IRCA needed amending, but having dealt with the immigration issue in 1986, Congress was unwilling to touch the matter again. And

President Bill Clinton was unlikely to push the issue. He had come to the White House bearing political scars from a skirmish that was indirectly related to immigration. As governor of Arkansas, he paid a heavy price when he lost his first bid for reelection after Cuban detainees from the Mariel boatlift rioted at a military base in his state. Two years later he made it back to the Little Rock statehouse, but he never forgot the lesson that immigrants and successful politics rarely mix well. Janet Reno had also been badly battered as district attorney of Dade County during the Mariel crisis. The new attorney general was not looking for a starring role in any new immigration drama.

The immigration-shy administration received a series of sensible recommendations from a commission led by the formidable and highly respected former Congresswoman Barbara Jordan of Texas. President Clinton warmly endorsed the commission's work but did nothing to implement its ideas. During the Clinton years, the White House strategy was to name a respected and serious expert, Doris Meissner, as head of the Immigration and Naturalization Service (INS) and to let her attempt to defend the net effect of poor legislation, underfunding, and the unwillingness of the White House and Congress to confront reality. Not surprisingly, the INS fell further and further behind in its work, earning the reputation as one of the federal government's least effective agencies.

If the political system had responded rapidly to IRCA's obvious weaknesses—for instance by toughening the employer penalties—the subsequent rise in anti-alien feeling might not have taken on the energy it did. But important and powerful political forces did not favor change. They rarely do.

In the early 1990s push for passage of the North American Free Trade Agreement, both Presidents Bush and Clinton inadvertently helped to foment anti-immigrant sentiment by encouraging false expectations. They promised that NAFTA would reduce migrant flows by promoting economic development in Mexico. Many economists at the time challenged the assertion. In the short term, they argued, NAFTA was likely to increase Mexican emigration from rural areas affected by U.S. farm exports and from urban areas hit hard by the competition from American factories. Not foreseen by those on either side of the debate was a series of shocks that rattled Mexican society in 1994, the year NAFTA went into effect. The developments helped produce a dramatic rise in illegal immigration.

On January 1, 1994, the Zapatista rebels in Chiapas began their guerrilla war against the Mexican government, helping to unsettle the economy. And when the new Zedillo administration took office in December 1994, it immediately stumbled into a financial crisis and a crippling devaluation of the peso. Across the country, Mexicans stunned by yet another drastic drop in their standard of living started packing their bags for the trip to El Norte.

The impact of NAFTA on Mexican emigration remains heavily debated. The dual magnets of the booming American economy and larger post-IRCA Mexican communities in the United States probably accounted for most of the influx. But clearly, at least a portion of the outflow of former Mexican factory workers and campesinos was stimulated by the inability of Mexican producers to compete with increasing and cheaper U.S. imports entering the country as tariffs fell. For many Americans, the NAFTA accord that had promised to reduce migration northward appeared to be having the opposite effect.

Just as events in Mexico influenced American perceptions of migration, broader international developments also played their role in promoting nativist sentiment. The bombing of the World Trade Center by Al Qaeda terrorists in 1993, eight years before their horrifically successfully September 11 attack on the same buildings, raised national security concerns about foreigners. The end of the Cold War and the resultant build-down of the U.S. armed forces hurt California's heavily defense-based economy: military bases were closed and arms manufacturers lost contracts. In a repetition of a familiar historical pattern, as the economy declined, anti-immigrant sentiment increased.

Adding to the souring environment was the unwillingness of the federal government to deal adequately with the added financial burdens that migration was causing many local communities. Higher outlays for education, health care, and social services outraged many California taxpayers. Republican Governor Pete Wilson saw the issue as a way to help his sagging 1994 reelection bid. He backed a referendum item, Proposition 187, to ban undocumented immigrants from receiving state benefits including health care and education. Proposition 187 passed but was later ruled unconstitutional. By then Wilson had already won reelection.

Anxiety about immigration was not limited to California. Elected officials from other states were also hearing from worried, and increasingly angry, constituents. Few in Washington were willing to stand in the way of Congress as it prepared for the 1996 elections by passing two pieces of legislation that reflected the impulses underlying Proposition 187. The Immigration Reform Act and the Welfare Reform Act blocked undocumented aliens from receiving certain welfare benefits. It banned Medicaid payments to poor legal immigrants for their first five years in the United States. It also raised the minimum requirements that sponsors needed in order to provide financial guarantees for the entry of their relatives. Those requirements were a response to the large number of relatively poor aliens who had taken advantage of the 1986 IRCA amnesty and were now seeking to bring their families into the United States, frequently without the resources necessary to support them.

These measures and Proposition 187 did much to organize the Mexican community in the United States, now millions larger owing to the 1986 amnesty. Presidential candidate Vicente Fox listened to the undocumented Mexicans he had met during his precampaign swings through the United States. They had complained about the daily inconveniences, slights, and injustices that constrained their lives.

There were more and more Mexican voices to raise those concerns. Close analysis of the 2000 census results revealed important new data about the number of undocumented aliens presumed to be in the country. The analysis began when the Census Bureau saw that it had been wrong with its projection that the census would find a population of about 275 million people. The estimate had been low by about ten million. The bureau attributed the major portion of the difference to a dramatic spike in the illegal population. By 2003, the Census Bureau and independent investigators concluded that approximately nine million people were living illegally in the country. Mexicans accounted for almost five million of them and that number was growing by about 300,000 per year.

Previously, Mexican authorities had estimated that no more than three million Mexicans were living without documents in the United States. They knew that number was inaccurately low, but they kept using the figure because it understated the enormity of the influx. I had long challenged it in conversations with Castañeda and others, largely based on my travels in the U.S. and discussions with visiting state governors. All of them reportedly massive increases in the percentage of Hispanics in their states. I felt vindicated by the revised figure, but it was a hollow triumph.

In addition to the five million undocumented Mexicans, approximately five million more people born in Mexico lived legally as American citizens or legal permanent residents. Another fifteen million or so American citizens traced their heritage to Mexico one or two generations back. Or, as in the case of some in the Southwest, to a time before the Mexican-American War. "We didn't come to the United States," I heard more than once, "the U.S. came to us." It was said usually in jest, but sometimes with an edge. The emotional links between Americans of Mexican ancestry and the newly arrived that could be mined for political purposes figured in the thinking of the new administrations that both countries elected in 2000.

At the embassy in Mexico City, we felt the pressure of the undocumented and the U.S. efforts to limit their number in several ways. Our biggest concern was our procedures for reviewing the thousands of requests for tourist visas that the embassy and the consulates received every day. We knew that a large percentage, maybe a third or more, of the nearly five million Mexicans living in the U.S. without permission had entered with tourist visas. They had convinced consular officers that they needed the document solely to go to Disneyland, attend a cousin's wedding, see a doctor, or celebrate a son's graduation. Then they overstayed their visa in order to stay with relatives and seek employment.

When I arrived in 1998, our visa procedures were chaotic, both in style and substance. There was no appointment system. People young and old started lining up at midnight, slept on the street, or paid someone to hold a place in line for them. Then, tired, disheveled, and in ill humor, they waited to meet a consular officer. Because the officers were frantic with work and tired of being lied to, they were occasionally rude. All interviews were conducted in Spanish, but some officers' language skills were limited by lack of experience. Almost always the rapidity of the interview made the officers seem abrupt, especially in a Latin culture where few conversations actually begin until pleasantries are exchanged.

After waiting for hours, the applicants generally had only a minute or two to explain why they wanted to travel to the United States—shopping, tourism, family visit, or whatever motive might make sense. Each had to convince a consular officer that there was a good chance that they were going to return home. Proof of established status in Mexico—a long-term decent paying job, a bank account with regular deposits, and an address in a wealthy neighborhood—could help. But the consular officers knew those documents were easily forged, so they looked for any little chink in the armor of the applicant's story.

In my view, the lies of the visa applicants did not make them criminals. I've stretched the truth at times without remorse in dealings with figures of petty authority—parking meter attendants, traffic cops, and others trying to stop me from doing what I took as a right. But taken together, millions of lies had changed the demographic face of America and made a mockery of U.S. immigration policy. It was the job of the consular officers to put a brake on that. They took their work seriously.

We improved the mechanics of the consular operation. We instituted an appointment system, built a comfortable waiting room, automated many of the procedures, gave the consular officers better training and more time away from the grueling and intense applicant interviewing line, and increased the efficiency of our record checks. We made the whole application process more humane for applicants and officers. But in the end, it all came down, as it always has, to whether the consular officer believed the applicant's story or not.

It was impossible to know with precision how often the staff were right or wrong, but, given the nature of the process, they were probably wrong a significant percentage of the time. When I did the same work more than thirty years before as a vice-consul in Guatemala, I concluded that 50 percent of the people to whom I gave visas probably should not have received them. And 50 percent to whom I denied visas should have gotten them. Adding the two 50 percents together, I joked that I had probably been wrong 100 per cent of the time.

Many Mexicans expressed appreciation for the speed and efficiency of the visa adjudication system. The embassy's operation compared favorably with the treatment usually received in a typical Mexican government office. But, taken as a whole, the process was demeaning. For those bona fide applicants who were refused visas because they could not overcome the consular officer's suspicions, it was especially insulting. But while the visa system might cause considerable ill will, at least it did not result in the loss of life. The same could not be said about our border-control policy.

C H A P T E R   E L E V E N

The Hole in the Wall

By the early 1990s much of the U.S.-Mexico border was simply out of control. Illegal aliens were crossing almost at will and in huge numbers. The situation was especially grave around the San Ysidro port of entry, connecting Tijuana and the road to San Diego. An estimated 25 percent of all illegal border crossings were made in that area. Residential neighborhoods on the U.S. side were turning into major thoroughfares for crossers every night. The vast majority of illegal entrants wanted to do nothing more than make their way up the highway to San Diego and from there to some destination where they could join friends and find a job.

But, as in any flow of humanity, individuals with other motives entered as well. Petty and serious crime, including home robberies, narcotics trafficking, and gang violence, roiled the district. Most migrants waited for nightfall to sneak through the porous fences. Others were more brazen. One technique adopted by immigrant smugglers was to mass hundreds of crossers on the Mexican side of the port of entry and have them rush the gates. Some were caught but many made it through. Several crossers were run over as they dashed into oncoming traffic. A decade later, traffic signs carrying the silhouettes of a man, a woman, and a pigtailed child rushing across the highway still warn drivers as they head down I-5 from San Diego to Tijuana. The chaos played into the already growing anti-immigrant sentiment in California that brought out the vote in favor of Proposition 187.

Against this turbulent background, the federal government was obliged to act. In 1994 Attorney General Reno announced a multiyear program to beef up the Border Patrol and close off the routes most frequently used by smugglers, generally through urban areas. Disrupting the traditional crossing routes, it was argued, would deter illegal aliens from making the trip. The Immigration and Nationalization Service and the Border Patrol launched Operation Gatekeeper near San Diego and Operation Safeguard in the Tucson sector. The program was later expanded to other urban areas surrounding ports of entry. The toughening of the border included the construction of fences and watchtowers and the installation of lights and remote sensing devices, all operated by a vastly increased number of Border Patrol personnel, many stationed no more than three hundred yards apart in new SUVs. By September 2000, the Border Patrol had been increased by about five thousand officers to a total of nine thousand, more than 90 percent of whom were serving on the southwest border from San Diego to Brownsville, Texas. The Canadian border, by contrast, was lightly manned, a fact that would assume significance and provide challenges after September 11, 2001.

Operations like Gatekeeper and Safeguard served an important political purpose. The flow of illegal migrants through urban areas near the ports of entry dropped sharply, thereby improving conditions in the most impacted communities. More importantly, from Washington's point of view, it removed a major point of contention in the anti-immigrant argument by creating the impression that the federal government had reestablished control of the borders. However, there is no indication that the program actually served to lower the number of crossers. The alien smugglers found new, less well-patrolled points of entry. In fact, each year the number of those detained by the Border Patrol increased, reaching about 1.6 million in 2000.

The number of detainees was seen as a rough indication of the immigrant flow, but, of course, it did not indicate precisely how many aliens were *not* caught on their way northward. The figure also included many individuals who were caught, released, and then tried again, often multiple times. The truth is that we had no idea how many migrants successfully crossed the border illegally each year. But the detention of so many persons annually was startling in its enormity. On an average night, nearly five thousand people—a total the size of many small towns—were detained, processed, and, with few exceptions, returned across the border by the INS and the Border Patrol.

While programs like Guardian and Safeguard may not have succeeded in lowering the overall number of crossers, they had a major impact on changing the routes of migrants, with unintended consequences. Unable to cross in populated areas, aliens ventured into inhospitable zones—deserts, mountains, rivers, and canals. Migrants had always faced danger in the crossing, mostly on the Mexican side, where there was no effective law enforcement and police officials were frequently corrupt. There they suffered depredations at the hands of gangs who robbed, raped, and sometimes killed, often with the connivance of local police. But the new INS strategy resulted in many more deaths on the U.S. side of the border as migrants succumbed to desert heat and mountain cold, drowning, snakebite, or other calamities. In 2000, Border Patrol data indicated that nearly twenty-five hundred had perished since Operation Gatekeeper had begun. One person a day was dying in the effort to go north to find a better life. The deaths became a rallying cry for Mexicans and others critical of American immigration policy.

One afternoon, as I flew in a Border Patrol helicopter from Laredo to San Antonio, I listened to the two pilots, one a Vietnam veteran and the other a young Mexican-American, talk about their efforts to find illegal aliens in the arid scrubland of southwest Texas before they succumbed to the heat. Of course, one of their principal functions was to detect illegal aliens and alert ground patrols about their whereabouts. But these were not cops looking for lawbreakers. They were lifesavers looking for human beings to save. Movingly, they talked about finding bodies and of their efforts to identify the dead. Many carried no papers or had their corpses stripped of all identification by the alien smugglers. The dedication of the pilots was impressive, but I could not help but think that, in their own way, they too were paying a heavy price for our border policy.

If the positions were reversed, the death of thousands of Americans trying to cross into Mexico would certainly raise a public protest in the United States. But the intensity of the Mexican response is only comprehensible when placed in the larger context of Mexican attitudes toward migration. There is probably no issue in the thicket of U.S.-Mexican ties in which the attitudes of the two countries contrast more sharply. For Americans, immigration is a question of law. Surely, some

Americans have attitudes about illegal migration that are tinged by prejudice, social concerns, or economic self-interest. Nevertheless, most can empathize with the plight of people who are simply trying to improve their lives. But almost all Americans feel that the matter of who can come into the country, how, and when is something that is rightly governed by legislation and administrative procedure. Waiting in line for one's turn to board a bus, mail a letter, or cash a check is as American as not cutting in front of someone at the supermarket to buy the apples for mom's pie.

Americans see the entrance of Mexicans or anyone else into our country without permission as a lack of respect for our laws and institutions. Americans are dedicated to principles of fundamental fairness and playing by the rules. The average Mexican is as decent a person as the average American. But a long history of unresponsive or abusive government has inculcated in that population a cynicism about government and its arbitrary rules.

On occasion, when I was feeling particularly peeved or mischievous in front of a Mexican audience, I utilized the most famous phrase in the Mexican historical lexicon to explain the American view. I did this once at a breakfast attended by about forty editors, government officials, and business leaders. I reminded the group that "respect for the rights of others," as Benito Juárez had said, "is peace." (*Respeto al derecho ajeno es la paz*). I suggested that, as opinion leaders, the attendees might consider using their positions to encourage their countrymen to respect American rights and laws and not to enter the United States without the appropriate permission. One female member of the audience, a high-ranking member of the Foreign Ministry, became nearly apoplectic. My use of her national hero's words to America's advantage offended her. I thought she was going to come after me with a butter knife. Not surprisingly, I did not receive any support from other members of the audience. Not that day, not ever.

At base the emigration phenomenon is largely the product of a massive increase in national population during the second half of the twentieth century. That growth rate has now slowed, owing to an effective government family-planning program. Forty years ago the average Mexican woman gave birth to 7.3 children. Today, the average is 2.4 and heading downward. Shortly after arriving in Mexico, I met a man who put the population growth into perspective for me. "You know," he told me at a typically overcrowded cocktail party, "fifty years ago when I was a teenager, the advertisement I heard most frequently on radio was for Bohemia beer. The announcer told us to drink Bohemia because 23 million Mexicans could not be wrong." In the space of his adult life his country's population had quadrupled to nearly 100 million. By 2000, the environs of Mexico City alone were home to a number of people almost equal to the entire country's population five decades before. All those new Mexicans needed to find work somewhere and the country's economy did not grow fast enough to provide the opportunities.

Mexicans see migration northward as a natural part of life for a portion of the population. For individuals, it provides a way out—a chance to find work and a better life, either temporarily or permanently. For successive PRI governments, emigration reduced the number of unemployed and generated a flow of remittances back toward Mexico, estimated at over $14 billion a year by 2003. Also, the outflow helped promote a level of domestic social peace as the discontented made their way northward. Emigration constituted a safety valve of sorts for the Mexican government. Basically, the phenomenon responded to the economic reality of both countries: Mexico had workers to spare and the United States had jobs to fill. Given the predictable nature of the migration flow, adding dangerous impediments to the crossing that resulted in deaths was seen as irresponsible at best, criminal at worst.

The accepted orthodoxy asserted that the Mexican Constitution gives every citizen the right of free travel in and out of the country. This is true, but it is only part of the truth. The assertion ignores other provisions of Mexican law that dictate, as in every country, that entrance or departure must be through established border ports and with appropriate documents. Leaving Mexico through the desert is unlawful. But no politician would try to punish such activity, nor even criticize it. Some might try to dissuade it, but none would attempt to prohibit it. On some level, Mexican public opinion regards migration to the United States as a fundamental human right.

Arguments that the migrants themselves bore some responsibility for the injuries or deaths that might befall them because they infringed on U.S. law or did not use common sense in choosing their routes carried no weight at all. Some Mexican activists took their resentment so far as to argue that the toughening of the border was intended to be deadly. They argued that it constituted a particularly noxious form of modern social Darwinism designed to ensure that only the strongest, and thus the best workers, make it through. The press carried almost daily accounts of reports of migrant deaths and made no effort to divorce incidents of violence, the handful of Border Patrol shootings of migrants, from the much larger issue of accidental deaths. And, in those cases of violent death, no effort was made to assess the situation. The victim was simply assumed to be innocent, and not, as occurred in some instances, an armed criminal or an uncontrollably violent drug freak high on amphetamines.

Clearly, the two governments had to take steps to try to calm the scene at the border. Some efforts worked and some did not. The Border Patrol and representatives of the Mexican federal police and the Ministry of Interior's Institute of Migration met frequently to seek ways to improve the safety of migrants. The United States continually asked the Mexicans to place more law enforcement officers on the frontier in the hope that they would move more aggressively against the organized bands of alien smugglers. The Ministry of Interior created a special force called Grupo Beta with the specific task of orienting migrants away from the most dangerous crossing points. But Grupo Beta never had more than 125 officials for a two-thousand-mile border. Even with automobiles and other equipment donated from the American side, it was not an effective mechanism. In addition to its limited resources, it did not have the legal authority to prohibit anyone from attempting a dangerous crossing.

The Border Patrol increased its own training in lifesaving and introduced new equipment, including inflatable river craft and more helicopters, to search for migrants in trouble. The U.S. Department of Justice established a new mechanism to review every incident of violence involving a U.S. official and a migrant to determine whether any violation of civil rights had occurred. Finally, as part of INS's Border Safety Initiative, the U.S. Information Service within the embassy worked with the Mexican government to produce public service television commercials to inform prospective immigrants of the dangers they would confront in attempting illegal crossings of the border. The efforts were multiple and, when there was decent and motivated local leadership, moderately successful. But the flow of migrants did not stop. The deaths continued.

As enforcement increased in one area, migrants moved elsewhere. And as traditional entry points were closed off, the numbers passing through other channels increased. It was as if many small garden hoses crossing the border were blocked. The result was that those that remained open discharged with the force of fire hoses. One of the most affected areas was Douglas, Arizona, a small border town of about 14,000 residents and a good entry point for migrants heading north to Tucson, Phoenix, and points beyond. In the mid-1990s residents reported seeing outnumbered agents nightly chasing groups of thirty or forty illegal aliens through town.

But once the Border Patrol was strengthened within Douglas itself, the alien smugglers diverted the migrants to the ranchlands outside the city. The ranchers complained that the migrants were destroying property and fences and allowing their cattle to roam. They asserted that some cattle had been stolen or killed and that ranch houses had been broken into and personal property stolen. The fact that only a few crossers committed crimes did not make the nightly parades of migrants less overwhelming. In the period between October 1999 and May 2000, more than 200,000 migrants were detained in an area accounting for no more than twenty miles of the border's length. Ten thousand kilos of marijuana were seized during the same period, much of it carried by migrants who paid the alien smugglers by serving as mules.

Some local ranchers decided to take matters into their own hands. They formed armed patrols, arrested aliens on their property, and held them until the Border Patrol showed up. They advertised their successes and used the Internet to invite others to participate in the "hunt." This was vigilantism at its worse, heavily tinged with racism and militia-like paranoia. The Mexican press went wild about the Arizona "immigrant hunters." It was not until a few weeks after the uproar had begun that I realized that the Mexican public actually believed that the ranchers were going out each night and shooting aliens like jackrabbits. That is what the headlines told them—the "hunters" were at work.

I tried to set the record straight. There had been no shootings. But I managed to step on my tongue on several occasions. At first I minimized the importance of the ranchers. I referred to them as a small group of *chiflados*, loosely translated as kooks or flakes. Years earlier, chiflados was the word that had been used to denote the Three Stooges—*los tres chiflados*.

My comment did nothing to calm things down in Mexico. But it earned me a collection of hate mail from Arizona, where the press reported that I had denounced the ranchers as, of course, stooges. "Mr. Ambassador," began one letter, "are you an American or a Mexican." Another e-mail sender told me that he intended to write to "my congressman and senator to inform them of my disgust of you. What country do you hail from anyway? Communist Russia?" Governor Jane Dee Hull of Arizona, who had done much to improve relations with Mexico, called and asked me to tone it down. I was not helping her keep the lid on, she explained.

But I still had to deal with the Mexican press and was no more successful there. I attempted to answer their questions about why the ranchers had not been arrested. I noted that, as long as they stayed on their own property, they were technically not guilty of any crime. They did not, as the press insinuated, remain free because U.S. authorities actually supported their efforts. I also made the point that the ranchers had not wounded or killed anyone. But it all came across as a defense of the vigilantes. I was able, however, to continually make the point that the Douglas area needed more law enforcement personnel on both sides of the border. The government of Mexico responded by sending some additional Grupo Beta and military personnel, and the INS promised a massive increase in Border Patrol members, who actually did show up over the following months.

The problem of illegal Mexican migration to the United States will not disappear in the near future. Ultimately, if Mexico's economy grows sufficiently, fewer people will head northward. This has been the pattern in Europe, where the economic development of the Iberian Peninsula has largely ended the once-significant flows of Portuguese and Spaniards to northern nations. It was also the case with Puerto Rican migration to the continental United States. As U.S. citizens, Puerto Ricans need no special permission to come to New York City or other American locales. Ultimately, 25 percent of the island's population moved permanently to the mainland. The flow slowed as Puerto Rico's economy improved.

The most optimistic estimates posit that demographic changes in both the United States and Mexico will mean that within fifteen years, a burgeoning economy to the south will have no excess workers to send to a post–baby boomer United States desperate for laborers. The Mexican demographic profile is rapidly approaching that of the U.S., with fewer youths and more old people. Fewer children were born in Mexico between 1995 and 2000 than between 1990 and 1994. And that downward trend will continue.

But the vision of a Mexico without an exodus is challenged by many, including Mexico's National Population Council, an agency of the Ministry of Interior. It asserted in a November 2001 report that, given the geographic proximity of the two countries, the increasingly integrated economies, and spiraling family ties, a significant growth in migration to the United States is inevitable. The Mexican-born population of the United States is expected to increase at an annual rate of at least 300,000 for the foreseeable future. By the year 2030, the report said, the number of Mexican-born individuals living north of the border will double. By its very nature, the migration issue calls for cooperative management efforts on the part of both governments. The ease with which the complex topic is politicized places a special responsibility on political leaders on both sides of the border to deal with the matter candidly and skillfully.

The situation in Douglas improved slowly as the Border Patrol presence in the area increased, but it remained tenuous. Mexican public attention to the matter waned toward the middle of 2000 as the country prepared for the July elections. Candidate Vicente Fox promised voters at home and the millions of Mexicans living in the United States that once elected he would speak for them all. He painted a new vision of a Mexican diaspora with continuing and strong ties to the motherland. He vowed to be its protector and advocate.

Mexico Changes Course

On my first night at my first embassy I saw an ambassador in agony. Nathaniel Davis was white as a sheet. He had bet heavily on the wrong horse.

Joan and I had arrived in Guatemala in the late afternoon of the first Sunday of March 1970, Election Day. Within a few hours I was in the embassy's Election Room, where I was introduced to the ambassador. He was the first high-ranking diplomat I had ever met. He put me at ease and gave me a job scribbling numbers on a blackboard. It was all pretty heady stuff for a twenty-seven-year-old rookie. As the results came trickling in, I could measure the ambassador's reaction. The apparent winner was a military man, Colonel Carlos Arana Osorio. Wanting to send a message of repudiation of the man and the thuggish methods of the Guatemalan military, Davis, after consultation with the State Department, had refused to meet with him during the campaign. He fully expected that the Guatemalan people in their infinite wisdom would choose another candidate, who had considerably better democratic credentials. Apparently, wisdom was in short supply in Guatemala that year.

Davis was a superb diplomat and a man of extraordinarily high character. Eventually, he would run afoul of Henry Kissinger over the Nixon administration's effort to involve the United States in Angola's civil war. But that was years later, and on this March night he got caught on the wrong side of the ballot box. It was a mistake I did not intend to make in Mexico.

Throughout 2000 I kept up a steady round of meetings with the three major candidates and all types of party theorists, activists, and hacks. I enjoy the company of politicians in campaign. Like dogs in heat, there is a simplicity and transparency to their objectives. Observing Mexican politicians is doubly fun because they truly enjoy backstabbing and gossiping, two of the world's great spectator sports. On occasion, my contacts with the candidates, usually over huevos rancheros early in the morning at my home, would make it to the press with the insinuation that I was favoring one over the other.

One magazine editor who bore a particular animus toward me because I had chosen to ignore him and his publication branded me "the proconsul." To him, my sins of interventionism were legion. For example, in my Senate confirmation hearing I had said, "the United States will encourage the highest levels of participation and political transformation in Mexico with the conviction that a vibrant Mexican democracy is the best guarantee of that country's social and economic progress." Mr. Editor found this declaration "one of the most brutish for its crude absence of diplomatic language ever made by an American ambassador." He also objected to my comment urging Mexican political parties to adopt rigorous internal financial controls to guard against the infiltration of drug money into their campaigns. He found that a flagrant intromission into the internal affairs of Mexico. I thought that if that was all he could find to criticize me about, I was doing my job well. For the rest of the press, neither the United States nor its ambassador became a campaign issue. It bespoke a discretion I did not think I had fully mastered.

In fact, there were no issues in the campaign, other than the fundamental one that Fox effectively controlled: the need for change. After seventy-one years of PRI rule, most Mexicans felt that need. It was to Fox's credit that he was never overly specific as to the alterations he would introduce. That left each voter to pick something to object to and then assume Fox would fix it. In fact, Fox had no intention of changing the Zedillo government's policies of economic reforms, with their steady diet of bitter but necessary pills. But he did little to get that view over to disaffected Mexicans who saw him as the catalyst for a course correction. Ironically, Labastida, the candidate of the party that was responsible for structural reform, and the leftist Cárdenas would both have made much more significant changes in economic policy, if either had been elected.

But that's not what the voters chose to hear: Vicente would make it right. Underlying Fox's entire approach was his argument that the PRI was corrupt, a view most Mexicans shared. His campaign posters featured two fingers held in a victory salute and forming the "Y" of the simple word ya which in Spanish can mean "now," or as it did for Fox, "it's about time." The message was clear. Fox would clean house.

Fox's focus on corruption and change did not guarantee him victory. He still had to face the organizational strength of the PRI, and the tools he had to work with were weak. Individual PAN-istas were as smart and as switched on as any Mexican politicians, but taken together the party was stuck in a rut. It had been in the opposition for so long, it really did not know how to win. Indeed, one problem Fox had to face early on was generated by a campaign biography in which he was quoted as saying that the PAN's candidate in 1994, the powerful party leader Diego Fernández de Cevallos, could have won if he had run a better campaign with more fire in his belly. The PAN leadership saw Fox as an outsider who had come to the party late in life after a career in business. The PAN preferred its members to have been born into the party. One PAN governor, a late-coming businessman like Fox, joked with me on a day that I visited his capital that the local PAN had just decided to admit him as a member. This was three years after he had won election on their ticket.

The PAN's stodginess and inability to take a broader view had caused me considerable heartburn when President Clinton visited Mérida in early 1999. I had arranged for the president to meet jointly with representatives of the three major parties. The meeting was in itself a message: the United States respects Mexico's new political plurality and favors no party over another. The get-together was scheduled for early morning on the day following the president's arrival. Late that evening the PAN informed us that it would not send representatives. A PAN spokesman griped to an embassy officer that a few weeks earlier, when the Pope had visited Mexico, the PAN, a heavily Catholic party, had not been given a role to play in the papal meetings. Not attending the session with the president was the party's way of getting back at the PRI for the alleged discourtesy of freezing them out of papal contact.

When confronted with abject stupidity, my general response is to leave it alone to fester in its own ignorance. If the PAN did not want to meet Bill Clinton, so be it. It would be their loss, not ours.

I was wrong again. Sandy Berger, the president's national security advisor, found me in a hotel bar at midnight drinking margaritas with Washington friends who had accompanied the president. Berger was concerned that the U.S. press was on to the story of the PAN's intended no-show. He believed the media would play it as a snub of President Clinton and as a demonstration that Mexico lacked confidence in Clinton and the U.S. pro-democracy position. Berger was insistent that the PAN's absence would turn into a major story that could tarnish the trip. He was right.

Over the din of the hotel bar, much of the noise being made by my margarita-ized friends, I cell-phoned the leader of the PAN, Felipe Calderón Hinojosa, at his Mexico City home. At first, he resisted, arguing that the PAN's position was a principled one—if the PRI would not let them meet the pope, they would choose not to meet the president. I told Felipe that if he thought it would be useful to the PAN in either Mexico or the United States to be presented in the American press as insulting President Clinton that was his business. But I also expressed the thought that he might want to rethink his party's strategy.

By 8 a.m., two PAN senators had been rousted from bed and appeared at the president's meeting. They did not have a clue as to what was going on, but the U.S. press was denied a juicy story and could, in Berger's view, now focus on the substantive achievements of the Mérida meeting. Of course, they did no such thing. The president's comments at an informal press gathering, at which he seemed to endorse his wife's potential run for the Senate, grabbed the headlines.

In order to circumvent a party that most observers viewed as not up to the task of winning the presidency, Fox created his own organization, the Friends of Fox. That group raised funds, helped promote him, and generally lived in uneasy harmony with the PAN's power structure. It was not a happy relationship, but Fox was not the only candidate who was having difficulty with his own party. Francisco Labastida was caught in a difficult bind. After the PRI December 1999 primary, Labastida sought to present himself as a reformer, not an easy trick for a high-level member of the PRI establishment. His campaign was run by Esteban Moctezuma, a young forward-thinking PRI-ista, but Moctezuma already had many enemies among PRI dinosaurs. They held back from fully supporting Labastida. "You know," one of Moctezuma's team told me one morning, "the very worst thing that will happen if the PRI loses is that we will become the opposition party, and for the PRI there can be no such thing as a loyal opposition. We will be terrible." The PRI never turned Moctezuma's concern into a campaign slogan. "Vote for us because we will be worse as the opposition than as the government" would not have attracted many voters. But they presented Fox and the PAN as inexperienced administrators who would have difficulty governing Mexico. Behind the "governability" issue lurked the unspoken threat that a PRI opposition would make governing impossible for Fox. Support for the PRI came not only from those who feared them in opposition, but from many millions of Mexicans who appreciated what the party and its governments had accomplished.

During the campaign, Federico Reyes Heroles, one of the most independent and acute of Mexico's political analysts, wrote an important commentary, the theme of which was "we are not idiots." He argued that for all of the PRI's sins, which he had catalogued publicly for years, Mexico had nevertheless progressed under its leadership. Economic growth, social development, generalized peace, and a growing middle class were all elements of a successful post-Revolutionary Mexico. Reyes Heroles asked the PAN-istas to stop treating the Mexican people like idiots by asserting that nothing good had come from the PRI.

Labastida attempted to bore into Fox's support among the relatively well-off, urban, educated sector of the population. One campaign theme that backfired was his argument that all Mexican children should learn computer skills and English in school. Though sensible, the idea that computers should be part of the lives of all Mexican children while so many of them still lived in rural poverty struck many as ludicrous. And the call for English instruction raised the specter of loss of cultural identity. To his credit, Labastida stayed with the argument even after it proved to be a dud.

The PRI's strategy depended heavily, as it always had, on securing an overwhelming majority of the votes of the nation's poor. Organizing the rural poor was an area where the party truly excelled. But as the campaign progressed I wondered whether history could be depended upon.

Fernando Gutiérrez Barrios, running for senator in Veracruz, told me that the countryside had emptied out since his last campaign a decade earlier. The men had gone to the cities or to the United States to find work. Many families had followed. It was arguable whether the PRI's hold on the rural poor had diminished, but clearly there were fewer of them to hold on to. And in urban areas, the once near-total control of information by the PRI had broken down. The urban poor were getting their news and views from television. The more they saw of Fox, the more they liked him.

Throughout the campaign, middle- and upper-class Mexicans, even many Fox supporters, would tell me that Fox was not sufficiently presidential. Mexicans expect formality and decorum from their leaders, they explained. This cowboy, with his boots, jeans, and occasional barnyard language, was not the image of Mexico that the people would want. "Could you imagine him visiting the White House dressed like that?" one wealthy matron asked me. Well, actually I could. In the end, they argued, the country would vote for Labastida, who was far more presentable. But his presentability always reminded me of Thomas Dewey in 1948. The acidic Dorothy Parker had snidely likened the mustachioed New York governor to the little groom figure on top of a wedding cake—too stiff, too perfect. Actually, there was a lot of the Dewey-Truman in the Fox-Labastida race, with Fox taking the "give 'em hell, Harry" approach.

Labastida tried to utilize Fox's own rough image in the first televised debate of the candidates. He criticized Fox for using foul and inappropriate language. (Fox had previously referred to Labastida as la vestida—"the dress"—a particularly crude effort to besmirch an opponent in the land of machismo.) Fox was clearly prepared for the thrust. He parried along the lines of Churchill's famous retort to Lady Astor in the House of Commons. ("You, sir, are drunk," the story has her saying. "Yes, madam, I am, and you are ugly; but tomorrow I shall be sober.") Fox responded that while he might be able to clean up his language, PRI politicians were corrupt cheaters who had governed too long and would never be able to change. The comeback was devastating. Labastida came out of the debate the clear loser.

Labastida's postdebate decline in the polls forced him back to his PRI organizational roots. Dinosaurs like Manuel Bartlett and other prominent political figures who had become emblematic to the public as the corrupt and unresponsive face of the PRI were given positions in the campaign. It reminded me of that scene in *Lawrence of Arabia* in which Lawrence, vilely tortured by the Turks, assembles every cutthroat in the land to ride off to battle at his side. Labastida tried to explain this away to me as being of little importance: they had volunteered, and he had simply found them campaign positions. Whatever the truth may have been, the reformist image that he was trying to convey was seriously tainted.

As May and June 2000 progressed, the campaign stalemated. Fox and Labastida each seemed to have, according to the polls, the support of about 40 percent of the electorate. Cárdenas was running a distant third, in the mid-teens. Fox tried hard to convince the public that a vote for Cárdenas was a wasted ballot in the effort to sack the PRI. The *voto util* ("useful vote") argument might have had some limited impact, but most of Cárdenas's supporters would have cast their ballot for him whether he was dead or alive. He was not simply a candidate. He was a social protest. His supporters did not really expect him to win. They were planning to fail gloriously.

Throughout the campaign, the Mexican press looked for evidence of partiality on my part or that of the U.S. government. They pored over every statement to discover our true intentions. The simple fact was that the U.S. government's interest in the election was in the process, not in the result. We could have lived easily with either Labastida or Fox as president. Even Cárdenas would have developed a decent working relationship with Washington. There really is no alternative, either for Mexico or for the United States. I talked ad nauseam about our interest in a clean process, but the reporters kept asking the same question, hoping that I would trip and say something indiscreet or highly revealing. It did not happen.

Both Fox and Labastida sought meetings with President Clinton in Washington. They, or at least some of their supporters, were not pleased when I passed the message back that the president would not meet with any of Mexico's contenders. He could not possibly have met with one and not the other two. In any event, the White House was not looking for a starring role for the president in another country's electoral struggle.

The electoral posture I adopted was to help increase Mexico's own self-confidence in its ability to hold a clean election. My view was not simply created for the occasion. I was convinced that it was accurate. The independent Federal Electoral Institute (IFE) headed by José Woldenberg was extraordinarily well funded and well organized. It had devised registration, voting, and tabulation schemes perhaps unequalled anywhere in the world for their completeness and impenetrability. The vote and the count would be clean, though many Mexicans themselves doubted it.

The PRI tried to use this lack of confidence to its advantage. It wanted the rural poor to think that their votes would not be secret. PRI hacks in the countryside dispensed food baskets or other gifts to encourage favorable votes. They asked the recipients for their voting identification numbers. The tactic was designed to leave the poorly educated with the impression that when the votes were counted, the PRI would be able to compare their ID numbers with the ballots and determine how they had actually voted. It was an insidious attack on democratic procedure, but it was never clear how effective it was. True, the PRI had spent seventy years indoctrinating the countryside, but the countryside had spent the same seven decades learning not to believe everything it heard. The PRI shenanigans reinforced a widespread belief that the party would simply not allow Fox to win. If necessary, the suspicion ran, it would doctor votes or pull the computer plug as it allegedly had in 1988. I did not see this as a possibility. First and foremost, President Zedillo did not want a fixed election to be his legacy. Second, IFE's system would protect against it. And, third, the large numbers of Mexican and international poll watchers and observers and the domestic and international press would not allow it. There may have been chicanery in the December 1999 PRI electoral primary, but the IFE had not run that election, and all of the poll workers and watchers had been PRI party faithful. Neither was the case in July 2000. The election would be clean and fair, I continually asserted. And it was.

The issue of drugs, which was such a critical element of the embassy's work, was hardly discussed by the candidates. But allegations of drug connections were brought to the embassy and had to be dealt with. I had had some early experience with the phenomenon while preparing to leave Washington in mid-1998.

The DEA had received information from the government of Mexico that Ricardo Monreal, a PRI politician who had left the party and was then running as the PRD candidate for governor of Zacatecas, was involved in money laundering. The Mexican authorities wanted to involve the DEA in a sting operation against Monreal in the final days before the state election. Attorney General Reno asked me to drop by her office. She asked for my opinion. I responded that if the guy was dirty, he would be dirty after the election as well. But I was suspicious that the information and the effort to collaborate against him might have been politically motivated. She agreed. We did nothing. Monreal won. The government never raised the issue again. Had the initial tip been a politically motivated falsehood or had the government decided that, once he was elected, it would lose more in terms of its international image by going after a seated governor? Whatever the truth, it was clear that allegations against candidates had to be screened carefully. Monreal sees himself as a presidential candidate for 2006. Assuredly, the allegations will surface again then.

Another drug-related allegation was brought to me by the DEA a few months before the 2000 election. Intelligence reported that a Labastida fund-raiser was trying to hustle millions of dollars in campaign contributions from drug dealers. Allegedly, he was promising the potential contributors that a Labastida government would serve their interests. I asked Washington for the name of the supposed fund-raiser. I wanted permission to take the information to Labastida himself. It would have been instructive to see how he would respond. But Washington refused. I never knew whether the refusal was to protect a source or because a reexamination of the allegation made it seem less firm than it originally had appeared. Or perhaps I had simply called the DEA's bluff.

Less than a week before the July 2 election, Attorney General Madrazo called and asked if I would see José Luis Reyes, the Fox family's personal lawyer, on a sensitive issue. Reyes came right over to the office. Over coffee he told me that the Texas office of the Fox vegetable export business had been visited by U.S. Customs agents who were investigating the discovery of narcotics in Fox frozen broccoli shipments. The Fox campaign was alarmed. Candidate Fox had little to do with the company, which was run by his brothers, but he and his campaign staff were concerned about publicity, and some were suspicious about the timing of the investigation. I contacted Janet Reno. She checked on the facts, and within a day I was able to assure Reyes that no announcement about the investigation would be made prior to the election. After Fox's July 2 victory, Customs continued to review the issue. Ultimately the agency learned that the Fox products were reboxed in Texas by other companies for shipment around the United States. The boxes still might carry the Fox brand name, but no culpability could be assigned to the family's Mexican wholesale firm. The investigation was terminated.

The embassy kept official Washington well informed of developments in the campaign, but the very heavy U.S. press coverage was already doing that. I became concerned that expectations were building in the United States that Fox was the guaranteed winner and that the only logical reason for his defeat would be PRI perfidy and corruption. I saw it differently. Labastida still maintained a good chance to win. In my briefings of visiting reporters and analysts, I went to extremes to note that while a Fox victory would be historic, he could lose in a fair fight. Labastida had a good chance to win.

Meanwhile Labastida's campaign was not going well. The tension between his initial team and the later add-ons from the traditional PRI was causing internal ruptures. The PRI was coming apart at the seams. In late June I traveled twice on Mexican government planes. Such trips were always fun and full of gossip. On a flight to Phoenix to attend a binational drug conference on a small PGR jet, none of the passengers, including two cabinet members, could convince me that they really believed Labastida was going to win. We compared estimates and the highest gave him a slender three-point margin.

From Phoenix I went on to Washington and New York for President Zedillo's victory lap. He was well received in both cities. A lunch hosted in his honor by the chairman of New York's Federal Reserve Bank was a cozy affair attended by Robert Rubin, Paul Volker, Pete Peterson, and a half-score of other former cabinet members and Washington heavyweights who had moved on to Wall Street. Let no one argue that Washington and Wall Street do not share the same boards of directors. I was planning to return to Mexico commercially. But Zedillo invited me on to his presidential jet. On the return trip there was considerable good-natured ribbing of Luis Téllez, Zedillo's secretary of energy, as he arranged the numerous business cards he had picked up from New York contacts. Zedillo yelled across the plane, "Estas en el job market, Luis?" The implication was clear. Zedillo's team had its own doubts about Labastida's ability to win, and thus their own political future.

In earlier years, the Mexican government had bridled at the suggestion that it allow outside electoral observers, but by 2000 it openly welcomed them. Numerous delegations came from the United States. The three most important were from the International Republican Institute (IRI), the National Democratic Institute (NDI), and the Carter Center of Atlanta. The IRI and NDI teams were led by two engaging and experienced Texans, former Treasury Secretary James Baker and former Governor Ann Richards. At breakfast at the house, they filled me in on some good American political gossip in the run-up to the two U.S. party conventions. Anne Richards was as piquant in her comments about the Bush family in private as she was in public.

They and others asked me my electoral predictions. It was a natural question, but I waffled. I told them that there were two most likely results. Labastida would win by a small margin or Fox would win big. In my gut I thought it would be the latter. After the results came in, I regretted that I had forfeited the opportunity to be brilliantly prescient. But there were just too many imponderables up to the last moment. One of the important questions for me was how effective the PRI machinery would be in turning out the rural vote. Indeed, as Gutiérrez Barrios had indicated, the vote might not still be there.

Given the margin of error, the polls were predicting a dead heat. An exhausted Vicente Fox dropped by the house for a drink two nights before the election. "The coin is in the air," he told me, by which he might have meant, as the phrase does in its English translation, that the race was a toss-up. Or he may have meant, as the saying connotes in Spanish, that all that can be done has been done and we will simply have to wait to see how the coin lands. I suspect that he meant both. Labastida in his final conversation said he was ahead by three points, but he knew, as did I, that his polls were suspect.

The three U.S. observer teams shared long experience in observing elections around the world. NDI and IRI had a more limited approach than did the Carter Center. Both had sent down observer groups during the late spring and summer. They were generally convinced that the mechanics of the vote would be clean and that the candidate with the highest tally would become the next president of Mexico. The Carter Center team, much smaller than the others, tended to focus more on the question of whether the surrounding atmosphere truly permitted a free exercise of Mexico's political will. Such estimations are infinitely more difficult to arrive at than the relatively simple task of seeing whether votes are truly recorded and counted. However, the Carter team did not shy away from its obligations as it saw them.

In the week before the July 2 voting day, the U.S. press had been led to a juicy story about apparent PRI electoral corruption. Governor Víctor Cervera Pacheco of Yucatán, an old-line PRI political lord, was giving out sewing and washing machines, food baskets, bicycles, and all manner of gifts to buy votes for Labastida. The story was heavily pushed by Fox's campaign team of Jorge Castañeda and Adolfo Aguilar Zínser. Having grown up in Boston and seen political machines at work, my reaction approximated Claude Rains's "shock" at being told that there was gambling going on in Casablanca. But it was an attractive story for the U.S. press and for the leader of Carter's team, Bob Pastor. Pastor's analytical independence was held suspect by the PRI and the government. He was a close friend of fellow academic Jorge Castañeda. The two had authored a book on U.S.-Mexico relations, and there was little doubt that Pastor's sympathy was with Fox. As Carter arrived, members of the IRI and NDI teams joked that they had seen the Pastor-Carter team at work before in other elections. They argued that Bob would come early, discover a problem that other observers had overlooked or not found worthy of indigestion, make a big deal out of it, and then organize a solution for President Carter to announce.

But things did not work as Pastor had expected. The report his team issued a few days before the election asserted that Mexican federal funds destined for rural social development and poverty alleviation had been diverted by Cervera Pacheco and others to buy votes. President Zedillo reacted negatively, taking the charge as a personal attack on his honesty. He had a long rebuttal hand-delivered to Carter by one of the Mexican security guards assigned to the visiting president. On Sunday, July 2, Election Day, I received an early morning call from a member of Carter's Secret Service detail. President Carter had given him firm instructions to deliver a counterrebuttal directly into the hands of President Zedillo. Receipt by a Los Pinos staff member would not do. It had to be given in person to President Zedillo. The Secret Service agent asked me to deliver it. I told him this was an issue between a private American organization, the Carter Center, and the government of Mexico. I saw no role for the embassy and wished him luck. The letter was delivered, but not directly to President Zedillo.

It probably was not federal money that Cervera Pacheco was using. He had access to plenty of state revenues and political contributions. As events later demonstrated, whatever kind of campaign fraud he was perpetrating was truly small potatoes. In mid-2002, Fox's government unveiled an immense scandal involving as much as $150 million dollars that had been passed by the state oil company, Pemex, to its labor union, which in turn had handed much of it over to the Labastida campaign. More than $50 million remained in a New York bank. That left open the ultimate question: what organization or group of individuals was going to carve it up.

On Sunday, July 2, we knew by late afternoon that Fox was going to win. Liébano Sáenz told me on the phone from Los Pinos that all the exit polls were moving in that direction. President Zedillo would make an announcement congratulating Fox as soon as the polls closed at about 7 o'clock. I called Baker, Richards, and Carter and gave them the news so that they could prepare their statements. All agreed that Election Day had gone smoothly, that votes were being cast in peace and tabulated honestly.

Zedillo asked Labastida to make an early concession speech. But he refused. The party hierarchy also rejected the idea, leading to later accusations that they had a plan to steal the election. Maybe some did, but Labastida and the party as a whole were simply reluctant to admit defeat. They wanted all votes fully counted and needed to be sure that the concurrent races for members of Congress, governors, and mayors would not be adversely affected by an early concession. Finally, Zedillo taped his message congratulating the people of Mexico and their new president, Vicente Fox. Labastida still balked, but Zedillo announced that he was going on the air at 11 p.m. Labastida had no choice. He gracefully conceded in televised comments after the Zedillo tape aired. Fox followed on television and then made his way to the symbolic center of Mexican political life—the elaborate statue of the Angel of Independence on Mexico City's main thoroughfare, the Reforma.

On his fifty-eighth birthday, Vicente Fox had swept to the Mexican presidency. The official election returns released a few days later gave him almost 16 million votes (42.5 percent) to Labastida's 13.5 million

(36 percent) and Cárdenas's 6.2 million (16.6 percent). The rural vote had declined as a percentage of the total vote. But more importantly, Fox had successfully challenged the PRI's hold over the countryside. In the 1994 presidential election, the PAN candidate had received only about 8 percent of the rural vote. Fox had obtained 5.3 million rural votes to Labastida's 6.3 million. Among the states he carried was Yucatán, where the governor's gifts had attracted so much attention.

It was over. And it was beginning. History had been made. Throughout the country joyous crowds assembled. The euphoria was palpable, as was the relief, as many had worried about a narrow electoral result that might have led to disputes and uncertainty. Adding all of the non-PRI votes together, the vast majority of Mexicans had cast their ballots for change. Fox had raised tremendous expectations. He told the cheering crowd at PAN headquarters on election night, "This is the moment of democracy, the moment of change that our country so desired." And they shouted back the rhyme, "Vicente, Presidente," and "Cambio ya"— change now. But at around 1:30 in the morning, the still-delirious mob at the Angel began a new chant as Fox addressed them. Even in the moment of triumph for so many, Mexico's traditional suspicion, skepticism, and fear of disillusionment showed through. Thousands shouted, "No nos falles! No nos falles!" Don't fail us! Don't let us down.

Incidents of Travel

"Señor Pollo called you." The desk clerk handed me the scribbled message when we returned from a morning bicycle ride through the ruins of Coba in the Yucatán jungle. I told Joan that a Mr. Chicken seemed to be trying to get in touch with me. Señor Pollo had left the phone number for the State Department's Operation Center.

It did not take a lot of imagination to realize that Secretary Powell had tracked me down on this Sunday morning. Although I knew I would not have to talk to a large fowl, I was still apprehensive as I waited for the call to make its way back to the Op Center and then to the Secretary's home.

It was late January 2001. We were traveling in Yucatán to take a break from the hectic schedule of visitors and other tasks associated with Vicente Fox's inauguration on December 1. Mexico had become the flavor of the month in the United States. The embassy was overrun by American legislators, businessmen, governors, politicians, and bureaucrats, all of whom just absolutely, positively, imperatively had to meet with President Fox and members of his new team. And they expected the ambassador to arrange their itineraries and obtain the requisite presidential meeting. Fox was infinitely hospitable, but I needed a break. Yucatán was relaxing.

The desk clerk handed me the phone.

It was only a few days after Powell had assumed office. My concern was that he was going to ask me to come back and take a position in the Washington hierarchy. I had already turned aside feelers that had come from his intermediaries in the previous weeks. Though I knew that working in the State Department under his command would be a worthwhile experience, I had already spent more than a dozen years of my career in Washington. I no longer had the patience for the interminable meetings, the interagency turf fights, the constant efforts to spin the press, and the tedious relations with Congress. But saying no to the secretary of state would take more courage than I felt like summoning on an otherwise pleasant Sunday morning.

"Jeff?"

"Yes sir, congratulations, welcome aboard."

"Don't worry. I'm not calling about what you think I'm calling about."

"Uh-huh," spoken with a certain apprehension and no intelligence.

"The president's chief of staff, Andy Card, was just on *Meet the Press* and let it slip that the president will visit Mexico next month. I didn't want you to be surprised. So I thought I'd better call you."

"Well, thank you. Of course, the Mexicans know the trip was being planned, but I'll let them know about the Meet the Press slip right away, so they can get out their own press release." Then I gratuitously added, "But, frankly, nothing Washington does can ever surprise me."

"Things will be different now," he responded pleasantly but with the tone of a commanding officer.

Getting away from phone calls from Washington was not the principal reason why we traveled frequently in Mexico, but it was a nice benefit. Most mortals will give up when told that the ambassador is out of town. But when the secretary of state picks up the phone and tells the senior watch officer of the State Department Operations Center to find someone, the officer will not rest until he has exhumed the missing person from his grave or found him in the Yucatán jungle, as the case may be.

It is useful for ambassadors and other diplomats to travel extensively in their countries of assignment. Often it is just not possible. Impassable roads, political uprisings, or bandits can be overwhelming impediments. And sometimes there just is not a hell of a lot to see or learn. Early in our postings to Zambia and Venezuela we had pretty much exhausted the travel possibilities of those countries.

But Mexico is very different. Travel is relatively easy and almost inevitably rewards the visitor with experiences that repay the effort many times over. Joan and I had the great benefits of a chauffeur and a security detail, but even without those significant smoothers of rough roads, it is not difficult to get around Mexico.

Some of my predecessors had faced considerably more difficulty. Travel in Mexico used to be dangerous, unhealthy, and difficult. Some of the best travel writing on Mexico and Central America was penned more than 150 years ago by John Lloyd Stephens, whom President Martin Van Buren had appointed to the diplomatic post of special confidential agent. His assignment was to close the American diplomatic mission in war-torn Guatemala City. But he had to pass through Mexico on muleback on his way south. Already a published travel writer, Stephens accepted the job primarily because he wanted to tour the area and write about it. He brought with him the British artist Frederick Catherwood, whose drawings of Palenque, Uxmal, and other Mayan ruins would enthrall Europe and the United States. The two volumes that Stephens and Catherwood produced, *Incidents of Travel in Central America, Chiapas, and Yucatán*, were best-sellers in the 1840s. They remain remarkably fresh and intriguing today. It was always interesting to have their books available when we were exploring the ruins that they had visited.

One of the most important advantages of getting out of the capital city was the opportunity to learn how people in the provinces think and act. A foreign diplomat who confines himself to Washington is not going to get the full story of America. And the same can be said of Mexico City. The Distrito Federal is too involved in intrigue and political chattering. The general tone of the capital media and public discussion is distressingly negative. To listen to Mexico City–based voices only, one would assume that the country was always on the brink of some horrible calamity, frequently attributable to the United States.

Outside of Mexico City, there is another nation. It is composed of vital, striving people who try not to pay too much attention to the capital city. There is a healthy tension between the provinces and the center. I could always guarantee myself a good laugh and appreciative applause by telling an audience in Colima, Tuxtla Gutiérrez, Puebla, Aguascalientes, or a dozen other places that I intended to move the embassy to their city. Everywhere I traveled I met governors, mayors, and businessmen full of ideas for the future and proud of their new highways, civic centers, and factories. As the American ambassador, I was always welcome. Local officials saw me as a potential voice for economic promotion. And, indeed, it was helpful to know enough to be able to direct an American investor to one state where the governor was particularly energetic and away from another where the bureaucracy seemed trapped in the doldrums.

I enjoyed meeting with officials at the state and local levels because, like their American counterparts, they were principally interested in getting the job done—building the road, opening the new university, attracting the investment. They were, for the most part, practical men trying to improve the welfare of their citizens. Some, of course, were rogues or picaresque figures consumed with political ambition. They often wanted to use the ambassador in some way to promote their personal aspirations.

On a visit to a small town in Zacatecas we were introduced to the "tomato king," a wealthy California farmer who had initially entered the United States as an illegal alien in the trunk of a car more than thirty years before. I thought the purpose of my visit was to highlight his public service work in his hometown. I did not understand, or did not listen carefully to my staff when they told me, that he was also a candidate for mayor. Before we knew what was happening, we were being paraded through town accompanied by a mariachi. I had become a prop in his campaign rally. The opposing political parties got heavy local press coverage with their denunciations of my "interference" in the election. I forcefully denied the allegation, telling the press that I had not been politically motivated. I did not tell them that I had just been careless, which was the truth. I also did not tell them that if I ever were going to get involved in Mexican politics, which I had no intention of doing in any event, my first foray would not be to support the leftist PRD candidate in a small town in Zacatecas.

One of the more colorful hijackings occurred when we visited the capital of Zacatecas for the first time. Newly elected Governor Ricardo Monreal met us at our hotel shortly after we pulled into town. An international folk dance festival was about to begin, and we accompanied the governor as he led a parade down the colonial-era main street. The star of the procession was not the governor, the mayor, nor the visiting U.S.

ambassador. A burro bearing a cask of tequila was clearly the crowd's favorite. He ambled from side to side of the street, stopping wherever he wanted. Little earthenware cups were handed out. The burro's tequila supply appeared endless. We had a great time, but were pleased to return later to our hotel, one of the more imaginatively constructed in Mexico. Its central courtyard had been a colonial-era bullring and later became the city's garbage dump. It was cleaned out in the early 1990s, and the luxurious Quinta Real appeared. It was a delight.

Travel can provide a better understanding of a problem that can only be partially comprehended from a distance. Within a few weeks of arriving in Mexico, I visited the two Laredos, the pair of border towns through which more than 50 percent of the two-way trade between the countries passes. I always had to remind myself that Nuevo Laredo was on the Mexican side, so accustomed was I to associate anything labeled new with the United States. It was founded by Mexicans who did not want to, or could not, stay in their Laredo homes when Texas became an independent republic in 1836.

I visited "the Laredos" because I was concerned about the time it took to move goods across the border. The process of exporting from Mexico by truck is something to behold. Goods leave a factory in Guadalajara or Monterrey and travel by modern long-distance haulers to Nuevo Laredo. There the trailers are detached and taken across the border by drayage vehicles, many of them on their last legs, spewing oil and smoke. Once across the line, the trailers are hitched to American-owned cabs for the long-haul runs to Chicago, New York, or other destinations. Over a distance of a few miles, every trailer is pulled by three trucks. Each movement requires a different set of papers to satisfy the customs authorities of both countries. The net effect of this convoluted system is that the cost of moving goods from Mexico to the United States, and vice versa (the process is as difficult heading south), is simply too high. Mexico's sales pitch to manufacturers is based on is its proximity to the United States. The border fandango erodes Mexico's competitive edge.

I met the truck owners and customs brokers to help them solve the problem. There was, however, a fundamental difficulty: they did not think there was a problem. The system was working very well from their point of view. All that extra work and form filling had provided a very generous living to their families for generations. All had homes in both cities, and the country club where we had dinner seemed more than comfortable. They were extremely cordial as they politely sent me on my way, my ambassadorial ego deflated. I realized that any improvement in border crossings was not going to be initiated by that group. They had too much to lose. When I left Mexico four years later, nothing had changed.

Getting out of the capital city also meant talking to different audiences and not hearing the same rehearsed phrases. It was not until I fielded questions from university students in Guadalajara that I realized how they and most Mexicans were interpreting headlines of the previous weeks about the "immigrant hunters" in Arizona. They thought that the vigilantes were actually hunting and killing illegal aliens as they crossed the border. It was a gruesome image that the Mexican press created by distorting what was in reality a horrible situation but one that had not involved violence. There were ranchers detaining illegal migrants on their properties, but there was no blood or massacre, only vigilantism, racism, and profound ignorance.

Occasionally, we heard wonderful stories. The young governor of tropical Yucatán—he had replaced Cervera Pacheco of the election fraud allegations—entertained us with tales about his eccentric grandmother, who as a young woman had saved the life of a baby crocodile. She brought the creature to her Mérida home, where it lived until its death decades later. The governor recalled his boyhood when he and his cousins would slide down the stairs on the eight-foot long creature. The only difficulty occurred during Mérida's frequent floods, when the household pet would go swimming in the street, much to the consternation of the local citizenry.

But not all travel was punctuated by Macondo-like tales of eccentric grandmothers or the boosterism of governors and mayors. I learned more about Mexico—the dimensions of poverty and disease in the countryside, the lack of rule of law, the power of drug lords, the strength of political parties and candidates, the state of the rural economy, the corruption of local officials and dozens of other topics—by moving around the country, talking, and, listening. I also learned to be cautious about false aesthetics. There is tremendous beauty in Mexico, but some of it masks ugly reality. The Madonna-like mother and child wrapped in a shawl begging by the side of the road may be strikingly biblical in appearance, but the romance of the ancient world has little to do with their poverty and does not help them put food on the table. Many Indian villages are picturesque in the extreme, but desperately poor.

Americans living and traveling in Mexico cannot help but be impressed by the almost omnipresent courtesy and hospitality. Only a few years after the conquest, Spaniards returning home added a new phrase to their country's lexicon—as polite as a Mexican Indian. Confrontation is discouraged and, to the American ear, forms of speech can be marvelously orotund. The Spanish language itself demands circumlocution. The Spanish side of a bilingual dictionary is about 15 to 20 percent thinner than the English portion, but the same business letter is one-third longer in Spanish. The source of much of the extra verbiage stems from the cultural obligation to be grandly polite and respectful in salutations and closings.

I particularly appreciated the small everyday gestures that went unnoticed by Mexicans but greatly appealed to me. When confronted with a befuddled foreigner who has obviously not understood directions, a Mexican will provide directions and then ask, "Si me explico?" (Am I explaining myself?) rather than the "Me entiende?" (Do you understand me?) more common elsewhere in Latin America. The speaker thus assumes, rhetorically at least, responsibility for any failure of communication.

I also marveled at how Mexicans would take the complications of their own language—notably the use of *tu* and *usted*—and work with them. For an American, the simple "you" suffices and, not incidentally, fits better in a society in which class has not been as traditionally important as it has been in Mexico. I found Mexicans much more willing to move rapidly to "tu" than many other Latin Americans. However, an important personage like a foreign ambassador must be the first to drop the formal form. When in doubt, Mexicans will use a somewhat tortured grammar that connotes a certain tentativeness. "Como estamos?" (How are we?) is a common greeting by someone who thinks he may be able to *tutear* the other person, but is not quite sure as yet. Usages like "me explico" and the subtle rules of the tutear are, of course, unremarkable second nature to Mexicans. But to a foreigner, they form part of the culture's charm.

Whether the adhesion to forms of courtesy is uniquely Mexican—a product of an arabized Spain mixing with native culture—is a question for scholars. Some argue that Mexico is a country of masks where true thoughts and feelings are disguised, in part by the excessive politeness. Whatever the historical or cultural roots might be, as someone who has been treated rudely on several continents, I found the Mexican attitude infinitely preferable.

The concept of masks, whether valid or not, is worth remembering for any diplomat. There is a special reserve in Mexico that closes some topics to discussion, as we saw during a weekend in the countryside with another couple. The conversation was free-flowing and interesting throughout several long meals and some sightseeing. It was only later that we learned that the host's father had been shot in the head by unknowns just a few days before and was recuperating in the hospital. I think that if my father had recently taken a bullet to the cranium, I would probably have mentioned it. It is often not difficult to conceal reality in a society that takes pride in its ability to hold things close to the chest. Mexico City's small Jewish community has long been a prime target of kidnappers. But rarely do stories of the kidnappings or ransoms become public. Of course, there is a practical reason to maintain secrecy—other kidnappers need not be tipped off to willing ransom payers.

Because there is so much about Mexico that is attractive, that which is ugly can be easily missed or overlooked. Bob Rivard, the editor of the *San Antonio Express*, spent years confronting the ugly side as he tried to piece together the story of the murder of one of his reporters. Phillip True had wanted to write about the culture of the Huichol Indians and the assault it faces from modern society. In 1998, he set out to backpack through Huichol land in Jalisco State. He was murdered by two Huicholes who he thought were befriending him. The case was complicated, and as Rivard delved deeply into it, he confronted police and judicial incompetence, defensive politicians, uncaring bureaucrats, untrustworthy guides, and lying witnesses.

The more Rivard looked, the more elusive justice became. The pressure of American public opinion, the embassy, and Rivard himself kept the case alive. Without outside intervention, the murder would have sunk into the Mexican legal system's miasma of unsolved crimes and unmourned bodies. Reflecting on his four-year search for justice, Rivard said that he was at once attracted and repulsed by Mexico, that its beauty and culture were captivating, but its dark side of deceit appalled him.

I empathized with his feelings, though I never could have expressed them so eloquently.

Whatever profound or semideep thoughts I might have entertained about the value of listening to new voices, and of understanding Mexican aesthetics and cultural masks, the truth was that we traveled widely because it was so pleasant and interesting. One of the great fortunate coincidences of world cultural history was the meeting of Iberia and Indian Mexico in the sixteenth century. Two cultures whose art was prolific, colorful, iconographic, and convoluted confronted each other to the artistic benefit of future generations.

How fitting it was that those dull seventeenth-century pilgrims of New England found Indian cultures not much more colorful than their own. Whatever the Indian societies of the American Northeast might have notably accomplished in terms of social or political structure—one thinks of the complex Iroquois nation—their artistic contributions were about as understated as that of the intruders who disturbed them. What would have happened to the treasury of world art if the Spaniards had come to New England and the English had met the Aztecs? It is too horrible to contemplate.

The merging of Spanish and Indian artistry produced exceptional work that rivaled the best that each culture had produced on its own. In the barren mountainous region of the central state of Queretero we visited the mission churches of the Sierra Gorda built in the 1750s by Indian artisans under the direction of Franciscan friar Junípero Serra. He was the same priest who then walked to what is today California and established its string of missions along the coast. Now carefully restored, the Mexican churches are a riot of color and rough but exuberant copies of baroque statues and paintings.

Joan and I were especially captivated by the charm of Michoacán, a state peppered with villages that continue to produce weaving, guitars, pottery, and lacquer work with techniques and designs first taught to them by the benevolent prelate Vasco de Quiroga in the mid-sixteenth century. Quiroga was much influenced by Thomas More's *Utopia* and sought to teach self-sufficiency to the Indian communities so they would not fall under the cruel domination of local Spanish landowners. The vision failed, but the handicraft tradition endured.

Joan, more than I, was attuned to the great impact of natural colors on the artistic development of the indigenous people. Mexico is a rainbow brought to earth—brilliant blue skies, endless rows of green cornstalks, the bright red hills of Baja California bordering vibrantly blue waters, the lush green hills overlooking Acapulco, the millions of orange and black monarch butterflies that come to Mexico from the north to breed, hot pink dragonflies, glistening hummingbirds of every shade, and white butterflies the size of small angels. And everywhere the land is monumental—snowcapped volcanoes, endless vistas of cactus, barren mountains, and fearsome deserts. The exuberance of color and the immensity of the terrain surely motivated the artistic and spiritual impulses of Mexico's native inhabitants, the Spaniards who disrupted them, and the mestizo culture of Rivera, Tamayo, Kahlo, and Siqueiros that inherited their traditions.

We became frequent visitors to pre-Hispanic ruins. We most enjoyed those locales where the ruins stood close to Spanish colonial architecture. The magnificent Zapotec mountaintop city of Monte Albán, for example, is but a few miles from the now-restored baroque wonder of the Dominican monastery of Oaxaca. From the colonial city of Mérida it is an easy drive to the Mayan center of Uxmal. And the magnificent remains of wall paintings in the ruins of Cacaxtla are close to the charming colonial town of Tlaxcala, which is only a short drive from Mexico City.

As an inveterate people watcher, I enjoyed finding a place to just sit and watch the world go by while Joan went shopping or engaged in more socially redeeming activities. The *plazas mayores*, the main squares, of Pátzcuaro, Mérida, Taxco, Oaxaca, or a dozen other places on a Friday or Saturday night are full of Breughel-like activity. While adults sit on benches and chat, the teenagers promenade and flirt. Often I found a seat on a park bench. Frequently I was approached—always respectfully—by people who recognized me from the photos that appeared too often in the press. We would talk of what was happening in their town, their concerns about their kids' education, and, almost always, about their relatives in the United States.

Everywhere we went in central and southern Mexico we found examples of crafts that sustained traditions that had flowered from a unparalleled sense of style and color mixed with inordinate skill. Early in our stay in Mexico we visited an exhibition put together by the cultural philanthropy of Mexico's largest bank, Banamex. The best work of Mexico's leading weavers, potters, embroiderers, woodworkers, and other craftsman was displayed in a breathtaking exposition of indigenous art. Banamex had the great good sense to publish a small book containing the addresses of the artisans. We used it as our guide as we moved around the country.

Visiting the artisans in their village homes was a superb experience. And those we visited gave us the names of others in the village or ran to the houses of their neighbors or brothers to bring out more wares for sale. At first, I thought that by eliminating the middlemen we would be able to buy the products at rock-bottom prices. But, in fact, the artisans' homes were generally so humble and we were such easy marks that I would inevitably agree to whatever price they asked even though I knew it was outrageous by local standards. It is hard to bargain when children and chickens are scurrying through your legs on a dirt floor.

By chance we found one village, Los Reyes Mexzantla, twenty miles off a paved road and deep in the desert of southern Puebla state, where the women had formed cooperatives to produce clay pots unlike any others we had seen. While these artisans certainly had mastered their art, they were profoundly ignorant of the economics of production. They were unable to determine their costs, never factored in their own time or energy, and would regularly sell their pots for cost or at markups of less than 10 percent. Joan was able to get them professional help by working with the state government, the embassy's office of the U.S. Agency for International Development, and Chip Morris and Lee Carter, two Americans who promote native handicrafts. Together they helped develop a system for charging reasonable prices; they also developed techniques to make the pottery waterproof, a quality of obvious importance for flowerpots.

The enduring Indian heritage of Mexico fascinated us. While we tried to avoid "events" and ceremonies because they were often too touristic and crowded, there were occasions when we could not avoid being part of a larger group. Sometimes the experience was magical nevertheless. The celebration of the Day of the Dead on November 1 and the predawn hours of November 2 in the graveyards near Pátzcuaro in Michoacán are unequalled in the country. The Indian families in Michoacán decorate the graves of their relatives with candles, orange marigolds—the flower of the deceased—and elaborate shrines. They bring food and drink and spend the night with the departed. In recent years, the state government has given families money to buy even more candles and decorations in an effort, unfortunately successful, to attract more tourists. Busloads of teenagers who show no respect for the dead or the living arrive for noisy and quick tours. The evening has taken on a carnival-like atmosphere with food sellers and tee shirt hawkers abounding.

But despite those distractions, the scene is moving. At two a.m. the graveyard at Tzintunzan is misty with the light and smoke of thousands of candles, redolent with incense, and blanketed with orange flowers. The families are courteous to foreigners and reverential to the dead. The noisy tourists have left. There is not a better moment in Mexico's year. We visited Pátzcuaro many times to browse its handicrafts and to stay in a pleasant, modest hotel we found there, the Posada de la Basílica, which overlooks the town.

In the predominantly Indian communities of Michoacán we found great pottery. In Chiapas we admired the textiles, particularly the huipiles of the Mayan women. But we also came across a world that, like some other indigenous cultures, has been debased by alcohol. As in other societies facing the same problem with alcohol, it is the women who keep life together in these Indian villages. They raise their families and work at their pottery or weaving to earn a few extra pesos. Protestant evangelical missionaries have won hundreds of thousands of converts throughout Mexico, particularly among Indian women, in large part because of their strong opposition to alcohol. Chiapas is now 40 percent Protestant, a figure of much concern to the established Roman Catholic hierarchy.

Oaxaca is one state in which Indian traditions and communities seemed exceptionally healthy. We noted less public drunkenness, and the villages near Oaxaca City were populated by families with a social cohesion that was admirable. The large Zapotec-speaking rug weaving clan of the Vázquez family in Teotihuacan del Valle and the women of the pottery cooperative in Santa Maria de Atzompa, not far from Monte Albán, were dignified, hardworking, and welcoming. As I thought of Oaxaca's Benito Juarez, Mexico's only full-blooded Indian president, I came to believe that there must be something in the Zapotec-Mixteca tradition that makes them different. When I tried this theory out on anthropologists and other experts, they received it with the bemused puzzlement that academics reserve for the unschooled.

The government of Mexico has done a good job over the years of researching, restoring, and making available to the public the archeological ruins of prior civilizations. In part that effort was motivated by a nationalist desire to present Mexico both to Mexicans and to the world as a millennial culture worthy of respect. It has succeeded. Millions of people each year visit Teotihuacan, Chichén-Itzá, Palenque, and other large, well-developed sites. We did so as well, but because we had four years to explore the country, we saw many more sites.

Sometimes the lesser known locales were even more interesting. The trip to Yaxchilan, a Mayan city that reached its peak in the eighth century, requires a forty-five-minute boat trip down the Usumacinta River, which forms Chiapas's border with Guatemala. As we ascended the steep hill that rises from the river to the ruin, we heard a loud roaring. Thinking jaguar, I started to plan our escape back to the boat. But the source of the racket turned out to be a group of enormously noisy, but not aggressive, howler monkeys. Reassured, I started to swagger like Indiana Jones as we trudged through the jungle. Other great sites we visited included a string of excavations leading inland from Tulum. It was at one of those locales, Coba, where Señor Pollo caught up with me.

We looked to Mexico's museums to deepen our understanding of the culture. The Anthropological Museum in Mexico City is justifiably famous, but I found its size and displays overwhelming. The much smaller museum at the Zócalo's Templo Mayor is more manageable, as is the strikingly designed Anthropological Museum in Jalapa, Veracruz. When visiting archeological sites or museums, we would try to sneak in without being recognized. Often, we could carry it off, but just as frequently a guard would summon the director, who would insist on escorting us on a tour. This often stretched a visit we had planned for an hour to double or triple that time, as we heard about each edifice and item in detail beyond our capacity to absorb. But we appreciated their courtesy and tried to reciprocate by showing interest even when exhaustion or boredom made it difficult to do so.

On occasion, the special treatment yielded experiences that were memorable. It sent a chill down my spine to descend steps into a tomb at Monte Albán and find an undisturbed and perfectly formed incense burner in the shape of a warrior's head. It was still mounted on the wall a thousand years after the tomb had been sealed. One morning we were spotted in the Museo Dolores Olmedo in Mexico City and Dolores herself invited us into her home. She was the doyenne of Mexico's artistic world. Her life had spanned the twentieth century, bringing her into contact with nearly every artist and political figure of note. Well into her nineties, dressed in a bright red gown with fierce black hair drawn tightly back, she served us champagne as she quite appropriately sat on the throne of the last Dowager Empress of China. Her face, perhaps attended to more than once by Mexico's ever-active plastic surgeons, had itself taken on a Manchu appearance. She regaled us with great humor about artists she had known as she sat under Diego Rivera's portrait of her as a strikingly beautiful young woman.

Our travels made our appreciation of Mexico grow, and perhaps our understanding as well. The return to Mexico City to face the accumulated problems of the embassy, to deal with the latest back and forth with Washington, or to confront the Mexican government was always a bit of a letdown.

The Fox Presidency

Vicente Fox found it was easier to become president of Mexico than to be president of Mexico. The euphoria that greeted his July 2, 2000, electoral victory began to evaporate quickly, and within a few months of his inauguration newspaper pundits and others were expressing disappointment in his government. Fox, a man of warmth and obvious good intentions, maintained high personal popularity in public opinion polls. But as it became increasingly apparent that he could not deliver on his bold campaign pledge of change, disillusionment with his administration began to sink in.

Fox did have some success in his first months in office. His handling of the Chiapas conflict demonstrated political courage and a willingness to take risks. He had bombastically declared during his campaign that as president he could solve the Chiapas problem in fifteen minutes. The former businessman was confident that embedded in the welter of charge and countercharge, grievance and response, protest and repression, there was a deal waiting to be made. But he had overestimated both his skill and the reasonableness of the protagonists: the Zapatistas on one side and the Mexican political establishment on the other.

When I arrived in Mexico in mid-1998, Chiapas was an issue of only marginal and periodic concern for the American government. However, the December 1997 massacre of forty-five peasants in the pro-Zapatista village of Acteal had revived concern and press coverage. It was a principal topic in my early conversations with Rosario Green, Minister of Interior Francisco Labastida, and other government officials. I urged full investigation and disclosure of the Acteal event. There was some of both, but it was far from full, leaving most observers with the suspicion that some element of the Mexican government had armed, encouraged, or at least condoned the work of the anti-Zapatista campesinos responsible for the killings.

I avoided travel to Chiapas for a while because I knew that my presence could turn into a media circus, with the Mexican press concocting some overheated fantasy about the United States scheming to interfere. It was seven months before a good opportunity presented itself. I accompanied a delegation of American businessmen and was generally able to avoid commenting directly on the conflict by stressing the need for economic development. My private meeting with Bishop Samuel Ruiz turned public when he tipped off the press and photographers caught me entering his residence. That picture flashed around Mexico, causing considerable consternation in the Zedillo administration. I had wanted to keep the meeting private to avoid the charge of political grandstanding, but I was not dismayed that the Mexican and American public would learn of the embassy's continuing concern about Chiapas.

Publicly, I espoused the U.S. government position that Chiapas was an internal problem and that Mexicans of goodwill could find a solution. Privately, I felt they could use some help, not from the United States, nor perhaps from any government, but from prestigious non-Mexican mediators. It was an idea that impaled itself on the quills of Mexico's obsession with sovereignty. It had no chance of acceptance.

Bishop Ruiz was what I had expected. He was articulate, charming, and dedicated. Tata ("father"), as he was called by the Indians, was a charismatic, powerful figure. He talked at length and with emotion about the injustices the Indians of Chiapas had suffered for five centuries. He recounted that when he had arrived in San Cristóbal de las Casas forty years earlier, Indians were still expected to step off sidewalks and allow unimpeded passage to those of European stock. That particularly noxious colonial-era vestige had disappeared, but Ruiz clearly felt that the Indians he ministered to were still suffering endemic discrimination, persecution, and poverty. His economic views were classic Latin leftist, but by the time I met Ruiz in 1999, he had been marginalized by the

Zapatistas. As good Marxists, they were reluctant to consider a Catholic bishop as one of their own. The following year, the conservative hierarchy in Rome, which had never been comfortable with Ruiz's activism, finally compelled him to leave Chiapas.

During the presidential campaign of 2000, Fox, much influenced by Castañeda, promised that human rights would take a central position in his administration. He was willing to take chances to advance that agenda. When the Zapatista leader, Subcomandante Marcos, said he would negotiate only if Zapatista prisoners were released and the military pulled back from positions surrounding Zapatista villages, Fox complied. And when he demanded that Fox pledge not to interfere as they traveled to Mexico City to address Congress and the public, the president agreed again.

That decision received broad support from the public. Mexicans, who see themselves as a nation of victims, naturally support the weak and oppressed. While most did not share the Zapatistas' radical agenda, they instinctively sided with the Indians whom the Zapatistas proclaimed to represent. The move to allow Marcos to come to Mexico City was therefore popular with the masses.

But not with former PRI government officials. In my conversations with Zedillo's team, I had been struck by their concerns about the country's security and stability. While presenting Mexico to their own public and to the world as a stable country, those who had the best information and access to intelligence privately revealed a real concern about threats to the state. They tended to see government as a necessary and organized conspiracy against chaos. The violence of the Mexican Revolution, which had claimed a million lives, had not disappeared from their historical memory. Several guerrilla movements were active, leftist students controlled some universities, and radical labor unions were a threat. For these experienced men, letting Marcos stage a triumphal march to Mexico City opened the country to the risk of chaos, a risk too great to take. They thought Fox should stick with Zedillo's Chiapas strategy, which they saw as a success. Marcos was no longer a military threat; his domestic and his international attractiveness was diminishing, they insisted. Why give him an opportunity to occupy center stage once again?

But that is exactly what Fox did. The "Zapatour" was a public relations success for Marcos. As the caravan snaked its way to Mexico City, it received large and tumultuous welcomes. In the end, however, the Zapatour did little to increase support for the Zapatistas. In fact, by allowing them to march freely across the country, Fox robbed them of their strongest argument, that Mexico was a repressive state that denied its people freedom of expression. When the PAN and the PRI opposed Zapatista plans to enter Congress with their masks on, Fox intervened. He persuaded the PAN to forge a one-time coalition with the leftist PRD that permitted the appearance.

Marcos did not come to Congress. He wanted the world to hear from the Indians, not from him, the son of a middle-class non-Indian family from Mexico's north. His Zapatista colleagues spoke from the country's most visible pulpit, but in the end they accomplished little. Legislation for a constitutional amendment to expand indigenous rights was passed. However, it was so watered down by the PRI and the PAN that the Zapatistas rejected it as insufficient and unresponsive to their concerns. Marcos returned to the jungle, and the Chiapas tension remained unresolved.

But with his display of moderation and tolerance, Fox had boldly secured a significant victory. Mexicans supported his move. Foreign critics were disarmed. His openness, and Foreign Secretary Castañeda's lobbying, helped to clear the way for the European Union to approve a free trade agreement with Mexico. As additional evidence of the centrality of human rights in Mexico's domestic and foreign policy, the agreement included a provision that would invalidate it if the EU determined that Mexico was turning away from democratic principles. That provision represented a major departure from Mexico's traditional insistence that foreign countries not interfere in its domestic affairs. The fact that the understanding was with Europe, and not with the United States, made the provision politically acceptable.

Though in many ways successful, Fox's strategy in dealing with the Zapatistas may have been an error in that it robbed him of valuable time and energy at the beginning of his administration, when he might have more effectively focused on other pressing issues. Fox's personal strengths kept his popularity high, even as public faith in his government diminished. Mexicans appreciated his honesty and respect for human rights. His efforts to promote greater credibility within government, his dynamism, and his rough-hewn good nature all served him well. Mexicans, even those who were his sworn political enemies, would tell me that they thought Fox was a decent man. Then, with a certain satisfaction, they would list his deficiencies as president.

Much was made in Mexican political circles of Fox's purported lack of political skill. While he was universally regarded as a superb, charismatic campaigner, he was widely criticized as a poor head of government. The subterranean skills needed to broker deals, dispense favors, issue threats, and organize the multiple forms of manipulation necessary for effective governing seemed beyond him. Many wondered if he was just too decent a human being to rap the knuckles or knock the heads of his opponents or even his own cabinet members when they got out of line.

Those judgments were overly harsh. They unfairly compared Fox to the PRI presidents who had governed in a far different environment. Those presidents had exercised enormous authority through the vertical chain of command that linked the presidency to the PRI majority in Congress and to every government agency and entity in the country. But now many Mexicans—especially political commentators who had spent years advocating a more open system of government—turned on Fox. They criticized him for not exercising the unofficial presidential authority—which had been based largely on threats, bribes, favors, and the use and misuse of power—that they had done so much to erode. Fox may not have been Mexico's most skilled politician, but it was patently unfair to condemn him as inept for acting in a transparent fashion and for abiding by the new rules of the game.

Fox's political problems began on the day he was elected. While he won a convincing plurality, the PAN did not. The PRI remained the largest party in both houses of Congress and was able to form a workable majority with the PRD to block Fox's initiatives. Because Fox attributed his victory less to the PAN than to his own organization, the Friends of Fox, he drew on businessmen, technocrats, and many others whose links to the PAN were thin or nonexistent to be members of his cabinet. Of the most important cabinet members, only Minister of Interior Santiago Creel was a high-level PAN politician. Fox's team was not sufficiently well schooled in the dirty arts of politics to succeed in Mexico's tough public arena.

The foreign secretariat was given to Castañeda, whom the PAN generally detested for his arrogance and leftist past. Treasury went to Francisco Gil Díaz, universally regarded as highly competent and a nominal, unenthusiastic PRI-ista technician. Commerce was handed to Ernesto Derbez, an international economist who had spent most of his professional life outside Mexico, working for the World Bank. And the new attorney general was an apolitical military man, General Rafael Macedo de la Concha. Even Fox's personal staff in Los Pinos was short on PAN functionaries. One of his key aides, Alfonso Durazo, had actually been a PRI stalwart for many years, but had left that party when his mentor, PRI presidential candidate Luis Donaldo Colosio, was assassinated in 1994. The net effect of the way Fox organized his government was that it lacked skilled political operatives who could forge the important congressional alliances that he needed.

When Fox moved into Los Pinos on Inauguration Day, December 1, he set up his presidential office with an awkward structure that brought him little advantage. He created three super advisors through whom the cabinet was instructed to report. Adolfo Aguilar Zínser was put in charge of national security affairs. Eduardo Sojo was given the supervisory economic portfolio. Jose Sarukhán, a distinguished former rector of the national university, was supposed to make sense of the government's social programs. The three were coordinators rather than supervisors, but, for the most part, the cabinet members either ignored or circumvented them.

Of the three, Sojo was the most successful, largely because he quickly gave up trying to referee the battles (more personal than policy in nature) among Derbez, Gil, and Guillermo Ortiz, the president of the Central Bank. Rather, he served Fox as an independent economic advisor. Sarukhán was never able to establish a role for himself, and Aguilar Zínser ran into major problems. Both left their positions relatively quickly. The model of the three super coordinators fell apart and the replacement structures seemed to function no better.

The PRI had been traumatized by its electoral defeat. Mutual recriminations were the order of the day and factions were multiplying. The PRI was so angry and upset that when President Zedillo came to Congress on September 1, 2000, to deliver his last annual State of the Nation message, the members of his own party refused to applaud him. It was an especially ungracious gesture directed toward a man who had done so much for the democratic transformation of his country. The party was so weak during the period between the election in July and his inauguration in December that Fox could have moved aggressively to split it and draw some of its elected representatives to his banner. But Fox chose not to. It was not his style. He did not want to start a major battle.

Fox could also have pushed for an agreement with the PRI, a set of principles and goals that both major parties would use to guide their work in Congress. The most politically plugged-in member of Fox's cabinet, Interior Minister Santiago Creel, argued for this, but he could not convince his boss. The president rejected the approach, largely because he assumed that the PRI could not muster enough cohesion to unite behind such an agreement. Fox also was not eager to be seen compacting with the devils he had just cast out of Los Pinos.

So, by default, Fox had no strategy either to fight or compromise with the PRI, which though hostile and paralyzed, still held a plurality of seats in the Congress. I often recalled my conversation with the Labastida campaign aide who had predicted that the PRI would be a much less responsible political force in the opposition than it was when it ran the government. He was right. The PRI was so divided by disputes and contradictions that at times it seemed the only thing its leaders could agree on was the lowest common denominator of saying no to the President. Many in the party wanted Fox's presidency to fail. Even if Fox had been the best politician in Mexican history, he probably would have not have had much success dealing with his opposition.

The very structure of the Mexican political system added to Fox's difficulties. The constitutional prohibition against reelection for all public officials means that members of Congress generally do not have to be concerned about their constituents' views or about paying a price for obstructing a popular president. They do not have to present themselves and their records for validation in another election. Moreover, 200 of the 500 members of the Chamber of Deputies have no identifiable constituents. They are elected from party lists, not from geographical areas, and have even less connection to the voters. The structural flaws of the electoral system meant that Fox could not translate his considerable public support into pressure on his congressional opponents.

Not all of Fox's political problems were of the opposition's or the system's making. Many were self-inflicted. The first press reports of his new tax proposals revealed that he intended to increase the value-added sales tax on all products, including food and medicine. A more inauspicious beginning to a national debate would be hard to imagine. The opposition parties launched vicious attacks, and the PAN ran for cover, even though nearly everyone recognized the need for fiscal reform. Mexico collects a much smaller portion of its gross domestic product to finance its government than most countries. As a result, the government lacks the resources to build schools and highways, pay teachers well, and accomplish a hundred other essential tasks. But Mexicans are no more inclined to pay more taxes than citizens of other countries. In fact, they are considerably less willing because they believe that so much of what they pay is misused or lost to corruption. Beginning a tax reform debate with the intention of taxing food and medicine was a devastatingly poor start.

Fox had no more success with his efforts to promote reform in the energy industries. His government moved awkwardly among a number of proposals, looking for a way around another artifact of Mexican history: the nationalization of the oil industry by President Lázaro Cárdenas in 1938, a pillar of Mexican sovereignty. At an early stage before he took office, Fox talked about privatization of the giant and inefficient Pemex, the government's petroleum monopoly. But he quickly fell back to less complete measures. State-owned assets would not be sold off, he asserted, but ways could be found to bring the private sector into areas of production and distribution of energy that were closed to it. However, any proposal to change the status quo was easily attacked as an effort to sell the national patrimony. Other countries, Venezuela being a prime example, had managed to open their nationalized petroleum sectors to outside investment without ceding control of the nation's subsoil treasure. But those examples carried little weight in Mexico's political world.

The Ministry of Energy estimated in 2001 that Mexico would need close to $120 billion worth of investment in hydrocarbon and electricity production in the following ten years. The figures were hotly debated, with foes of any sort of opening of the energy sector arguing that they were overestimates. Perhaps so, but whatever the total, it was clear that Mexico would need an enormous amount of investment to meet its growing energy needs. Advocates for reform noted that every peso the government spent on a new oil or gas field or electricity plant was one less peso to build a school, educate a child, or provide health care. They asserted that it would make sense to share the costs and risks of energy development with the private sector.

Most public figures in Mexico believed that the old system was too rigid and stunted economic growth. In private conversations during the campaign, all the presidential candidates, including Cuauhtémoc Cárdenas, acknowledged to me that change was needed. But few politicians were willing to publicly run the risk of being labeled as traitors, eager to sell out the nation's patrimony and independence. Zedillo's secretary of energy, Luis Téllez, had introduced a reform plan but ultimately had to pull back in the face of ideological opposition. Fox had no better luck. By mid-2002, his energy secretary was pushing a plan for shared risks and profits in the development of gas fields. But the plan was so limited that it gained little attention from the major oil companies. And he ran into the chorus of old nationalist sentiments led by PRI Senator Manuel Bartlett, erstwhile presidential aspirant and an aggressive obstructionist.

The state-controlled electricity sector had witnessed some changes in recent years. Private investors built generating plants, but the law demanded that the electricity they produced be sold directly to companies that had contracted for the plants' construction or to the government for resale. No open or free market in electricity was permitted and future private investment was in doubt. Stymied in its efforts to promote electricity, oil, and fiscal reform, the Fox administration was unable to bring about the change promised during the campaign.

Another of Fox's campaign vows was that he would confront past abuse and corruption. He came into office promising a clean sweep of the abuses of the past. Carlos Rojas, one of his principal aides, was given the job of identifying corrupt officials from the previous government so they could be put on trial. But justice was easier desired than delivered. It was not until mid-2002 that the Fox administration was able to uncork a major scandal: the siphoning of vast sums from Pemex into Labastida's campaign. But even that discovery caused problems for Fox as the PRI fought back, becoming even more recalcitrant and negative in Congress.

It seemed that almost everything the Fox administration attempted ran into political roadblocks. When Fox took on the thorny problem of finding a location for a new Mexico City airport, he wanted to demonstrate that his government could make and implement decisions rapidly.

The old airport is overcrowded and outdated, and the need for a new one has been obvious for some time. The Zedillo administration had not been able to find a way through the political thickets that seem to be an inevitable part of airport site selections throughout the world. Fox, who saw the mess as symptomatic of the negative effects of PRI cronyism, wanted to make the decision quickly and on the technical merits.

The site that was selected made sense, but there was a problem. A few thousand campesinos would have to be relocated. When they angrily protested and the government handled negotiations poorly, the left adopted the campesinos as their own. It was widely believed that the PRD was financing the protests. The fact that the new airport would not be constructed in the Federal District, which was controlled by the PRD, but in the neighboring state of Mexico, which was controlled by the PRI, lent credence to the suspicion. The public, with typical and instinctive support for the underdog, supported the protestors, who marched through downtown Mexico City angrily waving machetes in demonstrations that looked like a scene from a B movie about Zapata. It was great theater, but the march opened Fox to criticism from another quarter. Social conservatives, alarmed at the machete-wielding defiance, bemoaned the lack of order and control.

Some Americans joined the tumult. A dozen U.S. college students of the committed, sandal-wearing variety came to a protest with their American faculty advisor. Several took machetes in hand, somehow managing not to maim themselves or anyone else. The government stepped in and deported them for interfering in domestic politics. It was an ineffectual move on the government's part, but at least demonstrated to the social conservatives that it was capable of taking some action.

Rather than risk a bloody confrontation, Fox backed away from the airport site, reinforcing the growing public and press perception that his administration was short on political skill. As often happens in politics, that perception fed upon itself and was nurtured by the media. By contrast, when the gigantic National University, UNAM, was paralyzed by a long strike a few years earlier, the Zedillo administration had developed enough of an aura of competence that its inaction was generally perceived as prudent and politically astute. Had the strike occurred when Fox was in office and had he reacted in the same way, he would have been portrayed as indecisive and politically incompetent.

One serious problem completely beyond Fox's control was the downturn in the American economy, which hurt Mexican factories by depressing demand for exports. Fox had campaigned on a pledge to raise Mexico's annual growth rate to 7 per cent and to generate millions of new jobs. But the economic slide in the United States kept growth well below 2 percent. And unemployment actually grew as factories closed. Erosion of U.S. markets was not the only problem. Some manufacturers moved to China and to other countries that offered cheaper labor. Mexico was losing its competitive advantage, and the high cost of energy and transportation as well as a weak system of justice were as responsible for the loss of manufacturing jobs as were the low wages in China.

Even one of Fox's notable virtues, loyalty, turned out to be a liability. He seemed constitutionally incapable of firing anyone. Prior to the resignation of Jorge Castañeda in January 2003, no cabinet member was replaced, though several should have been shown the door for misbehavior or incompetence. Cabinet ministers publicly contradicted each other, sometimes out of ignorance, sometimes out of malice. The minister in charge of revamping the national police sued a high-ranking official in the attorney general's office for defamation of character. Castañeda quibbled publicly with Minister of Economy Derbez and with Minister of Interior Creel. He persuaded the president to abolish an independent office of migrant affairs that Fox had established. The press started to refer to the "Montessori cabinet," a group of children allowed to express themselves at will, with no concern for order or discipline.

The average Mexican's greatest disappointment with Fox had little to do with cabinet conflicts, failures to obtain structural reforms, or political brouhahas like the airport conflict. Fox was not blamed for the economic downturn, which most saw as beyond his control. What Mexicans most wanted was firm action to improve their personal security. They wanted to be able to walk the streets safely, to be secure in their own homes, to trust that the government was capable of turning back the rising tide of violent crime.

This was particularly the case in Mexico City, where crime had risen markedly in recent years, especially after the 1995 peso crisis caused unemployment to skyrocket. Crime rates did not diminish once the economic situation normalized somewhat. Other areas of the country—even where the problem was generally under control—took their cues from television, radio, and print media dominated by capital city concerns. Everywhere, public safety topped the list of national problems.

I once asked a gathering of Mexican employees of the embassy how many had someone living in their household who had been the victim of a crime in the past year. Nearly half raised their hands. They recounted tales of purse snatchings, muggings, and neighborhood toughs shaking down store owners. Several had been victims of express kidnappings in which they were abducted at gunpoint and held until their families came up with the demanded ransom.

Every class of Mexican society felt targeted by the rising crime. The upper class was particularly vulnerable to kidnappings. The middle class feared carjackings and home burglaries. But as in most societies, spreading crime most afflicted the poor, who had the least power to protect themselves and the least influence to demand that authorities step in. More than any other change they wanted for their country, Mexicans yearned to see the Fox government act decisively to roll back criminality. Fox tried, but without much success. The task was overwhelming.

The police remained poorly paid, poorly trained, and poorly motivated. For years, efforts to make them more professional had moved in fits and starts. Fierce competition among federal law enforcement agencies and between federal and state authorities blocked several attempts. To make matters worse, police forces suffered from a long history of corrupt management. We saw one example of the problem during the Zedillo administration, when the government allocated hundreds of millions of dollars to improve policing at all levels.

Responding to the need for secure radio communication at the state police level, the federal government set technical standards for the equipment that it would finance. But even the standards were riddled with corruption. They did not establish, as government guidelines normally do, specific criteria for production and performance. They had another purpose. They simply identified a French company from which the radio sets had to be purchased. Because an American company produced an identical product, I brought the issue to Alejandro Gertz, Fox's new cabinet minister in charge of the national police. He was able to get the criteria changed, and the American company got some business. A blatant example of institutional corruption, which probably involved a payoff to someone in the previous administration, was reversed. But it was only one instance, the tip of the iceberg.

The Fox administration achieved some improvements in law enforcement, but the lack of trust and cooperation among the different agencies continued to be a big problem. Fox chose Adolfo Aguilar Zínser to be his coordinator of national security, assigning him the task of forcing Mexican law enforcement agencies to cooperate with each other. Aguilar Zínser, a noted and honest gadfly, had built his career as a vociferously independent political figure by attacking all elements of the PRI regime. His targets included the national domestic intelligence agency (CISEN), the PGR, and even the normally sacrosanct Mexican military. Having lashed out so often at these agencies, he was not likely to win their trust.

The heads of the agencies Aguilar Zínser tried to coordinate generally ignored him, as I saw myself at a meeting in the Defense Ministry's war room shortly after Fox came to the presidency. Aguilar Zínser had arranged the meeting and his fellow cabinet members grudgingly attended. I brought with me the embassy's deputy chief of mission, as well as the heads of the FBI, DEA, Customs offices, and the CIA station. Across the table, Aguilar Zínser was joined by the secretaries of defense, navy, interior, national security, the head of CISEN, and the attorney general. It was clear he wanted to use me to assert his authority over the Mexican officials and to promote unity among them.

I was willing to play along because I wanted to improve our bi-national cooperation. There was too much freelancing and opportunism at work. For example, if the DEA found working with the PGR on a specific case impossible, it would take the case to the Mexican Navy or another agency. The Mexicans played the same game, usually in their search for equipment, information, or budgetary support. What they could not get from the DEA, they would hustle from the FBI or Customs. I quietly supported Aguilar Zínser's efforts to put some order into the ever-shifting kaleidoscope of allegiances.

At the meeting, I introduced each of the embassy officials. I explained the structure of their offices, their manpower resources, their legal responsibilities, how they operated within the embassy, their lines of command back to me and to Washington, and their contacts within the Mexican system. It was probably more information than any Mexican at the table, and most certainly Aguilar Zínser, had ever received from the embassy. I drew back the curtain of secrecy in order to convey our confidence in the new relationship with the Fox administration.

Aguilar Zínser thanked me and asked his colleagues to respond. The bunker-like room was kept at an uncomfortably cold temperature. As the air conditioners hummed loudly, the chill became worse. Not one had a word to say. The silence was deafening. For Aguilar Zínser it was also humiliating. He struggled through another half-hour of awkward conversation, but the meeting was a dismal failure. Nobody on his side had any intention of cooperating with him. Nobody intended to speak as frankly with his Mexican colleagues as they frequently did with the embassy officials at my side. Prior to the meeting, I had suspected that the supposed coordinator was doomed to failure. After it, there was no doubt. Soon he was gone.

The internal Mexican suspicions continued. In May 2001, Attorney General John Ashcroft visited Mexico, meeting with most of the men who had attended Aguilar Zínser's disastrous meeting. All received him cordially, but one sent his entire staff out so he could tell me and Ashcroft not to trust anyone in the Mexican government other than himself. He specifically suggested that the United States not deal with the other agencies, though he admitted that his own organization was corrupt as well. Ashcroft left the meeting perplexed. He agreed with me that the only thing we could do was to ignore the conversation.

Despite the continuing rivalries and suspicions, Fox's law enforcement teams made notable improvements on the antinarcotics front. Fox recognized drug trafficking for what it is: a grave threat to Mexican democracy and society. He knew that PRI administrations had often rationalized their hesitation to work more fully with the United States by making the bogus argument that cooperation meant a loss of national sovereignty. Too often in the past, nationalism had been used as an excuse to prevent outsiders from learning about police or judicial inefficiency or corruption. There had been many honest officials operating within the PRI governments, and Zedillo had been as concerned about narcotics as Fox, but the ideology, cronyism, and, in some cases, the corruption of individuals and party structures kept the drug fight from being waged as aggressively as it should have been.

Under Fox, the Mexican army started to work more closely with his attorney general's office, also headed by an army general. Old problems remained, however, as the attorney general himself acknowledged when, early in his tenure, he called his own organization, the PGR, "a den of corruption." Two years later, in January 2003, he had to disband an entire two-hundred-man branch of the antinarcotics unit after the Ministry of Defense presented evidence of rampant illegality. The minister of defense, under no illusions about the vulnerabilities of his own troops, pulled much of his narcotics investigations force out of the provinces and back to Mexico City. He wanted to keep a closer eye on his field commanders.

But there was impressive progress nevertheless. Mexico continued to field as many as twenty thousand soldiers a day for narcotics crop eradication. And small, carefully vetted army and PGR units had notable success in bringing down hundreds of narcotics dealers. Some enormously big fish were caught, including Mexico's most wanted criminal, Benjamin Arellano, who was captured in May 2002, and Gulf cartel boss Osiel Cárdenas Guillén, who was seized after a Matamoros shootout that left two soldiers critically wounded. It was Cárdenas who three years earlier had used his gold-plated AK-47 to threaten a DEA and an FBI official. The navy, while maintaining its near state of war with the army, turned a major corner when it boosted its antidrug efforts and increased cooperation with the U.S. Navy and Coast Guard. Fox's leadership won him deep admiration in the United States. At the beginning of 2003, the White House declared that the two countries had achieved unparalleled levels of cooperation in the antinarcotics effort. The death of the certification ritual had done much to remove the venom from the drug cooperation scene.

As Fox's first year in office ended, the professional class of political commentators and opposition politicians stoked the fires of public disillusionment. In fact, polls indicated that more Mexicans blamed the other political parties and the Congress for the lack of progress than they did the president. He was given credit for maintaining economic stability—interest rates fell, inflation was held in check, and the peso remained strong. He was also praised for the new freedom of information act, his intent to open the files on political repression in the 1960s and 1970s, and an improvement in Mexico's international stature.

But the criticism of the press and the pundits was self-fulfilling. A sense began to develop that Fox's best day may have been July 2, 2000, when he overthrew the PRI's hegemony. The public still honored him for that. But increasingly he was being seen as a transitional figure, someone whose most important achievement was behind him. With more than four years left in his presidency, Fox was being consigned to the historical shelf reserved for the noble but ultimately ineffectual.

Fox could obviously not accept such a verdict. He had to confront it. Among the many arguments government spokesmen made to assert that Fox had turned the country around and put it on a new path was that he had brought favorable international attention to Mexico. He underscored his relationship with President Bush and tried to push Mexico to the center of the world stage. The UN Conference on Development that Fox was scheduled to host in Monterrey in March 2002 offered an opportunity to showcase his country. It would not turn out as planned. Mexico's Caribbean three-step would come back to haunt him.

C
H
A
P
T
E
R

F
I
F
T
E
E
N

Fidel's Revenge

The fabric of Cuban-Mexican relations finished the PRI years in tatters, but under Vicente Fox it would be ripped apart. This was not Fox's intent. He would have preferred to marginalize the Cuba issue in Mexican politics. But that goal clashed with another plan advocated by Foreign Secretary Jorge Castañeda and accepted by Fox. His administration intended to put human rights at the center of both its domestic and international policies.

In an effort to demonstrate that he was not looking for a battle with Castro, in one of his first moves he named a member of the leftist PRD, Ricardo Pascoe, as ambassador to Havana. An urbane former Trotskyite with an American mother, a U.S. passport he tried to keep secret, and a degree from New York University, Pascoe had moved marginally closer to the mainstream left as he aged. But he remained a Castro sympathizer, and his appointment was clearly designed to protect Fox from criticism from the Mexican left. Fox undoubtedly also thought that Pascoe would provide him some protection from Castro and his Mexican claque. He was wrong.

Before leaving for Havana, Pascoe came by the residence for drinks and a discussion of U.S. policy on Cuba. I knew that I was not going to change his view about Castro, but I wanted to encourage him to reach out to dissidents and others who could help develop civil society on the island and ease the transition that will surely come. Our conversation was pleasant. But when he left, I had not dissuaded him from his belief that U.S. policy on Cuba was counterproductive. I finished the meeting with the strong impression that he would do nothing to alter Mexico's traditional policy of solidarity with Fidel Castro—rather than with the Cuban people.

During the transition period between Fox's election in July and his inauguration in December 2000, the word went around Mexican political circles that I (or, in some versions, the U.S. government) opposed Fox's expected designation of Jorge Castañeda as foreign secretary. The rumor, based on Castañeda's leftist history and past opposition to NAFTA, was false. But I was silently concerned that Castañeda might turn into a vulnerability for Fox. His intellectual arrogance, quirky personality, deprecation of most politicians, and tense relations with the Mexican press were already well known. Rumors to the contrary, neither the U.S. government nor its ambassador would be foolish enough to express any views about who should be in Fox's cabinet. We have had plenty of experience dealing with foreign officials who had previously been labeled communists, terrorists, anti-American, or any number of nasty designations. I knew that we could work with Castañeda. As time would prove, we did, though my initial private concerns also proved to have some foundation.

But while the Americans were maintaining a prudent silence about Castañeda, the Cuban embassy in Mexico City was hyperventilating. It stirred up Cuba's friends, supporters and paid agents against Castañeda, whom they regarded as a particularly noxious character. An admirer of Fidel in his youth, Castañeda turned on Castro as he matured, becoming so bold as to say that the Cuban "isn't relevant politically" to modern Latin America. His conversion was not of the type common to American intellectuals who abandoned the Communist Party and moved far to the political right. Castañeda maintained his credentials as an intellectual of the left.

In books and newspaper columns, Castañeda had coldly and critically dissected Castro's control of the island and his promotion of revolution in the rest of the continent. In his biography of Che, Castañeda suggested that Castro had been less than zealous in protecting the life of the man he had met when they were both young revolutionaries in exile in Mexico City and who had been killed in the Bolivian jungle by CIA-assisted local military forces. With the fall of the Berlin Wall, Castañeda argued that the only way Castro could save his revolution was to abandon power. Castro apparently did not appreciate Castañeda's career counseling.

In many ways, Castañeda's criticism of Castro paralleled that of other disaffected Latin intellectuals. But there was a special animus that came from his experience as an opponent of the PRI who longed for his country to be truly democratic. As a young man, Castañeda had accompanied his father, then Mexico's foreign minister, to Cuba, where Fidel allowed him to dress up in a camouflage outfit, shoot real guns and play guerrilla for a day. But as Castañeda matured, he came to see Cuba as an enabler for continued PRI control in Mexico: one autocratic regime supporting another.

For many on the left, Castro's most offensive demonstration of support for the PRI was his presence at the 1988 inauguration of Carlos Salinas. At that time, Castañeda and many others were still fuming that the PRI had stolen the 1988 election from Cuauhtémoc Cárdenas. Castro's decision to attend the inauguration confirmed for Castañeda that Cuba was more interested in supporting the PRI's hold on power than in helping the Mexican left assume the nation's leadership. When Carlos Salinas left Mexico in disgrace shortly after the end of his presidency, he accepted Cuba's offer of comfortable refuge, providing further proof that Castro identified with the PRI power structure.

In October 2000, Castañeda told me that he planned to invite Elizardo Sánchez, the same Cuban dissident that Rosario Green had met on her trip to the island, to Fox's December 1 inauguration. But Castañeda changed his mind. He preferred to avoid angering Castro and wanted to ensure that Fidel would attend the event. Like the Pascoe nomination, that decision was another Mexican olive branch for Castro, who then attended the inauguration of the man who had knocked the PRI from power.

At a sparkling dinner in Chapultepec Palace on the night of the inauguration, Castro sat at the head table with Fox and the other heads of state. I sat with Madeleine Albright, the head of the U.S. delegation, at another table right in front of him. At one point, Albright wondered aloud what kind of international stir she could create by going over to greet the bearded one. Jokingly, I encouraged her to do so and kept plying her with wine, but I knew that this serious practitioner of diplomacy would do nothing of the kind.

In recent years, the PRI's support for Cuba had been, above all, a tactic. It was a way of protecting its domestic left flank, differentiating Mexico from U.S. policy, and—not incidentally—pricking the American balloon from time to time. The limits Mexico put on that support, such as abstaining on the Cuba votes at the Geneva Human Rights Commission rather than voting in the negative, were nods in Washington's direction. By the late 1990s, the PRI strategy was essentially a hollow game, devoid of ideological content.

But Castañeda had to consider Cuba policy within the context of Mexico's proud new emphasis on human rights. Fox had promised in his campaign to investigate his country's human rights abuses and punish those responsible. He pledged to dissolve the secret police apparatus. He vowed to open the political system to those who had been shut out, including the indigenous people of Chiapas. Fox's Mexico wanted to earn international recognition as a modern democratic state. The problem was that Castañeda wanted to present Fox as a paladin of human rights while not roiling Mexico's traditional relations with Latin America's last remaining dictator. Something would have to give. And it did—at the annual vote on Cuba's human rights.

Preparations for the yearly Geneva Human Rights Commission meeting began early in 2001. The Czech Republic, supported by other Eastern European countries whose representatives had personally suffered the abuses of communist control, floated a resolution on Cuba's record. As in the past, it called for Cuba to adhere to internationally accepted human rights principles and to release political detainees. The United States strongly supported the resolution and sought cosponsors and affirmative votes. Given its determination to be a human rights advocate, Mexico's new government seemed to offer the possibility of another mark in the "yes" column. Nevertheless, I cautioned Washington not to expect a change to Mexico's traditional abstention. It seemed to me that a vote for the resolution would be difficult for Fox so early in his administration, when he still was trying to convince Castro that he was not going to be hostile.

But Washington's expectations reached new heights after Castañeda made his international debut on human rights with a powerful speech to the Commission in Geneva in March. Copies of Castañeda's words were furiously faxed around Washington and other capitals. Its thrust was clear: the new foreign secretary was rejecting all the formulaic arguments that previous Mexican governments had utilized to justify abstention. Castañeda declared:

> It has been said that the defense and furtherance of human rights is a matter pertinent to the internal affairs of each country, which should not be subject to outside scrutiny. Mexico does not share this opinion and asserts that human rights constitute values that are both absolute and universal. We are firmly convinced that the exercise of sovereignty cannot be used as an excuse to justify any violation of rights. We likewise reject the excuse which some states have used to attempt to justify the violation of human rights by pleading hostility or foreign aggression. With total conviction, we maintain that it is invalid to curtail the human rights of any society or violate its fundamental liberties under the guise of "state versus foreign interests" since there are neither legal nor ethical grounds to support this.

Clearly, anyone who heard or read these words had to assume that Castañeda was making a break with Mexico's past and was signaling Mexico's intent to censure Cuba. But I was skeptical and called Washington's attention to a less noticed portion of the speech:

> We must be clear . . . Mexico recognizes the fact that certain countries' positions on human rights have often been debated and condemned on a basis of selective criteria—stemming from political interests—and not because of genuine concern for the defense of those rights. It is important that we prevent ulterior motives from distorting any initiative to promote human rights.

This was a repetition of the traditional Mexican argument that U.S. government's pursuit of a Cuba resolution in Geneva had less to do with human rights than with our political goal of isolating and castigating Castro. Castañeda was giving himself a back door to use. Ultimately, Mexico again abstained from voting on the resolution, which passed anyway by a narrow margin.

But Castañeda's performance was worse than unsuccessful. He managed to disappoint the United States, other governments and the people of Cuba. But he also infuriated the Cuban government. Felipe Pérez Roque, Cuba's foreign minister, accused Castañeda personally of trying to serve the Americans. "He is dazzled by their power," Pérez sputtered in outrage. In a bitter reference to Castañeda's turn away from the left to support Fox of the conservative PAN, he added, "and he has a well-known political history of disloyalties."

Castañeda shot back in a style uniquely his own, conveying both ridicule and a desire for reconciliation. He acknowledged that the Cubans were "*un poquito ardidos*"—a bit pissed off. But, he added, Mexico should not pay too much attention to their huffing and puffing, and simply focus on building better commercial and other ties with the island.

Castañeda's ridicule got most of the ink, generating another tumultuous round of reaction from the press and the political class, who expressed outrage that Fox and Castañeda were being tough on Fidel. Even First Lady Marta Sahagún mildly chastised Castañeda, saying "ardidos" was "an unnecessary word." The leftist daily *La Jornada* made the most of Sahagún's comment, spraying it across the top of the front page under the headline "Rebuke for Castañeda."

The Havana–Mexico City relationship stumbled through the rest of 2001. Washington's attention focused elsewhere, particularly after September 11. But Cuba remained a difficult problem for Fox and his foreign secretary. In an effort to patch things up a bit, Fox scheduled a one-day trip to Havana in February 2002. He faced a difficult choice. A trip to the island without some demonstration of concern for the hard-pressed Cuban dissidents would be a retreat from his human rights rhetoric. Yet Ambassador Pascoe, unlike representatives of the United States, Spain, and several Eastern European embassies, had refused to meet with them. The Fox government seemed to be speaking out of both sides of its mouth.

The trip did not go well. While he was in Cuba, Fox told the press that he had given a list of political prisoners to Castro and asked for their release. Castro flatly denied that Fox had even mentioned the issue to him, though he acknowledged that the Mexicans had given the list to Pérez Roque. At a dinner with Castro, Fox noted in passing that Castañeda would meet with a group of dissidents the following morning at the Mexican embassy. He added that he might stop by the meeting for a quick hello. Fidel was not pleased, especially when Fox's quick visit turned into a half-hour discussion. Cuba's friends in Mexico howled that Fox and Castañeda had gone to Havana to insult Castro and the revolution.

A petulant Castañeda responded with a long press interview on his return to Mexico City. He talked more sense about the Cuban-Mexican relationship than any Mexican government figure had ever dared to do publicly. The old days are gone, he asserted. "In a world without a cold war, in a democratic hemisphere now with no dictators, in a Mexico without a regime that utilizes the romantic identification with Cuba in its own shadow game, it is time to recognize reality. Cuba is a country, not a protest song. Our relations with the Cuban Revolution are over and our relations with the Republic of Cuba have begun."

Castañeda spoke the truth. But the crafty Castro would exact a cynical price for such candor. The trouble began when Castañeda visited Miami to open a Mexican cultural center. The visit was part of a broader Mexican effort to reach out to Florida, where Governor Jeb Bush and his Mexican-born wife wanted to improve ties that had been strained by resentment within Miami's exile Cuban community over Mexico's ties to Castro. Responding to a reporter's question about Mexico's position on Cuban dissidents, Castañeda declared that the doors to the Mexican embassy in Havana "would be open, as they would be to any Cuban or Latin American citizen interested in visiting Mexico." It was a clear signal that Mexico wanted to maintain contacts with the dissidents. Castro, undoubtedly seething as Castañeda moved easily through the Miami he despised, responded immediately. Within hours, hundreds of unemployed young Cuban men were storming the Mexican embassy in Havana in search of political asylum.

Frazzled by the siege in Havana, the Mexicans lashed out at the United States. In an apparent reference to U.S.-government-run Radio Martí, which had repeatedly broadcast his remarks, Castañeda blamed "radical elements" in Miami for twisting his words. Castañeda called me in high dudgeon, blaming Radio Martí for spinning his words to create a massive misunderstanding. After checking, I told him that while the radio station had indeed given his remarks heavy coverage, it had not suggested that Cubans should rush to the embassy for a free pass out of the country. (In reality, there may have been some malicious intent in the constant repetition of Castañeda's words, even if they were not in any way doctored.)

After a more measured assessment, Mexican officials soon concluded that Castro's own internal security apparatus had passed the word in

Havana and stimulated the rush to the embassy. It would not have been the first time that the Cuban government had played that game. The embassy invasion came to an end when a shaken Ambassador Pascoe allowed the Cuban police to empty the building in a predawn raid, arresting twenty-one young men who had sought refuge there.

The events of 2001 were the opening skirmishes of what would become a battle royal between Fox and Castro in the first half of 2002. Mexico had lobbied hard to host the United Nations Conference on Development and hoped the meeting would be a summit for heads of state from around the world. The Fox administration was eager for President Bush to attend because he would draw other world leaders. But for months, Washington refused to give a straight reply to the invitation. Of course, the president was preoccupied with the war on terror. But the White House was also concerned that the conference would turn into another opportunity for poor nations to beat up on the rich, particularly the United States, with accusations of insufficient financial support.

It was not until late in January 2002 that Washington was satisfied that the conference documents would call on all nations to recognize that reform of their own economic policies was the key to development. The White House then announced that President Bush would attend the mid-March Monterrey conference. The Mexican government was pleased, and as predicted, the number of heads of state who said they would also attend increased notably.

Shortly thereafter I received a call from the National Security Council asking me to speak with Castañeda about Fidel Castro. I was asked to tell him that the president would be coming whether Castro came or not. But the White House did not want President Bush placed in a situation of having to share speaking time or a venue with him. Washington wanted the press to focus on Bush's new international aid initiative. It did not want to provide the evening news with a melodrama about the president and the Cuban dictator.

The American concern presented the Mexicans with a scheduling challenge. They had planned to host plenary sessions at which the leader of each country's delegation would speak for five minutes while the sixty or more other heads of state either listened or conducted business outside the conference hall. President Bush would not have to be in the session hall when Castro spoke. But they also wanted to host a lunch and informal discussion for all of the heads of state. That would be difficult because Bush would not want to have to share a meal with Fidel.

I suggested that the informal discussion could be divided into several small groups, thereby keeping Castro and President Bush in different rooms, and that President Bush would not necessarily have to attend the lunch if Castro was going to be there. Castañeda interrupted me and said that I did not need to be concerned because the Cubans had just announced that Castro would not be coming to Monterrey. Problem avoided. I reported it all back to Washington.

But on the day before President Bush was to arrive at the conference, I got an early morning call from the White House informing me that Castañeda was urgently trying to reach Condoleezza Rice. Before she took his call, she wanted to know why he was calling. Immediately after that, I received a call from the Department of State. Castañeda also wanted to talk with Secretary Powell. Something was up, and I was asked to find out the reason for all the fuss.

I managed to make contact with Castañeda, who told me about a new twist in the unfolding story at Monterrey. Castro had just written to Fox that he would be coming to Monterrey after all. Castañeda wanted to assure the White House that Mexico had taken care of our concern about throwing the two presidents into the same pit. He said Castro would leave Monterrey before President Bush arrived. He did not state Mexico's obvious concern: that President Bush would cancel at the last minute. I thanked him for the heads-up and reported back to Washington.

President Bush went to Monterrey, where he laid out an ambitious plan to increase U.S. funding for poor nations by $5 billion a year, targeted at countries that adopted sound economic policies. But the president's message got buried in the flurry of press accounts about another dramatic development: the mysteriously angry departure of Fidel Castro. As Castro finished his predictable speech—taking six times his allotted five minutes to accuse developing nations of dancing to the tune of the wealthy few—he withdrew a folded piece of paper from his chest pocket and began to read. In an agitated voice and with trembling hands, he declared that for reasons beyond his control, he was forced to leave the meeting. Then he marched out and headed for the airport, where President Bush was just arriving. The two heads of state, one coming and one storming away, were actually at the airport at the same time. But there was no meeting.

In the Mexican and U.S. press, Castro's theatrical departure became the big story of the conference, obscuring the more substantive developments. The press was thrilled by the drama of it all. Had the government of Mexico asked him to leave? Fox said no, and Castañeda echoed his denial. At a joint press conference with Fox, Bush was asked if the United States had pressured Mexico to force Castro to leave. He responded forcefully and accurately in the negative. When essentially the same question was asked again, he snapped that he had already given his answer. President Bush was telling the truth. Fox and Castañeda were not. Actually, they were lying. Castro had proof. But he would wait another month before springing it on them.

Once again the stage for the drama moved to Geneva, where the U.S. and its allies introduced a new tactic on the Cuba resolution that put Mexico in a difficult position. Instead of the usual document that listed all of Castro's sins, the 2002 effort was a very simple statement that Cuba was deficient in its respect for human rights and that a special representative of the Commission should be allowed to visit the country and make a report. This was a tactic I had previously advocated as a way of drawing additional affirmative votes from countries that had squirmed at the traditional long recitation of Castro's misdeeds. The Clinton administration had not accepted my idea that briefer was better. However, the Republican administration was more self-assured about its anti-Cuban credentials than its predecessor and could afford to be more flexible on questions of language. The resolution was so bland it would have been difficult for Mexico to maintain its abstention, given the Fox government's emphasis on human rights as an instrument of foreign and domestic policies. On April 18, 2002, Mexico joined the majority and voted yes on the resolution. Then all hell broke loose.

Mexico's vote caused another press and political uproar at home, with the usual charges of selling out to gringo pressure. The leftist daily *La Jornada* editorialized that Mexico had "submitted itself to the will of the State Department" and had acted "against the will and interests of the Mexican people." Castro came charging into the fray with an embarrassing tape recording of his pre-Monterrey discussion with Fox. He had held the tape in reserve, waiting for a moment like this. Maybe he had told the Mexicans about it in an attempt to extort another abstention in Geneva. Maybe it was just simple vengeance. In any event, it was devastating. It offered a fascinating peek into the conversation of two heads of state. But more importantly, it revealed that despite Fox's protestations to the contrary, he had indeed asked Fidel to leave the Monterrey meeting. Mexico's honest man had been caught in a lie.

The tape made clear the following account of events. Castro sent a letter to Fox on Tuesday, announcing that he would arrive at the conference two days later. Fox then called Castro and said his last-minute change of plans was troubling. Fox, obviously reading from notes, presented a plan:

> Fox: "You come Thursday and take part in the session and make your presentation, since the time for Cuba is reserved for 1 p.m. Afterwards we have a luncheon hosted by the governor of the state for the heads of state; in fact, I offer you an invitation to the luncheon, even to sit by my side, and once the event is over, and your participation is over, you return."
> Castro: "To the island of Cuba?"
> Fox: "Well, no, maybe you could find . . . "
> Castro: "To where? To the hotel? Tell me."
> Fox: "To the island of Cuba, or wherever you like. And that you leave me be. This is the favor I'm asking you—that you don't complicate Friday for me."

The two then discussed when it would be convenient for Castro to arrive. Then, assuredly dripping with sarcasm, Castro asked, "Tell me, how else can I help you?"

Fox: "Well basically don't aggravate the United States or President Bush, that is . . . "

Castro did not let Fox finish his thought. This suggestion to a man whose life work had been to aggravate American presidents was the last straw. Castro was insulted and outraged. He cut Fox off in midsentence and launched into a lecture.

> "Listen, Mr. President, I am someone who has been in politics for forty-three years and I know what I am doing and what I should do. Have no doubt that I know how to tell the truth and to do so elegantly. Have no fear. I'm not going to drop any bombshell there. Although the truth is that I'm in disagreement with the consensus that has been reached. Yes, I will limit myself to expound on my basic and fundamental ideas, and I will do that with all the respect in the world. I'm not going to use that as a podium to agitate or anything like that: I am going to speak my truth. And the only reason I don't [cancel my trip to Monterrey] is that now that I've made the decision to go it would be embarrassing."

Fox ignored the outburst, repeated the invitation for lunch, and told Fidel that the Governor would be serving goat, a Monterrey specialty. Then the conversation drew to a close.

Fox: "So, we're in agreement, Fidel?"
Castro: "We're in agreement and we remain friends, friends and gentlemen."

The transcript dropped like a bomb. Polling indicated that the vast majority of Mexicans felt that Castro's release of the conversation was anything but friendly or gentlemanly. But if the tape proved that Castro was not civil, it also showed that Fox had lied when he told the press he had not pressured Castro to leave Monterrey early. More to the point, he seemed to be lying in the service of the United States. A worse combination for a Mexican politician would be difficult to imagine. It provided more grist to the mill of the political opposition. Fox had his defenders in the press and on the political stage, but his handling of the Monterrey affair reinforced the perception, continuing to grow in Mexico by mid-2002, that his political skills were deficient at best.

The embarrassment could have been avoided. The White House would likely have accommodated to the minimal schedule changes that would have eliminated awkwardness in Monterrey. But Fox and Castañeda had erred twice—first in their response to Castro's change of plans and then in their clumsy cover-up of the Fox-Castro conversation. The Monterrey debacle was unfortunate on many levels. It tarnished Fox's image as an honest man. It obscured his government's sincere dedication to the promotion of human rights. And it placed Fidel squarely back in the center of Mexican political life.

Visits from Planet Washington

No one who visited the embassy during my four years there could match the disruptive talents Fidel Castro displayed in Monterrey. But we certainly had our hands full with the thousands of official travelers who passed through every year. Most of the out-of-towners came from Washington. Some were technicians coming to repair equipment or train staff. Others were bureaucrats from the headquarters of one of the more than thirty agencies with offices in the embassy. Cabinet members, governors, and high-level officials from the State Department and other agencies came on one mission or another.

The travel was constant, but tended to pick up in inverse proportion to Washington's winter temperature. The lower it plunged, the higher the number of visitors. Whatever the motive, workers and decision makers in Washington profited by gaining on-the-ground experience and knowledge of Mexico. Conversely, the embassy learned what Washington was thinking or worrying about. Embassies can be fairly isolated places, and the contact helps. The visits are also one of the few means Washington has to judge an embassy's efficiency, morale, or level of contacts with host country officials. So embassy leadership is usually more than anxious to make the traveler feel that the visit has been enjoyable and worthwhile.

An embassy that screws up a visit becomes a topic of conversation back home. While there is some charitable understanding for mess-ups that are beyond human control or due to the incompetence of the local government, other errors become topics for conversation in the State Department. Woe unto the embassy that forgets to preregister an important guest so he or she does not have to wait in the hotel's check-in line; or does not get a daily briefing book of intelligence reports to a big shot at the crack of dawn; or, most horrible of all, leaves a heavy- duty personage stranded as a motorcade pulls out. The deaths of many Foreign Service careers are automobile related—not from accidents but from disgruntled visitors.

One result of NAFTA was the new interest that American governors demonstrated in improving trade and other ties with Mexico. By the end of the century, Mexico ranked among the top three destinations for the goods produced in most states. The growth of the Mexican immigrant population in the United States and the fact that many were becoming citizens meant that votes were involved as well. Mexico was becoming a local concern across the country.

More than three dozen U.S. governors visited during our time in Mexico, some more than once. Bush of Florida, Davis of California, Shaheen of New Hampshire, Locke of Washington, Ridge of Pennsylvania, Whitman of New Jersey, and others led large delegations of business people, university presidents, and notables in their Mexican-American communities. The trade portion of the trips was usually paramount. The commercial section of the embassy, part of the Department of Commerce, did wonders in arranging contacts. When Jeb Bush came with a delegation of several hundred Floridians, the section organized more than one thousand meetings with Mexican businesses.

Joan and I hosted frequent receptions for the visiting state delegations. We invited local businesspeople, government representatives, resident alumni of the state university, embassy employees from the state, and others with real or potential ties. We brought in a mariachi band, which was always a big hit, especially with the Mexican-American visitors, some of whom got misty-eyed on their return to their roots. I enjoyed hearing from small businesspeople who were excited about contacts they had made, or contracts they signed for fifty or one hundred thousand dollars worth of goods—relatively small sums, but important to them. They had needed help breaking into the Mexican market, and the embassy had provided it. Sometimes there were much larger deals. Representatives of

Corona beer and the governor of Idaho sealed a deal over the mariachi music that saw Corona invest $75 million in that state to build a malting plant.

Some of the governors were particularly colorful. Former professional wrestler Jesse Ventura of Minnesota lived up to his reputation as a free spirit. He told a press conference that his state could use another fifty thousand workers and invited Mexicans to "come on up and get a job." The governor's impromptu offer caused considerable overload on the consular section phones for several days while our staff explained that, notwithstanding his kind invitation, governors could not make immigration policy. The consular staff explained that they could issue work visas only after the U.S. Department of Labor approved a specific contract— a long and onerous process.

The governors were generally well briefed, clear about what they wanted to achieve, and anxious to show their delegations and accompanying press that they were not wasting taxpayers' money. They were also attuned to Mexican sensitivities, or willing to learn about them. In early 1998, the Republican governor of New Jersey, Christine Todd Whitman, was about to use a press conference at Los Pinos—after a meeting with President Zedillo—to call for the impeachment of President Clinton. When I told the governor's aides that this would be an inappropriate use of the Mexican presidential palace, they were hesitant to tell their boss that she was out of line. But when I explained my thinking to Whitman, she not only understood my point, she was grateful I had told her. She saved the impeachment call for a later press conference at the delegation's hotel.

Members of Congress, on the other hand, ran a far wider gamut in terms of their seriousness and preparation. But we welcomed them all. We had to. Some, like Representative Jim Kolbe of Arizona or Representative Silvestre Reyes of Texas, were frequent visitors who regarded improving relations with Mexico as part of their responsibilities. Reyes, former chief of the Border Patrol's El Paso sector, was especially effective in discussing border and migration issues. Kolbe, with his ties to the Republican leadership, was always a useful interlocutor. Senator Chris Dodd, who learned his Spanish as a Peace Corps volunteer in the Dominican Republic, was one of the few members of the upper house with a continuing interest in Latin America.

Most veterans of the Foreign Service of a certain age have a stock of hilarious and sometimes frightening tales to tell about visiting congressmen. Drunks, women chasers, numbingly dumb golfers, and gauche perpetrators of acts of outrageous cultural insensitivity all have their place in the congressional travelers hall of shame. One of my most vivid war stories comes from 1980 when I was posted to Zimbabwe as it became an independent state. Like Mexico twenty years later when Fox won the presidency, Zimbabwe was, for a while, an important stopping point for dozens of congressional visitors. I accompanied Congressman Clarence "Doc" Long of Maryland into a small meeting with the prime minister of the newly independent country, Robert Mugabe.

Long, the immensely powerful chairman of the House committee that controlled foreign aid funds, gave the guerilla leader a long lecture on the evils of socialism, which was well known to be the core of Mugabe's political philosophy. When the prime minister got a chance to reply, Long promptly fell asleep. The stunned Mugabe did not know what to do. Neither did I. It would have been exceedingly awkward to nudge the congressman awake. So Mugabe made believe that he didn't see the closed eyes nor hear the soft snoring. He looked at the ceiling and conversed with me for fifteen minutes until "Doc" awoke with a jolt, stretched, thanked him for his views, and left.

Insensitive or rude congressional visitors—including some who delight in mistreating the embassy staff assigned to help them—are still a problem, but they are few and far between. Fortunately for the American republic, but unfortunately for later cocktail party conversations, visiting congressmen have become a generally colorless breed. They are serious public servants intent on working hard so as to not allow their opponents to accuse them of frivolous boondoggling. Too many members of both houses are so afraid of political criticism that they do not take full advantage of the travel opportunities available to them. That is unfortunate, because travel can be an important tool in educating Capitol Hill.

Some CODEL—congressional delegation—members caused awkward moments because they had been poorly briefed by their staffs. Six House members came down just as the Mexican press and government were working themselves into a frenzy over a new law that that required the Treasury Department to freeze the assets of businesses owned by or with ties to drug kingpins. This was a hot issue, with overtones of a new certification process, and the Mexican business community was alarmed, fearing that an innocent business that unwittingly was connected to drug money could be caught in a legal and financial nightmare. That was an unlikely possibility, as experience would show. But only days after the congressional vote, it was the principal topic when Mexican government officials met the visiting CODEL. Not one of the Americans had the slightest clue about the legislation, despite the fact that they had just voted for it. They simply did not know what the foreign minister of Mexico was talking to them about and were so unsophisticated that they did not even try to hide their ignorance.

The incident revealed once again the contrast between Mexico's intense focus on U.S. action directed toward it and the generalized lack of congressional knowledge about what is important in Mexico. While no one can expect members of Congress to remember every one of the hundreds of votes they cast every year, it would have been useful for at least one of the visiting members to have been briefed on the law. If the embassy had had the opportunity to hold a briefing, we would have made sure that the members knew what was on Mexico's mind. But in this case, as in others, the CODEL was too busy, tired, distracted, or involved in shopping to have any interest in a briefing.

The annual meeting of the Mexico-U.S. interparliamentary conference always generated controversy, a few good laughs, and some useful conversation. The conference brought together large delegations from both sides—one year in Mexico, the next in the United States—to assess the bilateral relationship. For the Mexican congressmen and press, the event was always a big deal that received heavy news coverage. The Mexican attendees were in constant competition with one another for the attention of the press, which was usually focused on how well they were defending national sovereignty. By contrast, when the event was held in the United States, it was difficult to generate even a small article in the host city's newspaper.

Almost always the annual meeting was hijacked by the hot issue of the moment. One year it was the Casablanca mess. On another occasion it was a plan to construct a low-level radiation waste dump at Sierra Blanca, Texas, not far from the border. In 2002, the issue was Mexico's failure to meet treaty obligations to provide water to the Rio Grande valley. Although the conversations inside the meeting room were generally civil, if at times boring, and the social events always pleasant, there was plenty of opportunity for public chest-beating for the press.

Sometimes even the private conversations would turn nasty. During the May 2000 conference in the provincial capital of Puebla, the Mexican side, notably independent Senator Adolfo Aguilar Zínser, blew up when an American participant referred to undocumented immigrants as criminals. The congressman thought that he was simply citing an obvious fact: people who break the law are criminals. But the Mexicans took his labeling of so many of their compatriots as a profound insult. Aguilar Zínser's outburst was supported by the other Mexicans, most of whom could not otherwise abide him. Aguilar was so emotional that he almost forgot to leave the room to give a blow-by-blow account to the waiting reporters. But he recovered his composure and got his headlines.

For all of their deficiencies, the interparliamentary meetings were a serious effort to bridge the gap between the congresses of the two nations. As the years went by, the events became less formulaic and more substantive, and, thus, of greater value. Each gathering would end with a commitment that the two sides would continue to work together during the following year. But unfortunately, little ever came out of the pledges, except a repetition of them at the next annual get-together.

By far the most interesting congressional delegation I received was led by Senator Jesse Helms of North Carolina in early 2001. The name of Helms was widely known and reviled in Mexico, where legislation he cosponsored—the Helms-Burton Act to punish foreign businesses that dealt with Cuba—was widely viewed as American unilateralism at its worst. His frequent bashing of Mexico as chairman of the Senate Foreign Relations Committee was always material for editorial heartburn. Political scientist Rafael Fernández de Castro wrote that Helms's criticism of Mexico—which he said was "heavy-handed, arrogant" and "lacked sophistication, had made him Mexican nationalism's favorite villain in the past two decades."

Helms rarely traveled outside the United States. But he had been approached by Foreign Secretary Castañeda via Senator Fritz Hollings, another southerner, who had known Castañeda since their anti-NAFTA campaigning days together. Hollings arranged for Helms to meet with Castañeda after Fox's electoral victory. No one knew what to expect of the encounter between the tempestuous Mexican intellectual who had scorned Helms-Burton as an "absurd tragicomedy" and the tough-talking conservative senator who had scorned Castañeda's Communist past. But Castañeda invited Helms to visit Mexico, and much to everyone's surprise, Helms accepted. In early 2001 Helms flew to Mexico City with four other senators. It was a heavyweight group that wanted to demonstrate that the election of Vicente Fox had changed the U.S. perspective of Mexico. Indeed, this was Senator Helms's only message. At times, he delivered it with breathtaking frankness, basically stating that prior to Fox, Mexico had been a corrupt state that the United States could not work with. But he also pledged "a new spirit of cooperation" and declared, "there is no end to what we can accomplish if we work together."

But Mexican suspicion of Helms was so great that I had my doubts how the message would come across when Senator Fernando Margáin, the chair of the Mexican Senate's Foreign Relations Committee, arranged for Helms and his delegation to visit the Senate. Fortunately, traditional Mexican courtesy trumped all. Even the PRI senators present (who, by Helms's definition, were most probably corrupt) and young Senator Lázaro Cárdenas, the son of Cuauhtémoc, representing the leftist PRD, kept their remarks blander than mush. The meeting ended in professions of true love and respect all around. But the Mexican press was not about to give Helms the same kind treatment. They did not understand that in a lifetime of politics he had met much tougher audiences. At a press conference, Helms simply said what he wanted to say, turned down his hearing aid, and relied on the horrible translation being provided to confuse everyone. He then blithely shuffled off.

I found Helms to be a southern gentleman, though he probably turned off his hearing aid when I talked to him, too. I tried to brief him on how Fox's victory should be seen in the context of a gradual evolution of Mexican society: not everything that happened before Fox was horrible; not everything that will happen in his administration will be wildly successful or admirable. In any case, his visit ended with all sides more or less content. And the embassy and ambassador remained in one piece. That is about as much as one can hope for from a CODEL visitation.

There was another CODEL mission that was as unpleasant and awkward as the Helms visit had been courteous and constructive. It involved John Mica, an intense Florida Republican congressman and a strong proponent of decertifying Mexico for its antinarcotics performance—or nonperformance in his view. Mica also came with a message: Mexico needed to leave behind its corruption and inefficiency and enlist in the drug war. The PRI government awaited him with an apprehension bordering hysteria when he arrived in early 1999, at the height of the certification debate in the United States. Usually very skillful in handling visitors, the Foreign Secretariat was so unstrung that it blundered badly. While the other congressmen in the delegation were given special appointments with whichever cabinet minister they wanted to meet—Commerce, Energy, or Treasury—no such offer was made to Mica. So by the time the delegation met with Foreign Secretary Rosario Green, he was in a belligerent mood. After listening to Green and her deputy, Juan Rebolledo, detail Mexico's efforts in the antidrug fight, Mica let them know that he did not believe a word of what they said. Becoming more and more agitated, his face turning beet red, he blurted out, "I'm just trying to help you save your damn country!"

It was, to say the least, an awkward moment. I thought of dropping a pencil and spending the next few minutes under the table looking for it. A violent coughing attack that would necessitate leaving the room could have also sufficed. I cannot remember how the conversation recovered and progressed, but somehow it did. Mica later apologized to me, but not to the Mexicans. I was upset and felt that he had treated Green and the other officials unfairly. They were really trying to improve the drug picture. But there were many days—when confronted with undeniable proof of corruption, mismanagement, or the rapid advance of the narcotics mafias—that I remembered Mica. His manners were terrible, but his message was based on a frustration I sometimes shared. I understood where he was coming from.

C
H
A
P
T
E
R

S
E
V
E
N
T
E
E
N

The Mothers of All Visits

All visits by cabinet members, governors, and congressmen pose special circumstances and difficulties. But, in the world of official travel, nothing can compare with a presidential visit. Counting the heavy security contingents, the communication experts, speechwriters, other White House personnel, the press, embassy support staff, and a few foreign affairs specialists, the number of individuals accompanying a president overseas is usually about one thousand. This is an invading army, and it falls to the embassy to serve as the advance scout and intermediary between invaders and invadees.

The Mexicans have had considerable experience dealing with American presidents and other high-level visitors. But there was always room for misunderstanding and friction. Most often this involved the Secret Service and their counterparts in the Estado Mayor Presidencial, the military group responsible for the protection of Mexico's president. Both groups had a very narrow focus, carried guns, and let nothing matter to them other than their protection responsibilities. They tended to run roughshod over everyone and everything else.

But the details of a presidential visit cannot be left in the hands of security personnel. Civil servants and politicians also have a role to play. Before President Clinton's early 1999 visit to Mérida, I traveled there to smooth the way with the local governor, Víctor Cervera Pacheco, who a year later would achieve fleeting international fame for questionable electoral practices. Cervera was one of the PRI's last *caciques*, a local political lord. He ran the state of Yucatán with an iron fist. He did not bat an eye when I laid out for him what the presidential delegation would need. Sitting at his desk with a bank of telephones in front of him, he responded to each of my requests with a mumbled phone conversation with an invisible aide. A thousand hotel rooms? "No problem." Tourists with reservations would be sent elsewhere. A multitude to line the streets from the airport? "No problem." Thousands would be bused in from the countryside. And so it went. Every request was met with a definitive "No problem."

Midway through our meeting, Cervera Pacheco decided that I needed to replace the suit I was wearing with the traditional dress shirt of the Caribbean, a guayabera. Up went the phone receiver and within minutes a gasping, sweating minion entered the room. The scene was surrealistic as the diminutive and obviously nervous tailor was instructed to stand on the governor's desk to measure me while I stood with my arms outstretched. It looked like I was about to be crucified, which also would have likely have posed "no problem." The guayabera showed up the next morning. The thousand rooms and the crowd lining the street came later, just as promised.

Only a small number of the multitude accompanying the president on a foreign trip have the opportunity to travel on Air Force One. The seats are fought over by cabinet officials, bureaucrats, politicians, and all sorts of other large egos hoping that the close proximity to a president will result in a conversation with him. Generally, protocol and common sense dictated that the assistant secretary of state for the region to be visited should be on the plane in order to brief the president, write last-minute speeches, or otherwise attend to some until-then forgotten detail. The communications crew could connect the plane with anyone in the world by phone or fax, and not a few passengers would concoct reasons to call their offices or their mothers, just to be able to tell them where they were calling from.

Traveling on Air Force One is as comfortable as one might imagine. Most seats are of first-class quality—wide with smooth, gray leather. The food is good, but not gourmet class. The service is attentive, and movies are available. I saw the movie Air Force One on the plane. And, no, in reality there is no ejection capsule like the one President Harrison Ford used to escape in the film.

But no matter how comfortable it might be, there is a truth about presidential travel that irks some who accompany the president. Everyone except the president—and his wife, if she is traveling with him—is simply an extra in the road show. Everything is designed to accommodate POTUS, the president of the United States, and FLOTUS, the First Lady of the United States. (I refused to use those terms because they sounded like characters in a children's story about bunny rabbits.)

When POTUS and FLOTUS are ready, the plane flies, the motorcade moves, the meal begins or ends. And not a second before. For cabinet members and other heavyweight Washington types accustomed to being their own parade, treatment as an add-on would occasionally prove irksome. It bothered Madeleine Albright no end. Several times she devised special visits she would have to make on the way to joining the presidential party. That gave her an excuse to requisition her own plane and avoid being one of the president's attendants.

Despite the enormous expense and logistical effort behind presidential trips abroad, they are seldom historical or diplomatic watersheds. The discussions usually do not approach the level of Stalin, Roosevelt, and Churchill at Yalta as they divided postwar Europe. But they do often serve more modestly important goals, as two heads of state ratify the results of the work that their bureaucracies have spent the prior few weeks feverishly producing. Thus there is an inevitable search for "deliverables" to show presidential statecraft at work. This deadline pressure for deliverables is useful because nothing better concentrates the mind of bureaucrats than a presidential trip. Tasks that should have been accomplished the year before finally get done. Programs that have been dwindling get reinvigorated. And funds promised elsewhere get hijacked. A bureaucracy aroused to meet a president's expectations is a thing to behold.

There is an irony that usually undermines the meticulously planned and elaborately staged presidential diplomacy. Though inevitably presented as an effort to improve relations with the foreign land being visited, the principal audience is the accompanying American press. The White House wants stories datelined London, Bangkok, or Mexico City reporting to American voters what a wonderful job the president is doing and how wisely he is spending their taxes. The press knows what the game is and tries to find a reason to avoid satisfying the White House media operatives. It is a big game in which the press will only write about the routine business if it cannot find something better to write about. Usually it can.

When a U.S. president goes to Mexico, the Mexican press will march to the heavy drumbeat of its national sovereignty worries. Meanwhile, the U.S. correspondents accompanying the president—to Mexico or other countries—look for a way to engage the president about something else on the world stage that is making more dramatic news. When the U.S. president joins a foreign leader for a press conference and almost all the questions deal with an issue that has nothing to do with his host, the event can be uncomfortable, even embarrassing.

The U.S. press that accompanied President Clinton to Mexico in 1999, just two days after the Senate failed to impeach him, was massively uninterested in his discussions with President Zedillo or in the important Brownsville-Mérida law enforcement agreement that had just been signed. A hot rumor was circulating that Mrs. Clinton might run for Senate, and the reporters insisted on knowing his thoughts on the subject. "She'd make a good senator," he said. That became the story from Mexico.

When President Bush visited Vicente Fox's ranch in February 2001, the story that hijacked the press coverage was the U.S. bombing of Iraq. U.S. and British planes had bombed similar targets in the no-fly zones on many occasions, but this was the first time that the newly inaugurated President Bush had sent the American military into action. Almost all of the press questions dealt with that, as did most of the coverage. Some Mexican commentators were convinced that that the United States government had purposely planned the bombing raid to wrest importance from the Guanajuato meeting. But none could offer a plausible reason why President Bush would have wanted to confuse the message of his first foreign trip. The bombing and the press focus on it cast a pall over the visit. One newspaper reported that President Fox's spokeswoman (soon to be his wife) shook her head slowly and asked why the Americans could not have waited one more day.

Other Mexican commentators were convinced that the show of force was really intended as an intimidating message to President Fox.

Mexican opinion, as usual, could accept any motive for our actions except the most obvious one: there was no connection between the bombing and the trip to Mexico, no desire to turn the spotlight away from President Fox, whose friendship Bush was anxious to highlight for the American public. The truth was far less complicated than many Mexicans wanted to believe. The new White House had not yet gotten its left and right hands working together. But such a mundane, nonconspiratorial explanation was of no interest to the observers who delight in looking at the chaos of world affairs to find an underlying plot, motive, or plan. These are usually the same people who can take a plan and turn it into chaos.

It would have been instructive for the conspiracy theorists to stand on the tarmac as the president was about to board Air Force One for the return to Washington. They might have overheard Condoleezza Rice, his newly appointed national security advisor, shout in anguish into her cell phone, "But, Don, surely you must have known about it!" Surely, Secretary of Defense Don Rumsfeld did know about the bombing. But apparently neither he nor anyone else in the new administration had given serious attention to what it might do to the coverage of the president's first foreign trip. As Rice poured out her frustration to Rumsfeld, Secretary Powell stood silently nearby, wearing the bemused expression of a seasoned veteran who had witnessed more than his share of governmental confusion.

It is precisely to avoid confusion that presidential trips are minutely choreographed. Every meeting, every speech, every movement from point A to point B is the subject of long memos, charts, and stage directions. It is far easier to put on a production of *Macbeth* than to organize one afternoon of a presidential trip. The president himself becomes a hostage to his staff and to the program they have devised for him.

On occasion, presidents rebel, but rarely for long and hardly ever successfully. When I was assistant secretary of state, Joan and I attended a state dinner at the White House for President Frei of Chile. As we passed through the receiving line, I had a brief conversation with President Clinton about a trip we were planning to Latin America to take place a few months later.

"I'm really looking forward to it, Jeff."

"Yes sir, the planning is going well," I said while moving slowly along the line. But the president did not let go of my hand and stopped my movement.

"Convince them that I want to stay longer."

"Sure," I said, and took another step. But then I stopped and turned back. I was confused. Certainly, his Latin American hosts would be thrilled to have him stay longer. They needed no persuasion. "Convince whom?" I asked. He must have thought I was as thick as three bricks.

"My staff. Tell my staff to let me stay longer."

"Sure," I repeated. Another step. Another turnaround. "Wouldn't it make more sense for you to tell them?"

"Oh, they never listen to me," he laughed.

President Clinton was not a meek prisoner of his staff. But White House schedulers are engaged in a constant battle over the president's time. It is sliced thinner than prosciutto. The president can and does express his preferences, but he has neither the time nor the energy to fight the continuing battle over his schedule. Planning foreign visits is left to others. Generally, the president spends little time thinking about the visit until he boards Air Force One.

But President Bush had clearly taken part in selecting the destination of his first foreign trip. He decided to head south to convey a strong message: Mexico, and by extension the Western Hemisphere, would figure prominently in his foreign policy. His desire to be well prepared for the visit merged with Secretary Powell's effort to make a point about the State Department's talent and professionalism. A few days before his departure, the president took the unprecedented step of visiting the State Department to attend a briefing session.

Building on his military tradition, Powell decided that the department's lieutenants should brief the generals, or, in this case, the commander-in-chief. The military love to brief each other—"death by PowerPoint" is a common expression—and they do it well. The State Department does not have the same culture.

But the junior and midlevel officers of the Office of Mexican Affairs did well. President Bush showed an extraordinary knowledge of the U.S.-Mexico relationship, having dealt with many of the issues as governor of Texas. The young officers skillfully answered his questions about road repair, water purification plants, and migration problems along the border. Certainly, there was some showmanship all around, but reports of the meeting traveled like wildfire in the State Department, providing a real boost in morale. That, of course, was exactly what the new secretary of state wanted.

Despite Vicente Fox's Marlboro man persona, his Guanajuato ranch bears no resemblance to the Ponderosa, or any other of the other sprawling cowboy domains of television and movie fame. There are no bucking broncos or herds of longhorns. The ranch is more like a midsize farm. Its chief activity is the raising and freezing of broccoli and other vegetables for export to the United States.

Advance teams from both sides had agreed on a plan. Bush would fly in for a brief meeting and lunch. The two presidents would talk for about twenty minutes with only one note-taker per side. Then they would join the rest of their teams of about six each for broader conversations and lunch. The event would end with a press conference. By the standards of a presidential visit, it was going to be a fairly straightforward event.

The Mexican side made a few suggestions to make the event more photogenic. They recommended that the two cowboy presidents mount horses and take a brief ride around the ranch. The White House rejected the idea. Once in the saddle, the tall U.S. president would be dwarfed by his much taller Mexican colleague. A photo could make them look like Quixote and Sancho Panza.

Fox's ranch house is pleasant but not overwhelming. When I visited it a few days before President Bush's arrival, it was still undergoing renovations and extensions. Painters and carpenters were scurrying around, putting the final touches on a new extension. When President Bush entered the house, the first thing he saw was a beautiful saddle mounted on a wooden stand. All hand-tooled leather with elaborate silver inlays, it was inscribed with Vicente Fox's name. It was obviously a gift that he had received along the way from supporters. President Bush eyed it appreciatively, but I quickly diverted his attention to the Mexican officials waiting to receive him. I knew that if the president had expressed admiration for the workmanship, Fox would have presented him with an equally beautiful saddle. But the previous week, I had been obliged to decline precisely such a magnificent present, which had President Bush's name embossed in leather and must have been worth five thousand dollars. My explanation of U.S. rules governing gifts to presidents undoubtedly seemed incomprehensible and churlish to most of the Mexican bureaucrats, who saw the gift as a gesture of hospitality and friendship. Fortunately, the upper levels of the Mexican government were able to assimilate the message, chalked it up to strange American habits, and arranged for the exchange of much less valuable presents.

Every gift that a president of the United States receives immediately becomes the property of the American people. Whether it is a collage of famous Indonesian sportsmen done in chicken beaks or a Saudi prince's solid gold Rolex table clock, the gift goes immediately to the State Department's Protocol Office, usually on its way to government collections or warehouses. If a president wants to keep it, he must pay a fair market price based on a professional appraisal. Before the trip to Guanajuato, the White House had told me that President Bush was not in the market for a five-thousand-dollar saddle, so it fell to me to break that news to our Mexican hosts. The new Fox team was puzzled, but accepted my apologies. I was not about to allow the president of the United States to mess up my hard work on his behalf by uttering some compliment about Fox's saddle. I hustled him into the living room for a round of introductions.

Leaving their teams, the two presidents went into Fox's study for a private meeting. It had been scheduled to last for only twenty minutes but went on for nearly an hour. They were accompanied only by their official note-takers, Condoleezza Rice and the foreign ministry's number-two man, Enrique Berruga. Castañeda, who would have liked to be in on the private meeting, was compelled by protocol to stay with Secretary Powell. The two foreign ministers and their teams discussed a long list of issues while waiting for their bosses to emerge from the study.

The issue of migration would be the lasting hallmark of the Guanajuato meeting, but it was not the principal or first theme the two presidents discussed. Water was the first concern. On his way to Mexico, Bush had stopped in Texas and had been given an earful of complaints about Mexico's noncompliance with a 1946 treaty that governs the sharing of Rio Grande waters. Drought had scarred southwest Texas for several years, and the Texans complained that Mexico was far behind on its water deliveries. The Mexicans, for their part, contended that they were suffering from the same drought and there was little water to share. It was a hot political issue in Texas.

But the two presidents were stymied in their discussion because of a translation confusion—not of language, as Fox speaks excellent English—but of numbers. The U.S. measures water flow with the archaic British measurement of acre feet—literally the amount of water it takes to cover an acre of flat land to a depth of one foot. It is not a particularly useful tool for, say, measuring water as it flows along a river course. The Mexicans more sensibly measure flow in cubic meters. Neither the presidents nor Rice nor Berruga could figure out how to convert acre feet into cubic meters. The conversation stalled, only to continue at the luncheon table where some of the best minds of both governments demonstrated that they were as mathematically challenged as their bosses.

Finally, I saw Bill McIlhenny, a brilliant young Foreign Service officer, hovering outside the ranch house. Using his cell phone, we called an expert in Washington who was able to tell us that a million cubic meters of water equals a little more than eight hundred acre feet. Getting the conversion right did not actually make the discussion go any better. The basic fact was that for the previous decade Mexico had been delivering less than half the water it should have under the terms of the treaty. Projections for the coming year were no more encouraging. Nothing was settled, but Fox agreed to make it a top priority. Perhaps not willing to recognize the depth of local opposition on the Mexican side of the border to handing over more water to the gringos, he told Berruga to work out a solution. From that moment on, every time he saw him, President Bush, who has a penchant for nicknames, addressed Berruga as "Waterman." I later told him that he was fortunate that the two presidents had not been discussing a manure deficit.

Moving on from the water issue, Fox turned to his priority topic—migration, or, more precisely, the status of millions of Mexicans living in the United States illegally. His focus on the issue did not come as a surprise. When he traveled to the United States in August 2000, after his electoral victory but before taking the oath as president, he had mismanaged the topic and allowed it to dominate much of the press coverage.

Prior to that trip, Fox had talked of open borders between the United States and Mexico. He did not advocate that as an immediate goal but rather as a long-term objective. But he did not explain himself well and the press jumped on him. Both Bush and Democratic presidential candidate Al Gore were obliged to tell the press that they opposed open borders. Though each understood that the press's portrayal of Fox's thinking was oversimplified and taken out of context, neither tried to set the record straight. That was Fox's problem. Taking a firm line against open borders was not a bad position for a U.S. presidential candidate.

The Mexican reporters, always looking for an opportunity to find a slight or insult, played the two candidates' remarks heavily and labeled Fox's visit a failure. It was this coverage that enraged Castañeda and propelled him to criticize Mexican journalists for being monolingual incompetents. All in all, Fox's first serious effort to push his migration theme in the United States had failed, but he was not going to give up on it.

Knowing this, President Bush and his team came to Guanajuato six months later prepared to give Fox a better hearing. As governor of Texas, Bush had seen U.S. immigration policy and practice at work. He was not impressed. The United States needed Mexican laborers for its economy, and, as he would repeat many times over, anyone willing to travel thousands of miles over inhospitable terrain to find a job is bound to be a conscientious employee. There should be a way, he thought, to "match willing workers with willing employers."

For President Bush, the only migration-related topic that was totally off the table was a general amnesty for those already in the United States. Bush had no intention of advocating another amnesty, given the popular and generally accurate perception that the last amnesty in 1986 had not stopped illegal immigration. Indeed, it had instead led to a major increase in the number of immigrants living both legally and illegally in the United States. But other immigration-related issues, including a new temporary worker program and the safety of those crossing the frontier, were fair game for further discussion.

Anxious to display support for Fox, President Bush accepted the Mexican proposal to create a high-level commission to develop solutions. To underscore the importance of the matter, Bush appointed Secretary Powell and Attorney General Ashcroft, in whose Department of Justice the Immigration and Naturalization Service resided, to be the American cochairmen. Fox named Castañeda and Minister of Interior Santiago Creel. This was a heavy-duty cast. Everyone at Guanajuato understood its symbolic meaning: neither president would expose his top associates to an enterprise unlikely to succeed. Both presidents, still at the beginning of their terms, were committed to action. Both were naïve and not yet aware of the limits of their power.

Bush and Fox left the Guanajuato meeting in good spirits, notwith-standing the Iraq bombing flap. Each had made significant promises to be as helpful as possible to the other—Fox on water, Bush on migration. Neither would be able to deliver. But at the time, neither of the new presidents understood that.

C
H
A
P
T
E
R

E
I
G
H
T
E
E
N

Enrique

The community center walls were covered with cheerful posters promoting various public assistance programs. Drawings by the preschool children who attended Head Start classes during the day jumped from the walls in exuberant primary colors. It was early 2003, just a few months after we left Mexico, and I had brought about forty university students to a heavily Hispanic part of Boston. The idea was to get out of the seminar room where we had discussed policy and talk to some flesh and blood immigrants. The students, some from Mexico, sat in silence as I interviewed Enrique and translated his story.

In his late thirties, Enrique was a stocky man with an engaging smile. Back home in Mexico City he had been a jack-of-all-trades, a good carpenter and plumber. But he could not earn enough to support his family, including a son who was attending a technical college. Another Mexican in Boston, someone Enrique had regarded as a friend, lent him two thousand dollars to make the trip north. At the border, he was part of a group that a smuggler assembled at a cheap hotel and took across the line before dawn. But the Border Patrol caught Enrique, who smiled as he recounted that a female officer said she knew he would keep trying until he made it. With a modicum of triumph and flashing a broad smile, he said he needed only one more try to get past the Patrol. The students were captivated by his sincerity and obvious decency. They nodded in appreciation.

Once in Boston, Enrique bought a counterfeit social security card and began working as a dishwasher in a Cambridge taco joint that was owned by another Mexican. Some of the students said they had eaten at the restaurant. Enrique had probably cleaned their table. He was paid less than minimum wage, worked fourteen hours a day without overtime pay, and at times was sent to his boss's home for housecleaning chores. The students shook their heads in disgust. When several interjected that they would not patronize that restaurant again, Enrique thanked them. He had been afraid to complain to any authority about the poor working conditions, fearing that his boss might report him to immigration officials.

Enrique came to the community center a few nights a week to learn English. He had recently gotten a better job as a busboy in another taquería. The bosses there were less rapacious, and, one of the students noted, the tacos were better. When Enrique talked of his family, he choked up. So did some of the students—particularly some well-off Mexicans who may not have heard the details of life as an illegal alien described with such clarity and pathos before. Sharing a dismal apartment with other illegals, Enrique was able to send back about seven hundred dollars a month to his family. That was more than he had been earning in Mexico.

But Enrique was not exulting in the freedom or bounty of America. He had found precious little of either. He wanted to work as a plumber or handyman, but his lack of English, his false documents, and general uncertainty in a foreign land were thwarting that dream. He had moved downward from Mexico's lower middle class to America's proletariat. Like most other undocumented aliens, Enrique lived every day on the edge of exploitation and abuse. Even a fellow immigrant, the "friend" who had lent him the money to come north, had taken advantage of him by charging heavy interest.

Enrique was well spoken and showed flashes of humor. But there was also bitterness in his words, and frustration that he had been diminished as a man even as he earned more than he could have at home to meet his family's needs. In another world, he would be a respected part of his community, the kind of guy who would volunteer to coach the kids' soccer team. But now he was a barely visible scrubber of pots and cleaner of tables whose very anonymity was his greatest protection. Enrique could not obtain a driver's license, open a bank account, enroll in a public technical school, or comfortably participate in a dozen other activities common to Americans. And while he was having social security payments and taxes deducted from his paycheck, he would never receive benefits, because he had used a bogus social security card to get the job.

Of course, Enrique's greatest deprivation was that he could not live with his family. He could not legally bring them north, and he did not want them to run the risks or costs of an illegal crossing. Visiting them was too expensive and would require that he sneak across the border once again on his return. His situation contrasted harshly with the immigrant folklore in the United States that tells stories tinged in a rosy haze of strong and unified families suffering, striving, laughing, and crying together as they make their way triumphantly into American society. Enrique could not share his new life with his family. He was alone, sad and disillusioned. His American dream had taken on a bitter taste. In terms of money, he was undoubtedly better off. But the other important elements of life—home, family, friends, human contact, a sense of place and importance—were missing.

Vicente Fox must have heard many stories like Enrique's as he traveled around the United States in the years before his electoral triumph in 2000. Even before Fox took office, he made clear that he was determined to press the United States government to deal seriously with the issues of illegal immigration. When he bluntly said that it was time for the United States to "get real," he meant that Washington should acknowledge the country's dependence on Mexican migrants and stop forcing them to live in a shadow land of illegality, uncertainty, and vulnerability. A decent, religious man, Fox was motivated by a real concern for the lives of his countrymen. In recognition of their willingness to sacrifice for their families back home, he called them "heroes." His rhetoric constituted a significant change in Mexican political discourse.

In his outspoken advocacy of immigrants, Fox was not encumbered by the inhibition that had muffled the PRI's concerns. While outrage at perceived American mistreatment of the migrants was potentially one of the sharpest arrows in the PRI's quiver of anti-American rhetoric, the party faced attacks by critics who charged that Mexicans would not have been forced to migrate if the PRI had managed the country with less corruption and more attention to the poor. To acknowledge the migrants as a major issue was painful for the PRI, because it was a tacit acknowledgement of responsibility for the predicament of a million "Enriques."

As a former governor of Guanajuato, one of Mexico's biggest migrant-exporting states, Fox was steeped in the lore of illegal migration. He was also much influenced by Foreign Secretary Castañeda, who had studied the immigration wave that had brought millions of Mexicans to the United States since the 1970s. Castañeda told Fox that important elements of American public opinion—labor and business—were shifting to more favorable, pro-immigrant stances. He said labor unions and employers were ready to accept the immigrants as a permanent part of American life, and he wanted Fox to pressure the American government to do the same.

As a politician, Fox also understood that immigration issues were becoming increasingly important political themes on both sides of the border. He was looking ahead to a time in the not distant future when Mexicans and Mexican-Americans in the United States would play a greater role in Mexican political life. And he knew that as Republicans and Democrats in the United States sought to appeal to Hispanic voters, they would have to respond to Hispanic concerns. At a time when many newly naturalized citizens wanted to help relatives get a foothold in the United States, illegal immigration was becoming a major campaign issue for them.

Fox was also encouraged by the election of a Texan to the U.S. presidency just four months after his own stunning victory. Texas has a bond with Mexico that is stronger than that of the other border states. This is ironic, for in the past no state was the scene of worse anti-Mexican racism, and even today there are pockets of horrendous discrimination there. But there is another side of the story as well. Mexican-Americans in Texas feel very much a part of the state. They call themselves "Tejanos," a term that proudly anchors them in a specific place. Meanwhile, much of the state's Anglo population embraces the reality that the state owes part of its identity to Mexico. It may be purely superficial for many people, but there is something about growing up eating tacos, speaking some kitchen Spanish, and maybe taking part in the occasional teenage trip across the border for mischief, that has produced a Texan affinity for things Mexican.

Texas political figures like Lyndon Johnson, James Baker, Lloyd

Bentsen, Ann Richards, and George H. W. Bush considered themselves knowledgeable about Mexico and wanted to be friends of their southern neighbor. As governor of Texas, George W. Bush followed in that tradition, reaching out to strengthen old ties and build new ones. When he was a presidential candidate and faced questions about his foreign affairs qualifications, he had pointed immediately to Mexico and his friendship with Fox. Bush also liked to reduce the complexities of large-scale illegal immigration to "an opportunity, not a problem." From the south, it looked as if the stars were aligning for big movement on migration.

Despite all these positive factors, Fox wanted to move carefully. Just weeks before the two new presidents would meet at his ranch, Castañeda assembled a small group of advisers to nudge Fox to seize the initiative. Fox was concerned that the timing might not be right. "Isn't it too early to ask so much of Bush?" he asked, according to one of the participants. Their answer was emphatic: Now is the time to strike, while both administrations are fresh and looking to make their marks. Fox was ultimately convinced. Once committed, he became his own best cheerleader.

Two changes in Mexican law also compelled Fox to pay attention to the migration issue. In 1998 Mexico changed its constitution to permit double nationality. Mexicans who had lost their citizenship by naturalizing in another country could now apply to have it restored. A child born abroad to a Mexican parent could also take Mexican citizenship, without having to renounce citizenship in his or her country of birth. In one stroke, Mexico had given the many millions of Mexican-born who had already taken U.S. citizenship and their U.S.-born children the right to be Mexican citizens.

Mexico took another big step when it granted Mexicans living out of the country the right to vote. For years the PRI governments had blocked this initiative, understanding that those so dissatisfied in Mexico that they left for the United States would be likely to vote against the PRI. But as Mexican expatriates became more numerous and often used their U.S.-acquired wealth to exercise their influence at home, the PRI succumbed and the law was changed. Nevertheless, the lawmakers who gave immigrants the right to vote did not take on the big logistical problem of providing them with the means to cast their ballots in the United States. The promise of the reform remains unfulfilled, though the politicians talk of figuring out the logistics prior to the 2006 presidential election.

The net effect of those changes in Mexican law is that millions of Mexicans and Mexican-Americans will be able to participate fully in Mexican elections. That enormous potential, of course, provides a big incentive for Mexican politicians to curry favor by arguing that the U.S. should legalize Mexican immigrants already living in the United States. Though Fox is constitutionally barred from seeking re-election, he could give his party a big boost and take his place in history if he could persuade the United States to grant legality to the undocumented. And the architect of Fox's immigration strategy, aspiring Los Pinos resident Jorge Castañeda, could reap the gratitude, votes, and financial support not only of the immigrants but also of those in Mexico who depend on their financial support.

So Mexico's new political realities made it understandable that Fox and Castañeda put legalization at the top of their immigration agenda. They were less interested in proposals to enlarge and improve the temporary worker program so that Mexicans could come and go, but not necessarily stay in the United States.

Castañeda, who wrote frequently for American newspapers, had been weighing in on immigration for years. As NAFTA was being debated in the United States during the early 1990s, Castañeda was one of its most vocal critics, arguing in the U.S. press that NAFTA was woefully incomplete unless it matched the free movement of trade with an equally free movement of people. He compared NAFTA negatively to the accord forming the European Union. The EU had provided not only for the free movement of persons among member countries but also for the transfer of funds for economic and infrastructure development from wealthy members to poorer members. Neither the United States nor Canada was prepared to agree to similar provisions, without which, Castañeda argued, NAFTA would not benefit Mexico.

Castañeda had another worry about NAFTA. He assumed that a strong Mexican economy would tie Mexico more closely to the United States and would bring benefits to the party in power. As a staunch anti-PRI-ista, he saw NAFTA as yet another way the United States could support the established order. In this, he was wrong. NAFTA helped open the Mexican political system by decreasing the economic power of the state and by demanding more transparent rules of conduct. By helping to crack open a closed economic system, it weakened the PRI's hold on power; it did not strengthen it. Without NAFTA, the stage would not have been as well set for the election of Vicente Fox. And, without NAFTA, that committed free trader would not have had the opportunity to select a former Marxist professor as his foreign secretary.

Castañeda kept a close watch on the immigration debate in the United States. In early 2000, he sensed that the ground was shifting. In February, the national labor confederation, the AFL-CIO, whose alarm about illegal aliens taking jobs way from Americans had scared the Clinton White House away from immigration reform proposals for eight years, made a dramatic shift. The labor federation decided that it would embrace illegal immigrants as a source of future members rather than as a threat to American workers. Its executive council not only called for a new amnesty, it wanted repeal of the portion of the 1986 that criminalized the deliberate hiring of illegals.

The AFL-CIO's decision was remarkable only in how long it had taken union leaders to publicly recognize reality. Since the mid-nineteenth century, successive waves of immigrants had given vitality and strength to the American union movement. The undocumented from Mexico and elsewhere were not joining unions as their predecessors had, because they were afraid of coming out of the shadows and becoming visible targets for employers and the INS. Organized labor needed the immigrant workers, especially in the service industries, to counter its losses among blue-collar factory workers and professionals. So it joined the call for amnesty, while maintaining its strong opposition to temporary worker programs that could keep wages down by expanding the supply of workers.

Another important voice heard in early 2000 was Federal Reserve Board Chairman Alan Greenspan, who cited the importance of immigration in limiting inflation. In his own way, Greenspan backhandedly justified the AFL-CIO's new posture by recognizing that undocumented (and un-unionized) immigrants depressed wages.

Castañeda, deeply involved in Fox's presidential campaign throughout 1999 and the first half of 2000, decided that a historical moment had arrived. In his push to bring immigration to the top of the U.S.-Mexico agenda, he was helped immensely by his half-brother and close friend Andrés Rozental. Twelve years older than Castañeda, Rozental had followed his stepfather into the foreign policy establishment and moved his way up the diplomatic career ladder. Some in the foreign ministry whis-pered about nepotism. But most recognized that Rozental was an accom-plished, bright, and bureaucratically skilled public servant.

Rozental had held important diplomatic postings overseas, including ambassador to the United Kingdom. And he had been influential with-in the SRE itself, earning the reputation among American diplomats as a general in the army of those promoting the hyperinflated concerns about Mexican sovereignty. When Ernesto Zedillo chose Rosario Green to be foreign secretary in January 1998, Rozental recognized that his way to the top of the foreign ministry was blocked. So he decided to retire and enter the business world.

With a style smoother than that of his often prickly and somewhat impetuous younger half-brother, Rozental moved easily in Washington. He used his government experience and private sector contacts to obtain Ford and MacArthur Foundation funding to form a private U.S.-Mexico commission to look at the immigration issue. He enlisted Thomas "Mack" McLarty to be the American co-chair. It was a clever choice. McLarty had been President Clinton's first White House chief of staff. When he left that position midway through the first term, he became the president's personal representative for Latin America. His easygoing Arkansas manner, demonstrable interest in the hemisphere, and close-ness to the president—he maintained a coveted and scarce West Wing office—made McLarty the indispensable "man to see" in Washington for Latin American leaders during the Clinton years.

In 2000, Mack was a well-plugged-in Washington consultant, respect-ed by both Republicans and Democrats and still an important point of contact for Latin America. He was a brilliant choice to co-chair the migration panel. The other panel members did not constitute a particu-larly heterogeneous group. All came to their work with essentially the same view: U.S. immigration policy in regard to Mexicans was inhu-mane, ignored reality, and needed to be fixed in a way that would invite millions of illegal immigrants to enjoy full participation in American society.

The panel issued its report in February 2001, not coincidentally just a week before the two new presidents were to meet at Fox's ranch in Guanajuato. It offered an analysis of the problem and suggested a set of principles for a "grand bargain" between the countries on immigration.

The basis for the grand bargain would be the acceptance of shared responsibility for the problem. It suggested solutions that would make migration from Mexico to the United States mutually beneficial, as well as safe, legal, orderly, and predictable.

The report recommended making legal status more widely available for undocumented immigrants who were established, employed, and tax-paying. It also called for expanding the number of permanent family visas for Mexicans, and increasing the availability of work visas. And it asked for action to build an economically healthy border region, target development efforts in regions of Mexico with high rates of emigration, and strengthen the Mexican economy to reduce migration pressures.

The report was predictable, given the initial views of its members. It reflected both the political savvy of the drafters and the essential weakness of their "grand bargain" argument. Cleverly, nowhere in the report was the word "amnesty" mentioned. "Regularizing" and "legalizing" the status of immigrants became the preferred terms of the advocacy community in Washington. The effects of the 1986 legislation had made "amnesty" an unacceptable term in Washington political circles. The commission eliminated the word from its vocabulary, but not from its goals.

The commission's plan offered less than it appeared to. In fact, without stating it, it recognized the reality that as long as the Mexican government was unwilling to take strong steps to block its population from migrating, its contribution to the solution would be far less than the grand bargain would demand of the United States. Mexico's efforts would focus on cracking down on alien smugglers, working to build a viable border region, and cooperating to promote economic development throughout Mexico, particularly in areas of high emigration. These were worthwhile intentions, but few believed that, even if successfully begun, much could be accomplished in the short run to lower migrant flows.

On the other hand, the grand bargain placed the onus for most of the important action on the United States. Regularizing the undocumented, developing better temporary worker programs, expanding the number of visas available for Mexican family members, and other suggestions were all actions within the purview of the American government. In effect, the imbalance in responsibility recognized the reality. In the absence of a multilateral agreement such as the one governing the European Union or treaties dealing with refugee rights, immigration law remains uniquely unilateral. Each country dictates who may enter, who may stay, and when each must leave. The panel's effort to convert American law into a grand bargain was mirrored in the Mexican government's position that the topic should be one of negotiation between the two countries. President Bush accepted this concept at Guanajuato and the Powell/Ashcroft-Castañeda/Creel commission was formed. Such a high-level group was an excellent "deliverable" that justified the visit for both presidents.

Bush's decision to go along with Fox was based on a desire to be responsive and helpful to Mexico's new president. But the new administration in Washington did little serious analysis of the issues before making the commitment. Little thought was given to the real possibility for success in an area that was so complex and politically volatile. President Fox wanted the issue at the top of the agenda, and President Bush wanted to help and to be seen helping President Fox. Moreover, President Bush was no fan of the current immigration policy. A joint effort seemed to make so much sense. But in reality, there wasn't much room for negotiation. One side, the United States, controlled almost all of the chips. The other, Mexico, had little to bring to the table for trading. Despite Bush's gesture of goodwill and his desire to accommodate his friend, time would show that the Guanajuato meeting would lead to little more than the typical response of the American government to an intractable problem: form a committee and study the problem into oblivion.

C
H
A
P
T
E
R

N
I
N
E
T
E
E
N

The Negotiation That Wasn't

Presidents Bush and Fox launched an historically significant but strange diplomatic exercise with their decision to begin immigration talks. They signaled a newly cooperative approach to immigration issues. For the first time, Mexico and the United States acknowledged migration as a shared problem and accepted shared responsibility for making it orderly, humane, and legal. Those general principles were admirable but the high-level commission would prove unable to bring them to life. The Mexicans insisted on calling the talks a negotiation, while the Americans preferred the more casual "conversations" or "discussions." The two sides did exchange some position papers, but they really did not negotiate with each other in the classic form of diplomatic bargaining.

The Mexicans talked more to the press, hoping to add a sense of urgency to the process and create an expectation that the United States was about to agree to major changes in its immigration policy. The Americans, meanwhile, were far less clear about what was politically possible or even desirable. They fell into long and inconclusive internal debates in which various government agencies adopted differing and ultimately irreconcilable positions. But for a few months after the Guanajuato meeting, there was a palpable feeling in Washington, particularly in the State Department, that change was possible.

At the heart of any immigration discussion between the United States and Mexico there are two seemingly intractable issues, the products of deeply held ideological and political positions. Unlike many national governments, the United States does not document its own citizens. There is no national identity card. There is no obligation to carry any sort of identification, though of course life in the modern world without a driver's license or a social security card is nearly impossible. But the inherent distrust of government in the United States, sometimes manifesting itself in paranoid fantasies about what would happen if Washington could track every citizen, is so strong that any effort to develop a national register of legal residents, including citizens, is politically impossible. The net result is that we really cannot know easily who is illegally living in the country because we do not know who is doing so legally. While there is no constitutional prohibition of a national identity card, the idea faces formidable political barriers.

On the Mexican side, ideology and politics prevent the Mexican government from taking steps to prevent its citizens from crossing illegally into the United States. Politicians argue that the constitution guarantees the right of travel, and it does. But it does not guarantee the right to leave the country at any point where one may desire to do so. Mexican law is clear that an individual must enter and exit the country only through established crossing points. If Mexico were able to enforce its own law, keeping emigrants from crossing where there is no border post, many lives could be saved, and U.S. authorities would be able to check the travel documents of everyone seeking to enter the country. However, so strong is the belief that every Mexican has the right to enter the United States, and so deep is the economic need for millions to do so, that any notion of limiting or even channeling that flow is politically deadly. A plan to do so proposed by the governor of Baja California in the heat of summer in 2001 was based on the argument that his state had the obligation to keep people from crossing in dangerous areas, much in the same way that police could prevent an individual from jumping off of a roof. It was quickly withdrawn in the face of fierce opposition by political forces more concerned about not appearing to be kowtowing to American pressure than in saving lives.

The net effect of the Mexican position is that Americans suspect that any agreement that might be reached about amnesty, legalization, temporary workers, or other issues would be undercut because the Mexican government would not stop those who would fall outside of the agreement from crossing illegally. Castañeda understood this fatal flaw and realized that Mexico would have to address the problem in order to get a deal. In 1989, while still in academia, he had written, "In all likelihood any understanding which would address Mexico's concerns would also involve some limit on emigration and shared responsibility for enforcing it."

But were Castañeda and Fox prepared to challenge Mexican orthodoxy and agree to physically prevent illegal border crossers if an agreement could be reached with the United States granting them everything else they wanted? The answer is unclear. After he had left his cabinet position, Castañeda asserted that he had told Secretary Powell and Condoleezza Rice that "we were willing to go the plate on this issue, if the [American] administration was also willing to go to the plate on the tough issues that it had to face." He also said that the details of what Mexico would be prepared to do would be the last piece to be placed in the jigsaw puzzle, and only after the United States had committed to its part of the bargain.

It is difficult to reconstruct exactly what Castañeda said in private conversations and what his listeners heard or thought they heard. The issue of the Mexican government preventing its citizens from crossing the border never came up in conversations at the level of experts. If Castañeda made the point to Rice and Powell, he may have been so elliptical in his words that they did not understand him. And if they did understand what he was saying, they probably doubted that he would be able to actually deliver. The U.S. side was, in any event, just as unwilling to reveal its bottom line before knowing what the Mexicans had in mind as the Mexicans were to make any commitment before knowing what the U.S. was prepared to do.

The ideological flaws were important, but they did not immediately deflate the euphoria that emerged from Guanajuato. Still, other problems became apparent. Contrary to Castañeda's conclusion that the moment was propitious for immigration reform, there was not sufficient support either in the White House or in Congress for a sweeping program to legalize millions of immigrants who had come illegally to the United States. Many politicians were opposed to rewarding those who had broken immigration laws. Others feared that another legalization program would encourage even more illegal border crossings. And a great number wanted to avoid a negative reaction from voters across the country who were becoming uneasy as the U.S. experienced the biggest wave of immigration—both legal and illegal—in its history.

The month before the meeting in Guanajuato, I heard from a powerful political figure with another reason to resist the Mexican push for legalization. When conservative Republican Senator Phil Gramm of Texas came to Mexico City with four other senators in January 2001 to meet with President Fox, I asked him if there was any chance of some sort of legalization program. He candidly responded, "No way. The Democrats just want to get more of these people into the country so they will become citizens and vote for them. That's not going to happen." Later, back in the United States, Gramm vowed that a new amnesty would happen only "over my cold, dead political body." His negativity was based on the widely held Republican belief that a large percentage of those who had received amnesty under the 1986 law and had years later become citizens were voting for Democrats. That perception was correct. Ronald Reagan had signed that law, but Republicans got very little electoral benefit from it.

But if Republicans like Gramm had their sleep disrupted by images of long lines of newly naturalized voters, Democrats were intrigued by that possibility. In November 2001, Senate Majority Leader Tom Daschle and House Minority Leader Richard Gephardt came to Mexico, determined to spread the word that despite Bush's flirtation with immigration reform it was the Democrats who were the true friends of Mexican immigrants.

Daschle and Gephardt traveled to Puebla, a major source of emigrants for the New York area. They met with the families of some of the sixteen Mexican busboys, janitors, and messengers who died in the World Trade Center. The meeting was both moving and awkward, as Daschle and Gephardt tried to make conversation with the poorly educated and taciturn wives and children of the dead. As professional politicians, they handled it well. I promised the clinging gaggle of press photographers that I'd make sure they got good photo opportunities later in the day, if they would leave us alone while we met with the families of the deceased. For once, they complied.

At the next stop, a village that had sent most of its working-age men to the United States, Daschle and Gephardt and their wives toured the local primary school. I stayed outside to avoid the reporters' pushing and shoving. The teachers had lined up the students on the patio, all deep brown eyes and shining black hair. I suggested to one of the teachers that they prepare a song for their visitors. I then placed Gephardt and Daschle in the middle of the kids while they all sang "Cielito Lindo." It was a fun minute, which I had spontaneously arranged with no political intent. I simply knew the visitors would get a kick out of it, and I owed the photographers a good shot. To my surprise, their photos appeared on American front pages. No one in the White House ever asked the embassy whose idea the photo session was. I would have pled ignorance in any event. The two Democrats also got heavy press coverage in Mexico with pledges to support a broad legalization of Mexican immigrants. But they told me that they saw no possibility for a bill to begin moving through Congress until after the November 2002 elections.

Immediately after the Guanajuato presidential meeting, each side designated leaders for technical-level discussions. Ambassador Mary Ryan led the U.S. side, which also included representatives of the attorney general's office, the INS, and the Department of Labor. Ryan was a legend in the State Department. She had already served six years in one of the department's toughest jobs, assistant secretary for consular affairs. She had revamped her bureau, instilled a new spirit among her staff, and brought it to the cutting edge of technological innovation. Her Mexican counterpart, Gustavo Mohar, had served in the Mexican embassy in Washington as its resident immigration expert and later as its congressional liaison. He was assisted by an accomplished demographer and student of migration, Rodolfo Tuirán.

From the outset, the Mexicans pursued the five themes developed by the McLarty-Rozental commission. They wanted legalization for undocumented migrants already in the United States; an expanded temporary worker program; revisions of U.S. visa policies so that Mexicans eligible for green cards could get them faster; funds for economic development in Mexico that would provide alternatives to emigration; and cooperation on safety at the border. The U.S. side was much less united than were the Mexicans and less clear in its direction. Among themselves, the American team agreed only on general principles. They wanted to devise an ambitious program to match willing workers with willing employees— a goal that President Bush explicitly endorsed. Many of those workers were already in the United States, but some on the team did not want to institute a program that would be seen as rewarding those who had violated U.S. law and jumped the line of those waiting to come legally.

Beyond that, they wanted to ensure labor rights and dignified treatment for Mexican workers in the United States. But there was little discussion of the mechanics of how that could be accomplished. And they wanted the Mexican government to take certain steps, such as increasing efforts to intercept migrants from other countries who used Mexico as a corridor to the U.S. Finally, the U.S. side wanted to limit any agreement to Mexico, but understood that it might become a model for a broader program involving other countries that sent large numbers of migrants to the United States.

I attended the meeting in April that brought the four cabinet members and their aides together for the first time. When I heard Castañeda press Powell to reaffirm that the talks constituted "a single undertaking," I stopped doodling. I knew that Castañeda wanted it understood that no part of the agenda would be solved until everything was solved and that solutions on all fronts would be announced simultaneously. Castañeda's strategy, which would later gain fame as the "whole enchilada" approach, reflected his apprehension that the United States would not budge on the issue that he and Fox most cared about: the legalization of several million Mexicans living illegally in the United States. Powell agreed that the two sides were indeed pursuing a single undertaking, but he had a different understanding of the term, which remained unspoken. Powell meant that all topics would be discussed simultaneously but not necessarily resolved contemporaneously. It was a classic case of two serious men speaking a common language, using identical words with different meanings.

In the following months, the two sides met repeatedly at the Ryan-Mohar level. While the technical-level talks proceeded, good progress was made on institutionalizing a number of steps to improve the safety of illegal crossers. Communication between authorities on both sides was increased, and the Border Patrol began training Mexican officials in life-saving techniques. Meanwhile, the Border Patrol buildup continued, lessening tensions in the area where the Arizona ranchers had pursued immigrants. And the Mexicans strengthened controls on their own southern border, intercepting many more Central Americans before they could head north to the United States. They also moved more army troops into the northern border area to patrol for narcotics traffickers, alien smugglers, and other criminals who preyed on the migrants.

Heavier Mexican military presence was probably helpful, but it caused some problems. On several occasions, the military crossed into the United States, and confrontation with Border Patrolmen who spotted armed men in the middle of the U.S. desert in the predawn hours was only narrowly averted. In one instance, when a Border Patrol agent in Arizona had the back window of his Chevrolet Tahoe shot out, the Mexicans blamed drug traffickers. But the agent identified his assailants as a Mexican Army unit traveling in a military-type Humvee. I did my best to calm down U.S. officials after such occurrences. I could only imagine how furious and disproportionate the Mexican response would have been if armed U.S. military had crossed into their territory.

Adding to the tension was the belief of many American officials working on the border that individual military officers were providing escorts to both drug dealers and the alien smugglers. There was no hard evidence for this. But the potential for corruption was also a concern for the Mexican Defense Ministry, which frequently rotated its forces at the border, precisely to prevent collusion with the criminals.

The deaths of migrants in the searing heat of borderland deserts, the winter cold of the mountains, or the treacherous currents of the Rio Grande were always on the minds of both countries' teams. The deaths usually came in ones and twos, but when fourteen bodies were found in the Arizona desert in May 2001, the story erupted on both sides of the border. The immigrants, mostly from the lush state of Veracruz, died of heat exposure and dehydration after their smugglers abandoned them. It was a shocking tragedy, which dramatically underscored the human toll of vast and uncontrolled illegal immigration. A truly horrified Attorney General Ashcroft, a profoundly religious man, called me, Castañeda, and Minister of Interior Creel to express his concern and his determination to find the culprits. The smugglers were later arrested in Mexico, extradited to the United States, tried, and convicted.

In the spring and early summer of 2001, the discussions continued. But on the central issues of regularization, temporary workers, and visa policy review there was little progress. The U.S. team divided along clear lines. The State Department advocated changes that were more open and generous than the Justice Department was willing to accept. But the big player in the debates turned out to be the Domestic Policy Council (DPC) of the White House, which took its cues from the president's

chief political adviser, Karl Rove. The DPC's job was to filter policy recommendations from government agencies and screen out those that were
likely to damage the president politically. It was here that the Republican
Party's plans to court Hispanic voters ran into harsh, vote-counting reality. Karl Rove, who had done much to increase expectation about
Republican efforts to attract Hispanic voters, nevertheless calculated
that any move that could be portrayed, correctly or not, as a legalization
of undocumented aliens would alienate the president's political base.
I assumed that Rove's major concern was the 2002 congressional elections. A president who had taken office with fewer popular votes than his
opponent could not afford to suffer the traditional mid-term loss in the
congressional vote. And immigration reform looked like a vote loser to
Rove.

When I traveled to Washington in the spring and summer of 2001,
I was struck by how stunted the internal debate was. One problem was
the difficulty of getting policymakers to understand the complexity of
immigration policy. The much amended and amazingly voluminous
Immigration and Nationality Act (INA) makes the U.S. tax code seem
like a case study in governmental clarity. The INA is the incomprehensible chasing the unenforceable through the thickets of confusion and
the narrow spaces of loopholes. It does not work, but it does provide an
excellent living for thousands of immigration lawyers and a harried existence for the government employees who try to make sense out of it.
Even Colin Powell, who was capable of understanding the most recon-
dite of governmental minutiae, would become glassy-eyed as Mary Ryan
would try to explain some arcane provision of the law. The secretary then
faced the truly daunting task of explaining it all at White House meetings with the president and other cabinet members, who were even less
capable of dealing with the complex issues.

There were other stumbling blocks. Several members of Congress,
mostly liberal Democrats, started to question why Mexico should be sin-
gled out for special treatment. After all, only about half of the nine or ten
million illegal aliens were from Mexico. Many congressional districts
were home to relatively few Mexicans but had large numbers of undocumented Central Americans, Haitians, or other nationalities. Why not
help them as well? This insistence on opening the gates even wider only
reinforced the conviction of many in the administration that the presi-

dent's magnanimity in Guanajuato had opened a Pandora's box filled with dangers, both of politics and policy.

While illegal immigration from other countries was certainly a significant issue, I joined others at the State Department in making the case for giving special attention to the problems of Mexican immigrants. In conversations with members of Congress and reporters I pointed out that migration was more important to our relationship with Mexico than with any other country. Mexico deserved a privileged treatment, we argued, because of its strong economic ties to the United States, its membership in NAFTA, and the simple fact that failure to address the problem would only worsen the challenges it presented to American law enforcement and society. This thinking led to a proposal that would principally help Mexicans but would also benefit immigrants from other countries. It concerned the millions of persons whose applications for permanent residence had been approved but who had to wait for years for the INS to issue the coveted green cards. Immigration law put yearly caps on those visas and also limited the number that could be given to citizens of any one country. The backlog was enormous and included about one million Mexicans, who were receiving green cards at a rate of less than one hundred thousand per year. But most of the applicants had jumped the line and were already living—illegally—in the United States.

The new idea, dubbed the North American Proposal, was to provide a special visa quota for our two NAFTA partners. Its backers noted that if Mexico received an annual quota of two hundred thousand, the backlog would be reduced and the number of technical illegals, i.e. those approved for residency but just waiting in the shadows for the papers to come through, would be lowered significantly. Additionally, others on the waiting list from countries other than Mexico would get to move up faster, thus speaking to the concerns of the congressional critics who wanted a universal, rather than a Mexico-specific, fix. It would not be the complete fix that Castañeda wanted, but it would be an important step nevertheless. It was so ambitious that it ran into stiff opposition from opponents who saw it as a disguised form of amnesty.

While State pushed its plan to give legal permanent status to more Mexicans, Justice and the DPC were intrigued by proposals for a broader temporary worker plan. The idea was to offer something new—"blue cards"—to two hundred thousand workers every year. The proposal raised major logistical problems. It would provide no guarantee that workers would be allowed to stay in the United States and, therefore, few immigrants would participate. Also, it would have to be administered by INS authorities, which were already swamped. And the proposed 200,000 were a drop in the bucket, given the total number of Mexicans already employed illegally in the country.

As the internal U.S. government debate continued through the spring of 2001, the Mexican side kept pushing for results. The cabinet-level commission had agreed to issue a preliminary report in July, but then the U.S. members backed out, claiming that a report would be premature and might raise false expectations. Meanwhile, the Mexicans' lobbyists in Washington kept Castañeda and company well informed about the intragovernmental conversations. The route of information appeared to be from White House participants in meetings, to friendly Hill staffers, to Mexican lobbyists (some of whom were former congressional staffers), to the Foreign Ministry—all in an elapsed time not exceeding six hours. I would usually hear the latest news about Washington discussions from Castañeda or someone else in the ministry before I would receive a report from Washington.

Castañeda did not like what he was hearing. He feared that Washington would opt for some quick fix, a partial solution that might look good politically in the United States, but not in Mexico. He pushed his single-undertaking concept. With the brash doggedness that was his style, he publicly insisted on the "whole enchilada" during a visit to Phoenix in late June. It sounded like an ultimatum and clanked like a broken bell in Washington. I had spent most of July in Washington and met with Powell just before returning to Mexico City. He gave me instructions to tell Castañeda that his pushiness was making the American secretary of state's job more difficult and would complicate the upcoming September state visit of President Fox to Washington.

I met with Castañeda in his office shortly after returning to Mexico City in early August. His lobbyists in Washington had certainly informed him of the heavy indigestion caused by the enchilada remark, so he knew what my message would be. In the no-nonsense style of discussing issues that we had developed since the time we first met during Fox's campaign, I told him frankly that it was a mistake to push so hard and that his public comments were raising expectations that would set the two presidents up for failure when they met again in September. I said he ought to listen to his lobbyists, who had to be telling him that the mood in Washington was demanding a go-slow approach. Castañeda gave as good as he got. He was frustrated and impatient. The momentum that he had built so carefully had been stalled. His dream of a triumphant immigration announcement during Fox's visit was slipping away.

I returned to my office and wrote a cable outlining the meeting. I also sent a separate back-channel message to the secretary of state, saying that we had to move in Castañeda's direction. Just eight months into his six-year term, Fox's presidency was stagnating and he was being labeled as a president who could not deliver. We needed to find a way, I suggested, to do something on the regularization front to help bolster Fox. A politically strong Fox could work with us more effectively not only on migration, but also on trade, law enforcement, and a host of other issues. It was in our interest to help him out. Friends in the secretary's office told me that he shared my back-channel message with Ashcroft and others. But the policy scene was just too confused for it to make a difference.

On August 9, Castañeda and Santiago Creel were in Washington again to meet with Powell and Ashcroft. I flew up for the talks. The two foreign secretaries met alone briefly before joining their colleagues. Powell reiterated the message he had sent through me the week before: slow down, we just cannot move too fast. Castañeda was gracious, seemed to understand, and after the larger meeting broke no new ground, he put on a good front for the press at the State Department entrance. We are making important progress to achieve a good agreement in whatever time frame is necessary, he gamely said. He even joked that although Mexico would not soon be eating the whole enchilada, maybe *chilaquiles* (day-old fried tortillas and sauce) would be on the menu. "The negotiation is very complex. We've never insisted on a deadline and we will not do so now," Castañeda said.

Secretary Powell accompanied Castañeda to the brief press conference. We're in no hurry, he said; we have to do this right. Powell observed that the two sides "began to flesh out some of the details of the ideas we have been looking at over the last several months." But lacking any specific agreement, he spoke in generalities, saying the two shared a commitment to a humane, family-friendly immigration policy. He indicated that some Mexicans who were illegally living in the United States but who had jobs and paid taxes could be part of an expanded temporary worker program. Somehow, the *New York Times* misunderstood. A headline in the August 10 issue was way off the mark as it erroneously declared "U.S.-Mexico Talks Produce Agreement on Immigration Policy." The story conveyed the misimpression that a deal on amnesty was imminent, and quoted a statement by State Department spokesman Richard Boucher that there was broad agreement in principle about what the two sides wanted to accomplish. But in reality that broad agreement had been reached six months earlier in Guanajuato, and there were really no new agreements on details.

Nevertheless, such a story in the *New York Times* was enough to make conservative Washington vibrate like a tuning fork, especially since the *Times* just a month earlier had run a front-page Sunday story declaring that President Bush's top immigration advisers were weighing plans to allow more than three million Mexicans living illegally in the United States to legalize their status. The story noted that many details of the plan were still unresolved. But the inaccurate suggestion that something big was in the air caused a fuss, leading some observers to conclude that the story had been a trial balloon sent up by the White House to take the Hill's measure. A more Machiavellian view was that the White House planted the story to cause problems so that President Bush could throw up his hands in dismay when President Fox came to Washington. The White House then told the press that while the president wanted change, it would have to be piecemeal and would have to wait until after the midterm elections of 2002.

The hyperactive Mexican information-gathering machine in Washington reported frenetically back to Mexico City throughout August. Castañeda asked me to his office to discuss a report he had received that President Bush might announce during Fox's state visit a new temporary worker program that would accommodate one hundred thousand Mexicans a year. The story might have been an echo of the temporary worker blue-card program that had been floated earlier. Castañeda said that if it was true it presaged disaster. He told me Fox would have to reject any move that did not address Mexico's principal concern, the regularization of the undocumented. Better to do nothing, he said. Three days later Fox asked me to visit him in his office, where he presented essentially the same message. If President Bush could not deal with the issue of the undocumented residents, it would be better to confine public statements to general framework approaches. We can wait, he said. There is no rush. Better nothing than something that will be seen here as negative. He said the same thing to reporters from the *Washington Post*, who duly reported that Fox "[expected] it will take four to six years to complete a comprehensive U.S.-Mexico immigration reform."

Fox thus set the background on migration for his visit to Washington from September 5 to 7. For Bush, the visit was intended to be a demonstration of the importance his administration placed on the friendship with Mexico and its new president. There would be an elaborate welcome on the South Lawn of the White House with a military honor guard, a twenty-one-gun salute and colonial-era fifes and drums. Bush was pulling out all the ceremonial stops for the first state visit of his presidency.

Then Fox, facing new pressure at home, dropped a rhetorical bomb. His comment that there was no rush had been distorted in the Mexican press as indicating that he was giving up his quest for an immigration agreement. So Castañeda quickly rewrote the protocol-heavy speech Fox was to deliver at the welcoming ceremony. He put in language that came out sounding like an ultimatum. "We must and we can, reach an agreement on migration before the end of this very year," Fox declared. That looked great in the Mexican press, where Fox appeared as the bold leader making demands on the U.S. president. But it surprised the hell out of the White House and me. In effect, Fox had set a new, completely unrealistic deadline after having just acknowledged the need to move slowly and carefully. The White House was upset by Fox's rhetoric, but the desire to make the visit a success was so great that there was no public backlash.

When the two presidents sat down to discuss immigration, their conversation was disjointed and incomplete. Neither man demonstrated a good grasp of the details of the complicated issues involved. They talked past each other. Bush did make it clear that he would have to move more slowly, as there was no consensus on reform in Congress. In what was an apparent reference to the blue-card proposal, he talked about a new temporary-worker program. In what appeared to me to be an evolution in White House thinking, he noted in passing that it could offer the opportunity for some illegal aliens already in the United States to become permanent legal residents.

However, Bush did not explain the still-skeletal plan well. Fox was clearly more interested in the regularization aspect of the idea than in the temporary-work scheme. He asked President Bush how many people would be involved. Bush, not capturing the intent of Fox's question, responded that he was thinking of two hundred thousand. He was referring, however, to the number who would participate as temporary workers, not those (certainly a much smaller quantity) who might ultimately pass through the program on the way to becoming legal permanent residents. Fox, not understanding Bush and still thinking that his American counterpart was talking about those who could become legal residents each year, said that two hundred thousand was too few; five hundred thousand would make more sense. The conversation continued awkwardly and then moved on to other topics with no real understandings reached.

The conversation indicated just how little had been accomplished in the immigration discussions since the heady days of the Guanajuato meeting. A few days later, the events of September 11 forced the United States to turn its attention elsewhere. It later became conventional wisdom in Washington and Mexico City to assert that the two governments might have reached an understanding on immigration if the terrorists had not struck. But this is not an accurate reflection of the likely possibilities at the time of the state visit. The Bush team had realized soon after Guanajuato that it had stumbled into a political minefield. In the first year of the Bush presidency, won in a contested election, and with congressional elections looming in 2002, the president's team decided not to risk support among his political base by developing a dramatic new plan on immigration.

In the aftermath of the attacks, U.S. attitudes about foreigners and borders darkened. In early 2002, a time when some in the United States were proposing to register all foreigners, Castañeda returned to Washington to tell Secretary Powell that the idea could fit nicely into prior thinking about regularization of Mexicans. Of course, he meant that once they came forward and registered, they should be allowed to stay in the United States. Powell did not take the bait, and when the time came for the U.S. side to respond, he turned to Mary Ryan and let her do the talking. That gesture itself was a powerful sign.

Each secretary of state has his own style of handling conversations with foreign leaders. Powell's was to engage them in easy conversation. Always well briefed before any meeting, he rarely referred to notes or asked others on his side to take a leading role. The image he conveyed was of a man totally in charge and totally knowledgeable. By asking Ryan to respond to Castañeda, he was sending a clear message: it was not yet time to reinitiate high-level discussions. He was not engaged. The country was at war.

But the immigration debate within the administration did not cease. It moved in fits and starts into 2002. As the White House prepared for President Bush's trip to the March UN development summit in Monterrey, Secretary Powell met with Ashcroft and Secretary of Labor Elaine Chao. The three agreed to recommend that the president ask Congress to reinitiate a little-known but important section of the Immigration and Nationality Act that had lapsed. Section 245(i) allowed immigrants who had been approved for residency to stay in the United States while their visas were processed. That was an enormous concession for those who would otherwise be expected to return to their home country and wait for the local American consulate to issue the visa. Immigrants much preferred to pay the thousand-dollar processing fee instead of the costs of a trip to their native country, where there was always the possibility that the consular officer might find a reason not to issue an immigrant visa.

The secretaries' conversation, obviously meant to be private, was well reported to the Mexican lobbyists within hours. And soon the government of Mexico took the nearly astonishing step of formally informing me that they wanted the president to stop his efforts in favor of 245(i). Castañeda called me on March 8, less than two days after the three cabinet members had met, to tell us not to waste our time on pushing for the reinstitution of 245(i). Then he had Undersecretary Berruga inform me in a letter that 245(i) was not a central topic of interest in the context of the migration negotiations. The Mexicans obviously feared that the White House was trying to use action on 245(i) as a way of showing that it was "doing something" on immigration without really addressing the Mexicans' most critical concerns. Several hundred thousand Mexican families that would have benefited from the president's proposal were injured by their own government's tactical decision not to help them.

The Bush administration was quietly furious at the Mexican decision and Mexico's efforts to get Democrats on the Hill to kill the president's initiative. But there was no public blowup. And in Monterrey the two presidents publicly committed to continuing the high-level talks on migration. But privately President Bush expressed displeasure with the position that Hill Democrats were taking. They come here and talk a good game, he told Fox, referring to the trip Daschle and Gephardt had taken to Mexico, but back at home they don't deliver. They won't even help me on 245(i). Ultimately, Republican conservatives and unhelpful Democrats who took their cues from Mexico City killed the 245(i) extension.

In the thirteen months from Guanajuato to Monterrey the two governments had come face to face with old realities and—after September 11—new challenges. Castañeda's "grand bargain" on migration was simply not possible. The need for change in U.S. immigration law and policies remained but would have to wait for another opportunity.

In January 2004, as he was preparing to meet Fox at yet another international conference in Monterrey, Mexico, President Bush announced the outlines of a new temporary-worker program. Fox's initial response to the Bush plan was highly favorable, reflecting his desire to obtain at least some victory in the tangled immigration picture. His seeming endorsement of the Bush idea engendered criticism of him in Mexico for apparently accepting much less than half an enchilada. President Bush's suggestion was criticized as an election-year ploy to attract Hispanic voters, but it did constitute the first public endorsement of a significant immigration policy reform by an American president in almost two decades. Observers assumed that the congressional and public debate on the Bush initiative could take years.

C
H
A
P
T
E
R

T
W
E
N
T
Y

The End of the Honeymoon

I thought that we would leave Mexico in the summer of 2001. Three years is the usual tour for an American ambassador, and we had arrived in 1998. I had assumed that whichever of the two candidates—Gore or Bush—won the 2000 election, the new president would want to send a new ambassador, probably a noncareer person, to Mexico. But immediately after he took office in January 2001, President Bush asked me to stay for a fourth year, that is, until the summer of 2002. Four years would be more time than I had spent in any one location since I was twenty-one years old. But when one is a disciplined member of the Foreign Service, a request from the president is more than a request. Like Don Corleone, he makes offers that cannot be refused. We continued to enjoy living in Mexico, but from September 11 onward, the job became less satisfying, and in some ways more frustrating.

One element of the mounting criticism of Fox was that his vaunted friendship with President Bush had produced no benefits for Mexico. This view was naïve, mercenary, and uninformed. Naïve, because it assumed that an amicable relationship with the United States, in and of itself, was of little benefit to Mexico. This ignored the fact that Mexico's stature in the world depends heavily upon the perception that it is an integral member of a harmonious North American community. Mercenary, because it reduced friendship and comity to a quid pro quo bargaining enterprise. And ill informed, because it ignored the fact that the American government, taking its cue from President Bush himself, had responded to the Fox administration with numerous examples of confidence, support, and assistance.

The impression that the relationship was not producing benefits fit well into the predisposition to believe that Mexico was getting the short end of the stick and was encouraged, inadvertently or not, by Fox and his foreign secretary. Castañeda had abandoned the Flower Wars rhetoric. He talked openly about working with the United States, and because this was a new approach, the public assumed that the level of Mexican cooperation had markedly increased. In fact, much of the cooperation had existed for a long time, but the PRI had obscured it so as not to be portrayed as too friendly to the gringos. The misperception was aggravated by the continual criticism of the United States coming from Fox and Castañeda, who complained about the failure to move ahead on an immigration agreement. I understood and empathized with their concern, but felt that the constant references to the problem only embittered important political actors in the United States and contributed to the Mexican popular perception of Fox as an ineffectual leader.

The assertion that Mexico had received nothing from the Bush administration was simply wrong. Indeed, relations with the United States had improved to Mexico's benefit. In the wake of Fox's election victory, the U.S. Congress eliminated the insulting certification process, and U.S. law enforcement's confidence in its Mexican counterparts reached a new high. This permitted Mexican authorities to achieve some considerable successes. The arrest of Mexico's most wanted drug lord, Benjamín Arellano, only a few days after the shooting death of his brother Ramón, was a major achievement. The Mexican military deserved credit for the arrest. But, in part, the successes were the result of information that U.S. authorities had passed to their Mexican colleagues.

On the commercial side, some long-standing trade disputes involving sugar, cement, and tuna remained deadlocked. But the Bush administration opened more U.S. markets to Mexican agricultural products, and was moving as rapidly as electoral politics allowed to open the border to long-haul Mexican trucks. The new Partnership for Prosperity, announced during Fox's visit to Washington in September 2001, promoted several specific improvements in the economic relationship. For the first time the United States accepted a role in promoting economic development in Mexico beyond NAFTA-generated growth. When President Bush announced new temporary tariffs on imported steel, he specifically exempted Mexican and Canadian exporters, recognizing the special place that the two countries held in America's commercial relations.

On the immigration front, there was some progress, despite the absence of an agreement. Life was improving for some of the undocumented. Taking their lead from President Bush's continual professions of friendship, many state and local governments softened their restrictive policies. An ambitious Mexican program to provide identity cards to citizens abroad received increasing acceptance among American public authorities, including local police forces. Many banks accepted the new documents, allowing illegal migrants to open accounts for the inexpensive dispatch of funds back to Mexico. In some areas the cards also helped undocumented aliens obtain driver's licenses or access to higher education. Some in the U.S. government expressed concern about the reliability of the cards as identity documents. But, for the most part, the *matriculas consulares*—as the ID cards were called—were a success.

Even in the sensitive area of homeland security, a generally favorable attitude toward Mexico helped limit some of the negative effects on the border of post–September 11 security measures. From the outset, the attitude of the U.S. government as voiced by President Bush and by Governor Tom Ridge, his point man on homeland security, was that the two countries had to find a way to maximize security without strangling the flow of goods and people across the border. And though crossing problems on the border did increase, the overwhelming attitude at the top of the U.S. government toward Mexico was friendly and accommodating. While some Mexican voices asserted that the country should trade security cooperation with the United States for an immigration deal, the Fox administration wisely never seriously considered such a move. The post–September 11 mood in the United States was so anxious that public opinion would have fiercely demanded rejection of such a proposal.

Fox designated Secretary of Interior Santiago Creel to be Ridge's counterpart. Creel relied heavily on the chief of the national intelligence service, CISEN, Eduardo Medina Mora, for day-to-day contact with American authorities. And there was a great deal of it. The governments quickly agreed to improve cooperation at border crossings. The two customs services increased the exchange of information. Mexican authorities rapidly responded to U.S. security alerts.

It is true that while Washington was dealing with Mexico as a cooperative ally in the war against terror, American actions on the border were having a negative effect. The U.S.-Mexico border was crossed nearly one million times a day by 2002. North to south, south to north, often several times by the same person, the movement was endless and intense. The net effect of September 11 on the border was to give the INS, Customs, and the Border Patrol a free hand, which they used to tighten procedures. Terrorism was the justification, but in reality the targets were the familiar ones: narcotics and illegal aliens. The average search time for an automobile went from twenty seconds to more than a minute. Waiting times for pedestrians and automobiles increased significantly, with waits of two hours or more becoming customary. The incremental effect on delays for truck traffic was less severe because the economic downturn in both countries reduced freight shipments. Those who had to cross to the north to visit family or doctors or, in the case of several border communities, to work on the other side, began lining up well before dawn. But many for whom crossing was discretionary stopped making the trip.

The principal victim of the continuing crackdown was the special life of *la frontera*. Fewer U.S. residents wanted to go south when they knew they would have to wait in line for hours to cross back over. And fewer Mexicans were inclined to put up with the long waits, if they could avoid them. The economies of border towns on both sides suffered precipitous drops. Still, though there was no indication that terrorists had ever used Mexico to enter the United States, appropriate vigilance was necessary. But the special and appealing culture of the region, neither entirely Mexican nor entirely American, but a unique blend, was damaged, perhaps forever.

In the embassy we were frustrated by our inability to convey to the Mexican public that the bilateral relation was good, getting better, and bringing benefits to Mexico. For instance, during one week that was intense but by no means unusual, we announced a new fifty-million-dollar scholarship program for Mexican university students, three million dollars in grants to finance feasibility studies for port development, upcoming meetings of the binational commissions on border safety and the Partnership for Prosperity, and visits by three U.S. governors who would be accompanied by large commercial delegations looking to do business in Mexico. But little of this registered with the Mexican press, which remained obsessed with the notion that the United States was not returning Mexico's affection. Much of the Mexican media was incapable of seeing the relationship as anything other than a melodrama in which Uncle Sam was the bad guy and Mexico his victim. That was its story and it stuck with it, despite mounting evidence to the contrary.

The criticism that President Fox obtained nothing from his friendship with President Bush reached a climax in April 2002 when the Mexican Congress denied him permission to travel to the United States. It was not the first time that the Congress had invoked its constitutional authority in this manner. In 1999, when a recalcitrant Congress threatened to deny permission to President Zedillo to travel to the United States as it tried to shake more budget concessions out of him, Zedillo withdrew his request. But Fox did not withdraw his, and an alliance of PRI and PRD legislators killed the trip. In reality, the congressional hostility was aimed more at Castañeda than at his boss. The foreign secretary had angered Congress by refusing to appear at committee hearings. The opposition wanted its pound of flesh and chose to take it by denying Fox the right to go to the United States and Canada.

The PRI's bill of particulars against Fox was interesting less for the validity of the charges than for the reflection of traditional Mexican oldthink about the dangers of getting too close to the United States. Fox was accused of reaching agreements with the United States on post–September 11 border security that violated Mexico's sovereignty. The charge was false. There were no formal agreements, and the informal plans to cooperate in no way challenged Mexican sovereignty. Reflecting suspicions that the United States had dictated the treatment of Castro in Monterrey, but not yet privy to the full story that would be revealed by the telephone transcript, PRI critics accused Fox of pursuing a "confused" policy toward Cuba. Fox was also criticized for allowing the Mexican Navy to participate in a hemispheric training exercise with the U.S. and other navies. And, ironically, he was attacked for not defending strongly enough the rights of immigrants in the United States.

When Fox finally made the trip a month later, he responded to the political opposition in a distressing manner. At a May speech to business leaders in New York, he issued what seemed to be another ultimatum. His language was almost identical to words Castañeda had used a few weeks earlier in a little-noted California speech. Fox's words (written by Castañeda) lacked the necessary fingertip appreciation of the American mood. They demonstrated the same insensitivity that had produced the "whole enchilada" outburst and other unfortunate comments. "There cannot be a privileged relationship between the United States and Mexico without a real advance in substantive affairs in our bilateral agenda," he said. "And there cannot be a substantive advance without addressing, in an integral way, the theme of migration."

For Americans, the implications of Fox's words were stunning. He seemed to be saying that the special relationship between Mexico and the United States could no longer exist. Fox and Castañeda had managed to reduce the entire relationship to one variable: progress on an immigration accord. It was as much of a mistake as the one many in the United States had made for years by centering the entire binational relationship on the single issue of narcotics. Mexico and the United States had a lot more to deal with than migration or narcotics. To ignore that was a mistake.

By the time of the Fox New York speech, I was preparing for my departure from Mexico. President Bush had named Tony Garza, a young, attractive Texas Hispanic Republican, to succeed me. Freed of some inhibitions by my imminent departure, I let the word filter to the press that I had told Castañeda that I thought the focus on immigration was becoming unproductive. It may be a mark of my own personal denseness, but I never quite understood why Fox followed Castañeda and continued to use the theme. When most politicians are confronted by a problem that they cannot quickly resolve, they begin downplaying it so as not to draw attention to their inability to deal with it. The politically ambitious Castañeda had his personal reasons for pushing the topic, but Fox adopted the stance of aggrieved suitor as his own. That was a mistake.

The perception that the Fox-Bush relationship had cooled was reinforced in June 2002 when Fox canceled a long-scheduled visit to Texas. Once again he painted himself into a corner. The facts before him were straightforward. A Mexican citizen convicted of murder was scheduled for execution. There was no question about his guilt, but his lawyers argued that when arrested he was not given the opportunity, guaranteed by international treaty, to call the Mexican consul and ask for help. The lawyers correctly noted that consular notification is an important obligation.

Fox made every effort to convince Texas Governor Perry to spare the convict's life. He did so frequently, publicly, and vociferously. Of course this was popular with the Mexican public. But Fox had other options he could have used without diminishing his government's advocacy. He could have, for instance, pushed Castañeda or his attorney general out front on the issue. Perry, about to enter the height of his reelection campaign, could not comply. Fox cancelled his visit. Again, by making the issue his own and converting it into a cause célèbre, Fox robbed himself of flexibility. Canceling the trip became inevitable, but only because Fox made it so.

Another motive for canceling the Texas trip was the unresolved issue of Rio Grande water. This was the first theme President Bush had raised at the Guanajuato meeting fifteen months earlier, when the two presidents had revealed themselves to be mathematically challenged. But there had been no significant progress in the interim, and the farmers in South Texas were angry as hell. They had a right to be. Mexico's performance for years had been deficient to the point of outrageousness. For more than a decade Mexico had annually delivered less than half the water from the Rio Grande to Texas reservoirs than it was obliged to send by an international treaty. The Texas farmers demanded that Mexico pay its liquid debt. Their anger was magnified by the widespread and accurate perception north of the border that Mexico was taking a disproportionate share of the admittedly drought-reduced flow.

After the Guanajuato meeting, U.S. and Mexican negotiators worked out an agreement guaranteeing partial deliveries by the end of July or, in case of adverse weather, by the end of September 2001. But Mexico reneged once again. By June 2002 the political heat had risen measurably on both sides. Fox was facing open rebellion on the issue from the governors of several of Mexico's northern states. For the PRI governors, attacking the central PAN government for trying to send a vital natural resource to the gringos was an issue made in heaven. PAN governors were no more helpful, if a bit less confrontational. The U.S. ambassador was pilloried in the press for suggesting that Mexico was not as dry as it claimed. I pushed the idea that the spirit of the treaty demanded an equitable sharing of resources no matter how reduced the quantity might be.

As in the immigration issue, public and political opinion were unwilling to recognize that the United States might have legitimate interests and concerns. Public opinion also ignored the hard facts of law, in this case a treaty obligation. The Mexicans were acting with as little sensitivity and as much arrogance as they normally associated with the American style of operation.

Mexico delivered no water to Texas during all of 2002. The approach of the Bush administration throughout this period was remarkably sensitive to Fox's predicament. Obviously, Washington wanted to help Texas, but at the same time it did not want to add to Fox's domestic problems. It ignored demands emanating from Texas that the U.S. reduce the flow of Colorado River water to Mexico—also covered by the same treaty—until Mexico loosened up on its northward deliveries of Rio Grande water to Texas.

In some ways, Fox's inability to carry through on his good intentions about water paralleled President Bush's difficulty in making change in the immigration scene. Both presidents understood that the policies of their respective countries were unproductive and unresponsive to the other's needs. But their mobility was limited by the political straitjackets they inherited. Unwilling or unable to confront strong domestic political forces and negative public opinion, both chose not to risk their political capital. Neither was able to deliver.

Relations with the United States were also complicated by Mexico's posture in the United Nations Security Council. At Castañeda's urging, Fox announced on the day of his inauguration that he intended to seek a two-year seat for Mexico on the fifteen-member Council. The Dominican Republic had been well on its way to becoming Latin America's consensus candidate. But when Mexico entered the fray, the Dominicans were overwhelmed. Fox's decision was a major shift from Mexico's traditional wariness about membership on the Security Council.

While Mexico had held a Council seat early in the UN's history, it had avoided membership for many years in order not to place itself in the position where friction with the United States in a multilateral forum could translate into bilateral conflict. In 1981 other Latin American countries convinced Mexico to take a seat as a compromise when

Colombia and Cuba were at daggers drawn and neither would give up its candidacy. In terms of U.S.-Mexico relations, its tenure was a disaster. Mexico's flamboyant, uncontrollable, and leftist UN ambassador, Porfirio Muñoz Ledo, engaged in mortal combat with Ronald Reagan's representative, the ultraconservative Jean Kirkpatrick. That tension increased the already considerable ill will between Reagan and President Lopez Portillo during the latter's final years in office. The Mexican foreign secretary at the time was Jorge Castañeda, Sr., the father of Fox's new foreign minister.

Despite what was clearly a difficult chapter in his father's career, the young Castañeda wanted to risk Security Council membership again. A seat on the council would burnish Mexico's global stature, and Castañeda believed that, as the world's tenth-largest economy and most populous Spanish-speaking nation, Mexico deserved a brighter place in the international sun. A two-year stay on the Security Council would also give the new Fox administration the opportunity to pursue an ambitious human rights agenda. And perhaps most importantly, the United States would have to take Mexico more seriously. Castañeda focused more on the benefits that Mexico might obtain from greater visibility than on the potential negatives. Perhaps he thought that Mexico could trade its Security Council vote for a particularly favorable payoff from the United States, a new immigration agreement, for example. He was wrong.

It was a risky gamble. Although Fox and Castañeda were not as encumbered with foreign ministry old-think as had been their predecessors, they still embraced their nation's traditional values and concepts. Moreover, the foreign policy elite of Mexico within the ministry, the press, Congress, and academia had not lost its inherent suspicion of U.S. motives and its fervent dedication to anti-interventionism. Castañeda was playing the game with limited running room on a rough field. His problems multiplied when Fox named Adolfo Aguilar Zínser as ambassador to the United Nations.

Aguilar Zínser had been unhappy and ineffective in his job as coordinator of national security. He wanted out. At first, Castañeda suggested sending him to New York, but then dramatically changed his mind when Aguilar Zínser agreed that it would be a good move. Perhaps Castañeda felt that giving Aguilar, a powerful writer and speaker, the New York pulpit would reduce his own primacy in foreign affairs. He may also have realized that, in his outspokenness and unpredictability, Aguilar Zínser resembled Muñoz Ledo, who had caused so many problems for his father. Castañeda may have changed his mind because the decades-long friendship between the two men fell apart. Or maybe the relationship dissolved because he had changed his mind.

In any case, their personal turbulence had public implications. In late 2001 Castañeda was going through a difficult personal transition involving a divorce. Aguilar Zínser, who had known both Castañeda and his wife for decades, offered his views and somehow insulted his old friend. Their friendship fell apart in a very public manner. Castañeda fought his ex-friend's nomination to New York, but a loyal Fox insisted on rewarding the man who had played a crucial role in his campaign and election. Castañeda then decided that he would never speak to the new ambassador again. For the next year, the foreign minister of Mexico spoke not one word to his ambassador to the United Nations. Needless to say, coordination problems abounded. This left Aguilar Zínser with a freer hand than he should have been given. Naturally excitable, he exacerbated tension with the United States by his overly aggressive approach. When he purposefully sought a high-visibility role in thwarting the U.S. effort to gain UN support for the 2003 attack on Iraq, relations between the two governments reached a low point not witnessed in years.

As I prepared to leave Mexico in September 2002 after four years at the embassy, I met separately with Fox and Castañeda. I knew that over the years I had aggravated them on several occasions. But both were aware of my affection for Mexico and my strong desire to improve bilateral relations. Both were their most charming selves in our good-bye meetings. I met with Fox in his inner office in Los Pinos. There was no indication of any chill in the relationship, and he was abundantly generous in thanking me for always trying to understand the Mexican position. He expressed the intention to maintain close ties with the United States and to push for improvements. My last meeting with Fox reminded me of the time almost four years earlier when he was just gaining strength as the likely PAN candidate. This was a decent man, representing the very best of the Mexican character.

Castañeda dropped by the house for a final drink. He made it clear that he wanted to leave his job. He was resigned to the fact that an immigration agreement was unlikely. There would be no crowning achievement, no Castañeda Plan that would go down in Mexican history. I was sorry to hear that he wanted to go. He had fallen into many errors of judgment and rhetoric. He was never able to shed all of the intellectual baggage of the left and academia. He overstated his own importance. He frequently saw international relations through an overly simplistic and conspiratorial prism. But he had done much to bring a new honesty and clarity of purpose to Mexico's international position. He broke with ingrained tradition and ignored established shibboleths. He saw the direct link between international and domestic policy and acted upon it. He sought a new relevance and centrality for Mexico in the world. Regrettably, in doing so he had also managed to annoy many in Mexico City and Washington.

Castañeda talked openly about moving over to the Ministry of Interior or to the Ministry of Education. The first move would have forced Fox to remove Santiago Creel, his best link to the PAN, on the eve of a congressional election year. Impossible. Castañeda probably saw the Ministry of Education as a place where he could get wide publicity, travel throughout the country, establish new coalitions with political and labor forces, and prepare for his own presidential candidacy. But Fox, ever unwilling to change his cabinet, refused Castañeda's requests. In January 2003 Fox finally accepted his resignation. In his comments to the press, Castañeda cited his disappointment over the lack of an immigration agreement with the United States as the principal cause for leaving government.

Joan and I said good-bye to Mexico in September 2002 with the traditional flurry of *despedidas*—farewells. We held one of them for ourselves. Friends at the Ballet Folklórico of Mexico sent a large group of dancers and musicians to entertain more than one thousand guests. The dancers' presence underlined our appreciation and respect for Mexico's culture. We were sorry to leave. So much remained unfinished. But four years was a good run, and it was time to move on. Much of the effervescence and sense of possibilities that had buoyed the relationship as the two new presidents met at Guanajuato had dissipated. But the chill at the end of the honeymoon was still much warmer than the frigid Casablanca weather I had found on my arrival. Each government maintained a firm appreciation for the importance of the other. Both presidents remained committed to finding ways to bring their nations closer together. But all involved had learned that this was going to be far more difficult than either had imagined.

E
P
I
L
O
G
U
E

2025

"Dios mío," President González mumbled under his breath. He was worried. "That Canadian son of a bitch." He was also angry. His morning intelligence brief had confirmed his suspicions. Prime Minister LeBlanc was about to renege on promises to him and, instead, cut a deal with Canada's small Green Party. The Greens would trade votes on the budget in return for Le Blanc's dropping his request that the Parliament approve the entry of the five countries of Central America into the North American Union. The Greens viewed those nations as an ecological disaster zone. All the more reason, González thought, to get them inside the great North American tent.

The Canadian's gambit was understandable in terms of LeBlanc's domestic politics, but devastating nevertheless. Four years of González's efforts to give equal status to Central America could come crashing down. He was upset. "Two can play this game," he thought and called his aide. "Juan, set up a Los Pinos–White House phone call."

González took the call on the secure red phone in his back office, the one the press and public never saw. There he kept his collection of valuable Spanish colonial snuffboxes and a statue of the Virgin of Guadalupe, his mother's Inaugural Day gift. She had taken it with her from her small village in Jalisco, and certainly had never imagined it would someday grace a president's office.

The two presidents—of Mexico and the United States—discussed how they would handle the Canadian's perfidy. The conversation moved easily back and forth between English and Spanish. Finally the two agreed on a plan. They would issue a joint public statement urging the Canadian parliament to fulfill the dream of one North America from the Yukon to Darien. Both would make private phone calls to LeBlanc offering support. González would offer to make a state visit to Canada just before the next Canadian election. Not by coincidence, he would meet with LeBlanc in Toronto, which had become North America's fifth-largest Spanish-speaking city after all borders were opened in 2012. His colleague suggested that the two presidents instruct their representatives in the North American Parliament to increase their contributions for environmental assistance to Central America by 500 million vespuccis (1 vespucci = 1 U.S. dollar). González agreed. As the conversation neared an end, the two complained jokingly about their schedules for the remainder of the day.

President González walked back into the Oval Office to continue his schedule of events.

A U.S. president named González? Possible? Yes. A common currency? Open borders? A North American Parliament? A large Spanish-speaking community in Canada? It is too soon to tell. In 1979 a North American Free Trade Agreement seemed impossible to me. The world changes, options develop, the impractical becomes the logical, the inconceivable emerges as the commonplace. Doors should be left open, not closed.

The factors weighing against a North American Union are obvious. North America is not Western Europe. For advocates of convergence, the EU is a seductively successful role model. But in reality, it does not offer true parallels. Most obviously, North America lacks the most significant impetus for the process that ultimately led to the EU's creation: the two devastating twentieth-century continental wars that scared Western Europe to its senses. Further, the relative parity of the anchor economies of the United Kingdom, France, Germany, Italy, and, to a lesser degree, the Benelux countries, is absent. The gross domestic product of the United States is about twenty times Mexico's and seven times Canada's. Finally, it would be difficult to find three contiguous nations more concerned about protecting their own sovereignties. Of course, nationalism existed and exists in Europe, but it is of a different type. Mexicans and Canadians define themselves substantially in terms of their opposition to American cultural and economic domination. The nationalism of the United States basks in a sense of uniqueness and largely ignores its neighbors. In sum, the three nations are not yet a team suited up and waiting to take to the field together.

But there are other factors, some not yet visible, some only dimly perceived, that support the belief that a greater level of convergence is inevitable and advisable. Inevitable, because that is the direction that current forces—economic, cultural, and demographic—are pushing the three countries. Advisable, because greater integration will bring all three countries the benefits of cementing our economic base in this hemisphere, while we confront greater bloc economies in Europe and Asia. Integration will also make us more cosmopolitan—less torn by our ethnic divisions and more comfortable on a global stage. And we will be better able to confront the problems that do not respect borders—disease, drugs, crime, and environmental degradation.

What can be done? The simple answer is that we should get serious. The amount of noble rhetoric over the last fifteen years produced by the leaders of the three nations of North America about our joint future could easily fill a volume—not necessarily one that anyone would want to read, but a volume nevertheless. But words and pledges, if not backed up by conscientious effort, will lead to little change. Numerous studies and commissions have made endless recommendations. Some are impractical, either too complicated or well beyond the carrying capacity of the current political context. However, other suggestions make sense. The near-term goal should be to build a stronger institutional framework, a thicker rope that will tie us together. In doing so, we would keep ourselves open to the possibilities of the uncharted future. The following is just a small selection of steps that could be taken now, if sufficient political will existed. We could:

• Adopt the North American visa proposal that would create special, larger quotas for Mexicans and Canadians waiting for their documents as legal U.S. permanent residents.

• Recognize that the U.S. service economy is heavily dependent on foreign labor and raise the currently unrealistic numerical caps on non-agricultural temporary workers.

• Make the current program for temporary agricultural workers less onerous for employers and more attractive to workers.

• Revamp the current method for trade dispute resolution, which is often misused to avoid solutions and enables governments to ignore or endlessly challenge the decisions of arbitration panels.

• State as a policy goal the creation of a customs union with common external tariffs. This could begin with industry-wide agreements. Iron and steel are likely candidates for an initial agreement.

• Adopt common tactics and goals for the ongoing negotiations for a Free Trade Area of the Americas, which are scheduled for completion in 2005.

• Create a financial stabilization fund with contributions from the three governments to be drawn upon in case of serious exchange rate fluctuation.

• Expand the area of control of the current binational body that manages border rivers to give it executive control over those rivers' watersheds.

• Adopt continental minimum standards for air quality, toxic waste disposal, and management of nuclear materials within one hundred miles of borders.

• Broaden the mandate of the existing North American Development Bank and the Border Environmental Cooperation Commission to cover financing of irrigation and water management schemes.

• Create a fund to be managed by the three governments for developmental projects in the poorest sections of each country.

• Establish common visa issuance policies for citizens of countries outside of North America to facilitate travel, tourism, and security.

• Jointly plan and fund international highways, border crossing points, and ports.

• Develop a North American electrical grid and facilitate the permitting procedures for cross-border electricity lines and gas and oil pipelines.

• Pass legislation making extradition automatic when a North American government requests that one of its citizens be returned to face a criminal charge.

• Create a joint legislative commission with the obligation to hold hearings and legislate separately on common issues.

• Form a government-financed North American Research Institute to study joint problems and recommend policy options.

Most of these steps would require legislation in each of the countries. Some, such as the monetary stabilization and economic development funds, would obviously benefit Mexico more than the other two and thus might be challenged by opponents as give-away programs. Others would require the ceding of some degree of national sovereignty, and, as such, could be easily attacked by foes waving the bloody banner of nationalism. Necessary for the completion of all or some would be a firm political commitment of each of the governments to a greater level of North American integration. It is a commitment that has, as yet, not gone beyond rhetoric.

But even with political commitment, a greater level of integration will depend heavily on Mexico's ability to grow its economy and narrow the gap between its standard of living and that of its wealthy northern neighbors. That progress, in turn, will depend on its ability to maintain competitiveness, attract foreign investment, and use its own resources productively. In recent years, hundreds of businesses have closed factories in Mexico and moved their production to China or other countries where wages are lower. That loss made some Mexicans bemoan rising hourly wage costs, though, in truth, they had not increased significantly in a decade. In any event, the answer for Mexico is not to try to compete with China's wages.

But Mexico must trim the costs of other elements of production. Those costs are now too high even by world standards. Insufficient ports, highways, and border-crossing points coupled with high gasoline and diesel costs make transportation expensive. The lack of competition in electricity supply keeps that expense elevated as well. Truck hijackings, kidnappings of executives, and robberies at plants make security an onerous expense. The convoluted legal system also exacts its toll, frequently making the paper costs of doing business—contracts, deeds, building permits—exorbitant. But even if these deficiencies were addressed, Mexico would still need many more better educated workers at all levels. The key to economic success in the modern world is not low wages. It is trained workers and well-educated scientists, inventors, administrators, and engineers who introduce technological innovation. Mexico is short in all categories.

Certainly, the public and private sectors of Canada and the United States could help confront all of the above deficiencies. But, in the end, it will fall to Mexico to get its house in order. The irony is that open borders will only come into being when the pressure to cross them decreases. Foreign and domestic investment will flow more powerfully to productive activities only after the causes of stagnation are dealt with.

Indeed, many of the reforms for which Fox could not find political support were designed to increase competition, lower costs, and give the government more resources to build the human and physical infrastructure the country will need to compete in the future. The failure of the Mexican political system to face the looming reality of the future is putting the country at risk. It is also limiting the possibilities for North American integration, as is the generalized lack of vision about North America in the United States and Canada. It is one thing to mess up the present. That is not uncommon and all governments do it sometimes. But it is unforgivable to deny opportunities to the future.

The preceding suggestions for action are only a few of those that have been discussed in recent years. Some may make sense. Some may not. At base, what is most necessary is that the political leaders of North America offer a unified vision of the future to their citizens. The vision need not be complete in every detail, but it should offer the hope of a future in which the three countries live their individual national lives in greater cooperation with their neighbors. This will mean that the porcupine will have to act less like a porcupine and the bear will have to act less like a bear.

Index

Agee, Phillip 106
Aguilar Zínser, Adolfo 103, 142, 164, 171–72, 192, 241–42
Albright, Madeleine 21–22, 24, 26–27, 31, 36, 39, 102, 109–11, 177, 197
Álvarez Macháin 60, 82
Andrews, David 42
Arana Osorio, Carlos 131
Arellano, Benjamín 173, 234
Arellano, Ramón 234
Ashcroft, John 172, 204, 223, 227, 231

Babbitt, Bruce 42
Baker, James 141, 143, 210
Barros, José Luis 37, 103
Bartlett Díaz, Manuel 72, 76–77, 136, 167
Batista, Fulgencio 98
Bentsen, Lloyd 210–11
Berger, Sandy 19–22, 134
Berruga, Enrique 202–203, 231
Bin Laden, Osama 4
Boucher, Richard 228
Brayshaw, Charles 23, 39
Bush, George H. W. 82, 115, 211
Bush, George W. 1, 4–6, 9–11, 174, 182–85, 198–205, 211, 216–217, 220–221, 228–235, 237–240, 255
Bush, Jeb 181, 188

Calderón Hinojosa, Felipe 134
Camarena, Enrique 59–60, 76, 82, 89
Canales, Enrique 14–15
Capetillo-Ponce, Jorge 63
Card, Andy 146
Cárdenas, Cuauhtémoc 69, 70, 72, 75–76, 78–79, 133, 137, 144, 167, 177, 193

Cárdenas, President Lázaro 166
Cárdenas, Senator Lázaro 193
Cárdenas Guillén, Osiel 88–89, 173
Carrillo Fuentes, Amado 62
Carter, Jimmy 104, 142–43
Carter, Lee 155
Castañeda, Jorge 3, 18, 34, 37, 103, 117, 142, 161–63, 169, 175–84, 186, 192–93, 202, 204, 210–13, 219, 222–23, 225–32, 234, 237–43
Castro, Fidel 97–105, 175–87, 192, 237
Cervera Pacheco, Víctor 90, 142–43, 150, 195–96
Chao, Elaine 231
Chrétien, Jean 8
Christopher, Warren 36
Clinton, Bill 20–22, 46, 61–64, 78, 82, 86, 105, 111, 115, 133–34, 137, 189, 195, 199–200
Colosio, Luis Donaldo 164
Constantine, Tom 25, 60, 86, 89, 110
Coverdell, Paul 23
Creel, Santiago 8–9, 163, 165, 169, 204, 223, 227, 235, 243

Daniels, Josephus 68
Daschle, Tom 220, 232
Davis, Nathaniel 131
Derbez, Ernesto 164, 169
Derham, Jim 39
Díaz Ordaz, Gustavo 75
Díaz, Porfirio 23–24
Dillon, Sam 94
Dodd, Chris 8, 23, 189
Durazo, Alfonso 164

Fernández de Castro, Rafael 14, 192
Fernández de Cevallos, Diego 79, 133

Fleischer, Ari 18
Fox, Vicente 1–11, 18–19, 34–35, 37, 47,
    54–55, 70, 72–73, 78–79, 92, 96, 105,
    117, 129, 132–45, 159, 161–78, 180,
    182–86, 190, 192–93, 198–99,
    201–205, 209–14, 216–17, 219–20,
    222, 226–30, 232–35, 237–43, 250
Freeh, Louis 86, 95
Fuentes, Carlos 4, 105

García Márquez, Gabriel 103–105
Garza, Tony 238
Gavin, John 68–69
Gephardt, Richard 220, 232
Gertz Manero, Alejandro 170
Gil Díaz, Francisco 164
Golden, Tim 61–65
Gore, Al 63, 110, 203, 233
Gramm, Phil 220
Green, Rosario 24, 27, 31, 36–37, 39,
    101–102, 160, 177, 194, 214
Greenspan, Alan 112, 213
Guevara, Ernesto "Che" 98, 176
Gurría, José Ángel 36, 72
Gutiérrez Barrios, Fernando 97–99, 136,
    141
Gutiérrez Rebollo, José de Jesús 49, 62,
    86–87

Hale, William Bayard 33
Helms, Jesse 21–22, 192–93
Hernández, Silvia 8
Higuera, Ismael 89
Hollings, Fritz 192
Hull, Jane Dee 128

Ibarrola, Eduardo 84

Johnson, Lyndon 210
Jones, Jim 20–21, 23
Jordan, Barbara 115

Kelly, Raymond 86
Kerry, John 21
Kirkpatrick, Jean 241
Kissinger, Henry 131
Kolbe, Jim 189

Labastida Ochoa, Francisco 71–75,
    77–79, 97, 132, 134–37, 139–44, 160
Long, Clarence 190
Lott, Trent 27
Lozano, Antonio 25

Macedo de la Concha, Rafael 164
Madero, Francisco I. 14, 24
Madrazo, Jorge 25–26, 46, 61, 64, 81, 84,
    88, 90, 95, 139
Madrazo Pintado, Roberto 72, 75, 77–78,
    97
Madrid Hurtado, Miguel de la 69–71
Maisto, John 18
Marcos, Subcomandante 161–62
Margáin, Fernando 193
Marshall, Donnie 110
Mazzoli, Rom 113
McCaffrey, Barry 25–26, 50, 63, 74,
    86–87
McIlhenny, Bill 203
McLarty, Thomas "Mack" 22, 214
Medina Mora, Eduardo 235
Meissner, Doris 115
Meyer, Lorenzo 7
Mica, John 193–94
Moctezuma Barragán, Esteban 75,
    134–35
Mohar, Gustavo 221
Monreal, Ricardo 138–39, 148
Monsiváis, Carlos 12
Morris, Chip 155
Morrow, Dwight 68
Mugabe, Robert 190
Muñoz Ledo, Porfirio 241

Nixon, Richard 131

Olmedo, Dolores 158
Ortiz, Guillermo 164

Pascoe, Ricardo 175, 180, 182
Pastor, Robert A. 34, 142
Patiño, Jesús 89
Paz, Octavio 13, 17, 104
Pérez Roque, Felipe 179–80
Perry, Rick 239
Perry, William 93–94
Pershing, John "Blackjack" 14
Peterson, Pete 140
Pinochet, Augusto 99
Poinsett, Joel 13, 23, 68
Powell, Colin 6, 11, 145, 183, 199–200,
   202, 204, 219, 222, 224, 226–27,
   230–31

Reagan, Ronald 35, 104, 220, 241
Rebolledo, Juan 34, 36–37, 41, 194
Reno, Janet 25–27, 39, 45–46, 48, 64–65,
   83–84, 86–87, 109–10, 115, 122, 139
Reyes, José Luis 139
Reyes, Silvestre 189
Reyes Heroles, Federico 135
Rice, Condoleezza 9, 11, 18, 183, 199,
   202–203, 219
Richards, Ann 141, 143, 211
Ridge, Tom 188, 235
Riera Escalante, Pedro 106–108
Rivard, Robert 152
Robinson, Mary 73
Rojas, Carlos 167
Rosenthal, Andrew 63–64
Rove, Karl 224
Rozental, Andrés 213–14
Rubin, Robert 25, 45, 140
Ruiz, Samuel 160–61
Rumsfeld, Donald 199
Ryan, Mary 221, 224, 230–31

Sáenz, José Liébano 32, 61–66, 143
Sahagún, Marta 180
Salinas de Gortari, Carlos 69–72, 100,
   103, 177
Sánchez, Elizardo 102, 177
Sarukhán, José 164
Scott, Winfield 14
Simpson, Alan 113
Smith, William French 113
Sojo, Eduardo 164
Styron, William 105

Taft, William Howard 23
Téllez, Luis 140, 167
True, Phillip 152
Tuirán, Rodolfo 221

Vargas Llosa, Mario 16
Ventura, Jesse 189
Villa, Pancho 14
Villanueva, Mario 90
Volker, Paul 140

Weld, William 21–23
Whitman, Christine Todd 188–89
Wilson, Henry Lane 23–24, 68
Wilson, Pete 116
Wilson, Woodrow 14, 33
Woldenberg, José 138

Zapata, Emiliano 16, 168
Zedillo, Ernesto 17, 22, 26–29, 32–33,
   36–37, 45–46, 61–62, 64, 67, 69–72,
   74–75, 78, 82, 89, 95, 101–103, 138,
   140, 142–43, 161, 164, 172, 189, 198,
   214, 237

About the Author

Jeffrey Davidow is president of the Institute of the Americas in La Jolla, California. After serving thirty-four years in the State Department, he retired as America's highest ranking diplomat, one of only three people to hold the personal rank of Career Ambassador.

During his Foreign Service career, Ambassador Davidow focused much of his efforts on improving relations with Latin America. He served in increasingly senior positions in the U.S. embassies in Guatemala, Chile, and Venezuela, and then later returned to Venezuela as ambassador from 1993 to 1996. From 1996 to 1998, he was the State Department's chief policy maker for the hemisphere, serving in the position of Assistant Secretary of State. He then served as ambassador to Mexico from 1998 to 2002. Initially appointed to that position by President Clinton, he was asked by President Bush to remain in his post for an additional eighteen months.

Early in his Foreign Service career, he served as a congressional staff aide in a program organized by the American Political Science Association. In that capacity, he organized in 1979 the first congressional hearings on the possibility of establishing a free trade area for North America. On another occasion, he spent an academic year at Harvard University's Center for International Affairs where he wrote a book, later published by Harvard, on negotiation. After leaving Mexico in September 2002, he returned to Harvard to become a visiting fellow at the John F. Kennedy School of Government and the David Rockefeller Center for Latin American Studies, working extensively with undergraduate and graduate students during the 2002–2003 academic year.

Jeffrey Davidow graduated from the University of Massachusetts (B.A., 1965) and the University of Minnesota (M.A., 1967). He also did postgraduate work in India (1968) on a Fulbright travel grant. In 2002 he was awarded an honorary doctor of laws by the University of Massachusetts. He has been married since 1969 to the former Joan Labuzoski.